OHIO
TRAVEL ✦ SMART®

OHIO
TRAVEL ✦ SMART®

Second Editon

Marcia Schonberg

John Muir Publications
A Division of Avalon Travel Publishing

John Muir Publications, A Division of Avalon Travel Publishing
5855 Beaudry Street, Emeryville, CA 94608

Printed in the United States of America.
Second edition. First printing April 2000.

ISSN 1096-6137
ISBN 1-56261-512-2

Editors: Ellen Cavalli, Laurel Gladden Gillespie, Mary Lea Ginn
Graphics Editor: Bunny Wong
Production: Scott Fowler, Marie J.T. Vigil
Design: Marie J. T. Vigil
Cover design: Janine Lehmann, Marie J. T. Vigil
Typesetting: Scott Fowler
Map style development: American Custom Maps—Jemez Springs, NM
Map illustration: Julie Felton, Kathleen Sparkes
Printing: Publishers Press
Front cover photos: small—©Marcia Schonberg/Viewfinders (Lucas, Ohio)
                    large—©T.J. Florian/Photo Network (Columbus, Ohio)
Back cover photo: ©Marcia Schonberg/Viewfinders (Parade the Circle, Cleveland, Ohio)

Distributed to the book trade by
Publishers Group West
Berkeley, California

OHIO TRAVEL•SMART:
A GUIDE THAT GUIDES

Most guidebooks are primarily directories, providing information but very little help in making choices—you have to guess how to make the most of your time and money. *Ohio Travel•Smart* is different: By highlighting the very best of Ohio and offering various planning features, it acts like a personal tour guide rather than a directory.

TAKE THE STRESS OUT OF TRAVEL

Sometimes traveling causes more stress than it relieves. Sorting through information, figuring out the best routes, determining what to see and where to eat and stay, scheduling each day—all of this can make a vacation feel daunting rather than fun. Relax. We've done a lot of the legwork for you. This book will help you plan a trip that suits you—whatever your time frame, budget, and interests.

SEE THE BEST OF OHIO

Author Marcia Schonberg has lived in Ohio for all of her life and has written extensively about her home state. She has hand-picked every listing in this book, and she gives you an insider's perspective on what makes each one worthwhile. So while you will find many of the big tourist attractions listed here, you'll also find lots of smaller, lesser known treasures, such as the Zane Grey Museum in Norwich, or McKinley Street, the world's shortest street at 17 inches long, in Bellefontaine. And each sight is described so you'll know what's most—and sometimes least—interesting about it.

In selecting the restaurants and accommodations for this book, the author sought out unusual spots with local flavor. While in some areas of Ohio chains are unavoidable, wherever possible the author directs you to one-of-a-kind places. We also know that you want a range of options: One day you might crave lobster, steak, and a selection of wines from a Western Reserve vineyard, while the next day you might be just as happy (as would your wallet) with "three-way chili," a Cincinnati specialty, mounded atop spaghetti and finished with shredded cheddar. Most of the restaurants and accommodations listed here are moderately priced, but the author also includes budget and splurge options, depending on the destination.

CREATE THE TRIP YOU WANT

We all have different travel styles. Some people like spontaneous weekend jaunts, while others plan longer, more leisurely trips. You may want to cover as much ground as possible, no matter how much time you have. Or maybe you prefer to focus your trip on one part of the state or on some special interest, such as history, nature, or art. We've taken these differences into account.

Though the individual chapters stand on their own, they are organized in a geographically logical sequence, so that you could conceivably fly into Cleveland (Chapter 1), drive chapter by chapter to each destination in the book, and end up close to where you started. Of course, you don't have to follow that sequence, but it's there if you want a complete picture of Ohio.

Each destination chapter offers ways of prioritizing when time is limited: In the Perfect Day section, the author suggests what to do if you have only one day to spend in the area. Also, every Sightseeing Highlight is rated, from one to four stars: ★★★★—"must see"—sights first, followed by ★★★ sights, then ★★ sights, and finally ★—or "see if you have time"—sights. At the end of each sight listing is a time recommendation in parentheses. User-friendly maps help you locate the sights, restaurants, and lodging of your choice.

And if you're in it for the ride, so to speak, you'll want to check out the Scenic Routes described at the end of several chapters. They take you through some of the most scenic parts of the region.

In addition to these special features, the appendix has other useful travel tools:

- The Planning Map and Mileage Chart help you determine your own route and calculate travel time.
- The Special Interest Tours show you how to design your trip around any of number favorite interests.
- The Calendar of Events provides an at-a-glance view of when and where major events occur throughout Ohio.
- The Resource Guide tells you where to go for more information about national and state parks, individual cities and counties, local bed-and-breakfasts, and more.

HAPPY TRAVELS

With this book in hand, you have many reliable recommendations and travel tools at your fingertips. Use it to make the most of your trip. And have a great time!

WHY VISIT OHIO?

Ohio offers a treasure chest of unique attractions, backlit in shades of changing seasons. Whether you are spending a day or two or planning a longer vacation, Ohio's lush scenery, rich history, and dynamic cultural opportunities provide all the ingredients for a stimulating and relaxing getaway. Whatever destination you select, you will leave behind a wealth of possibilities for a return visit.

LAY OF THE LAND

Ohio does not have an ocean or major mountain range to attract vacationers, but with a Great Lake to the north, the Ohio River to the south, and a magnificent topography formed by ancient glaciers in between, the state offers scenery as spectacular as many more famous and crowded sightseeing venues.

Generally, it was glaciation during the last Ice Age that provided Ohio with its hilly southern terrain, plains, and multitude of lakes and streams. When you visit Kelleys Island in Lake Erie, look for the massive scars and grooves etched into the limestone. At John Bryan State Park in southwestern Ohio, marvel at the beautiful sandstone-faced cliffs. Hike through gorges cut into the Blackhand sandstone at the nature preserve of the same name in Licking County, then climb amid natural rock bridges and formations in Hocking Hills.

FLORA AND FAUNA

Keep a lookout for white-tailed deer as you travel about Ohio. Depending on which area you are visiting, you will also spot birds of prey and wading birds and hear a cacophony of songbirds and bullfrogs.

From footpaths and biking trails, visitors can easily spot wildflowers, monarch and swallowtail butterflies, and abundant waterfowl. In the evening cicadas serenade you along with choruses of frogs in the marshes. Cyclists looking for beaver dams can often be seen along old rail bridges, especially along the towpath trail winding through the Cuyahoga Valley National Recreation Area.

Garter snakes and water snakes are common sights, and Ohio does have three poisonous varieties of snake: timber rattlesnakes, swamp rattlesnakes, and copperheads. The latter are most commonly sighted while exploring the rocky surfaces in the Hocking Hills region. In the same hills you will need to duck to avoid disturbing the bats hibernating in the area's caves.

You may not expect to find an African savanna in central Ohio, but at the Wilds in Cumberland, grassy open ranges covering 14 miles of reclaimed strip-mining land now protect endangered species from around the world as well as native wildlife. Rhinos, giraffes, mountain zebras, gazelles, and Asian wild horses, to name only a few of the Wild's animals, graze throughout this huge expanse of land donated by American Electric Power. The Wilds is the largest wildlife conservation and research center in North America. If you go, leave your safari gear at home but do not forget a camera.

Generally, even from the interstate, you can expect to travel through a patchwork of farmland where neat blocks of corn, soybeans, and wheat sit against a hilly background of green forests. Freshly painted red, white, and blue Ohio bicentennial emblems on barns easily visible along Ohio's byways are de-signed to attract interest in 2003's big celebration. Grazing dairy cattle and deep red barns (along with a few classic "Mail Pouch" originals) complete the pas-toral collage. Colorful splashes of wildflowers, such as those west of Wooster on U.S. 30, are the result of the Ohio Department of Transportation's Wildflower Program.

In southern Ohio, look closely for tobacco barns. Their distinctive open sides provide a view of the drying leaves inside. In the grape-growing regions along Lake Erie, you will spot acres of densely laden arbors. In other areas you may wonder about the neat rows of pine trees (they may be Christmas trees awaiting the seasonal harvest). Octagonal barns are rare, but at least one can be found in Ashtabula County.

Lake Erie, the walleye capital of the world, lures anglers from all over the country. Inland lakes full of bass (both small- and largemouth), muskies, and crappies attract fishers, too. More than 200 boating areas over 50 acres in size dot the state, while both public and private sites stocked with trout satisfy those who enjoy fly-fishing. Licenses are required for enthusiasts 16 and older to fish in Ohio waters and Lake Erie.

Bird-watchers flock to the Erie shores. The lake is located at the cross-roads of two major flyways, the Atlantic and the Mississippi, and migratory birds rest on the open lake, islands, and shoreline wetlands during their journeys. More than 300 species have been identified between Oak Harbor and Lorain, in an area known as the Lake Erie Wing Watch. A list of annual birding events, hotels offering discounts to bird-watchers, and an informative brochure containing a bird checklist are available by calling 800/255-ERIE.

HISTORY AND CULTURE

While family genealogies often include early settlers who traveled through Ohio to explore lands farther west, most of the state's early residents came here to stay. They farmed, as did their predecessors—the prehistoric Hopewell and Adena—who likely hunted the giant mastodon. Those ancient dwellers farmed efficiently and created a rich collection of earthen pottery and burial and ceremonial mounds.

Later, Native Americans from other tribes—including the Wyandot, Ottawa, Chippewa, and Delaware in the north and central portions of the state and the Shawnee and Miami in the south—arrived. You will find remnants of these nations in the names of counties, rivers, parks, and monuments throughout the state, as well as at historic sites. The state's name itself is derived from the Iroquois term *oheyo*, meaning "great river" or "beautiful."

As New Englanders arrived in the Western Reserve (the northeastern portion of the state) other settlers arrived in southern Ohio by flatboat, establishing Marietta at the confluence of the Ohio and Muskingum Rivers. Marietta, populated largely by Revolutionary War veterans from Massachusetts who received Ohio land parcels as payment for their war efforts, became the seat of the Northwest Territory in 1788.

On February 19, 1803, Thomas Jefferson approved Ohio's statehood, making it the first state from the Northwest Territory. It was not until 1953 that legislators realized statehood had not been voted on by Congress. President Eisenhower later signed the bill legally approving Ohio's statehood.

In Ohio's early history, capital cities included Marietta, Cincinnati, Chillicothe, and Zanesville, before Columbus was permanently chosen in 1816. Recently, the exemplary nineteenth-century Greek Revival statehouse was restored to its original elegance.

Ohio became a melting pot of ethnic backgrounds as more and more immigrants moved westward. They settled in Cleveland and went on to develop the canals and, later, railroads to connect the ports along Lake Erie with the Ohio River.

Many citizens held staunch abolitionist views long before the Civil War. Their commitment grew, often at grave personal risk, to help slaves reach Canada via the Underground Railroad, which was neither a railroad nor underground. Rather, it was an antislavery network shrouded in secrecy that helped thousands of slaves escape owners and bounty hunters. In all corners of the state, visitors can view and sometimes tour more than 200 dwellings that once harbored runaways.

Also of interest to history buffs is Ohio's "presidential path," which led eight favorite sons to the White House. National monuments to and birthplaces or homes of Presidents Ulysses S. Grant, Rutherford B. Hayes, James A. Garfield, Benjamin Harrison, William Henry Harrison, William McKinley, William Howard Taft, and Warren G. Harding dot the state and highlight not only their presidential years but also the political and social atmosphere of their eras.

THE ARTS

Because of the early influx of settlers from New England, you will find town squares and covered bridges that resemble those in Connecticut. Town names are often clones of New England ones, too. Architecturally, Ohio provides an eclectic hodgepodge. It ranks third in the nation in the number of sites listed on the National Register of Historic Places, according to the Ohio Historic Preservation Office. Victorian mansions, Greek Revival houses, Italianate farmhouses, art deco museums, and Frank Lloyd Wright homes can be seen throughout the state. Cincinnati, Cleveland, and Chagrin Falls are just a few of the many cities offering walking or driving tours to help visitors appreciate the state's architectural diversity and preservation.

Ohio's leading art museums own vast holdings from myriad eras, and some, such as Youngstown's Butler Institute of American Art and the Kent State University Museum (of fashion design), focus on a specific period, school, style, or medium. The Ohio Craft Museum in Columbus showcases works by some 2,000 Ohio artists; the National African American Museum and Cultural Center in Wilberforce (outside Dayton) offers changing exhibits by African American artists; and the National Heisey Glass Museum, a 5,000-piece collection of decorative and functional glassware, recounts the company's history in Newark from 1896 to 1957.

Performing arts venues are found in major cities and small burgs as well. You will find professionally cast performances, including Broadway series productions, in grandly restored showplaces such as Dayton's Victoria Theatre, Cleveland's Playhouse Square (which houses three unique theaters), Columbus's Palace Capitol Theatre at the Rife Center, and the Southern and Cincinnati's new Aronoff Center for the Arts. On the smaller stages theatergoers will find community and semiprofessional entertainment. Period melodrama can be seen aboard the *Becky Thatcher* showboat in Marietta.

During summer, Picnics with the Pops take place in Columbus, the renowned Cleveland Orchestra heads to its summer home at Blossom Music Center in Cuyahoga Falls, and the Cincinnati Symphony and Pops Orchestra sets up at the Riverbend Music Center on the banks of the Ohio River. The annual Lancaster Music Festival, held each July, combines fine and performing arts during a 12-day montage of festivities. You can find live regional jazz and rhythm and blues, as well as touring groups, throughout the state no matter what the season.

CUISINE

If you think the music and art in Ohio are eclectic, wait until you sample the restaurant fare. Cleveland's ethnic neighborhoods offer diverse eateries. An authentic neighborhood ambiance in Little Italy makes dining there special. The same goes for Asia Plaza. Even President Bill Clinton stopped in Parma, a Polish community on the city's west side, to sample pierogi; and some Ohioans think the best corned beef and rye bread in the world come from Cleveland.

Though Columbus does not have the ethnic pockets found in Cleveland, it still provides an international smorgasbord. Spanish cuisine can be found both west and north of downtown, outstanding soul food and ribs on the near east side, and authentic New Mexican cuisine on the northwest side, just to whet your appetite.

As Ohio is part of the Midwest farm belt, you will find plenty of hearty meat-and-potato fare, with many restaurants boasting "homemade," "made from scratch," and "fresh-baked" selections. Nowhere are these descriptions more prevalent than in Amish communities. Here you will dine on pot roast, chicken, mashed potatoes with gravy, and buttery rolls before finishing off the meal with a slice of—you guessed it—homemade pie. If you stop in one of the many bakeries, you will undoubtedly leave with cinnamon rolls and cookies for later.

Some of us take a few Ohio favorites for granted, such as the buckeye confection, named after the state tree. It is a mixture of peanut butter and powdered sugar rolled into a ball and dipped in semisweet chocolate to re-semble the inedible nut of the Ohio buckeye tree. Lake Erie walleye and perch fill many freezers and attract hungry motorists longing for a fresh lakeside fish platter. Far from the lakeshore you will find restaurant menus featuring the catch of the day, but the best places add the waterfront view.

At the other end of the state, restaurateurs and customers alike continually argue over who offers the best ribs. If you are traveling in summer, you will run into annual rib cook-offs throughout the state.

Cincinnati is known for its chili, boasting several ways of serving it and too many chili parlors to count. "Three-way chili" is served over spaghetti and topped with shredded cheddar; for "four-way chili" add chopped onions; and for "five-way chili" add a scoop of kidney beans on top of "four-way." Please be forewarned: Cincinnati chili has a different taste, even before you add the "ways." Perhaps it is the cinnamon, or maybe the allspice, in some of the "secret" recipes.

Another peculiarity you will find on some Cincinnati breakfast tables is goetta: a combination of seasonings, sausage, and cornmeal. You may get to sample the dish if you stay at the Amos Shinkle House B&B, across the river in nearby Covington, Kentucky.

You can learn a lot about a community's history just by scouting out the beer names at the various brew pubs. Burning River Pale Ale and Moondog Ale are in Cleveland, and Lake Erie's Gale Warning Ale in Marblehead.

If you prefer sampling wines, Ohio (believe it or not) ranks fifth nationally, behind California, New York, Washington, and Oregon, in the number of wineries and sixth in annual wine production. More wineries are joining the 40-plus already in operation, so those statistics will likely jump.

Several wineries offer year-round dining or summer cookouts. Others pro-vide scenic picnic grounds in pastoral settings. You will find friendly vintners eager to provide tours, samplings, and horror stories about Ohio winters. Each summer dozens of wineries, with the help of corporate sponsors, cele-brate during Vintage Ohio. Music stages, craftspeople, and dining attract wine enthusiasts to Lake Farmpark in Lake County during the first weekend in August. A similar festival attracts thousands in Dublin (west of Columbus) each spring.

OUTDOOR ACTIVITIES

Outdoor activities abound in Ohio, especially in summer, when more activities are available than time permits. It is the season for leisurely entertaining and vacationing.

Because of the myriad inland lakes and rivers, plus Lake Erie to the north and the Ohio River to the south, many popular pastimes center on the water. Canoes, pontoon boats, fishing charters, and paddleboats are available for rental. Dinner cruises, river hops, canal boat rides, and fishing trips are among the most popular outdoor summer activities.

Hiking, walking, and bird-watching sites are abundant in Ohio, perhaps because of the seemingly endless number of managed trails. If you are so inclined, you can hike the Buckeye Trail, following the blue blazes completely around the state and putting 1,200 miles on your pedometer. The North Country National Scenic Trail cuts a U, with most of its 277 miles hooking up with the Buckeye Trail. Hiking is popular during all seasons, but winter hiking amid frozen waterfalls and pristine ice formations sets a different mood. Add a crackling fire in a cabin in the woods, and you may have the most romantic weekend ever.

Any season is perfect for a self-guided walking tour through a quaint community or an architectural stroll in a metropolitan area. If you enjoy the company of others, join a volksmarch. The state association of walkers plans free walks that lead participants through fields or city streets.

Horseback riders are easily accommodated by the numerous camps and trails. Unique spots, such as the Smoke Rise Ranch for overnight camping and the Heartland Country Resort, are particularly interesting.

No matter where you live or visit in Ohio, a biking trail is nearby. Most of the "Rails to Trails" paths and those that follow the towpaths of old canals are relatively flat. If you are riding in the Cuyahoga National Recreation Area, you might want to hop aboard the Cuyahoga Valley Scenic Railroad for the ride back. Some trails, such as the Kokosing Gap from Mount Vernon to Danville, travel through interesting towns filled with antique shops and eateries. Most trails are multiple-use systems, suitable for in-line skating and walking.

Outdoor festivals are favorite pastimes, too. Communities honor their largest pumpkins and tomatoes as well as bratwurst, popcorn, Swiss cheese, ice cream, and sauerkraut. You can spend the day reliving the past at living history sites.

Amusement parks and professional sports will fill any gaps in your outdoor leisure plans. Whether it is water parks, roller coasters, baseball, football, soccer, hockey, or car racing, you can do it or watch it in the Buckeye State.

PLANNING YOUR TRIP

Before you set out on your trip, you will need to do some planning. Use this chapter in conjunction with the tools in the appendix to answer some basic questions. First of all, when are you going? Local events, the weather, and other seasonal considerations may play a role in that decision. This chapter discusses all of that, while the Calendar of Events in the appendix provides a month-by-month view of major area events.

How much should you expect to spend on your trip? This chapter addresses various regional factors to consider when estimating your travel expenses. How will you get around? Check out the section on local transportation in this chapter. The Planning Map and Mileage Chart in the appendix can help you figure out routes and driving times, while the Special Interest Tours outlined in the appendix provide several focused itineraries. This chapter concludes with some reading recommendations to give you various perspectives on the state. If you want specific information about individual cities or counties, see Resources in the appendix.

WHEN TO GO

Each season brings its own beauty to Ohio's favorite destinations, and each one offers unique reasons for a visit. Visitors often choose to repeat their trip during a different season for a totally new experience.

Ohio enjoys all four seasons, although some residents complain that one is too short or another too long. Summer is the most popular time for visiting Ohio, but the other seasons should not be eliminated from your travel plans. From winter hikes and ice fishing, spring maple-sugaring days, and summer cooldowns at popular water parks to fall harvest festivals, all seasons have something to offer.

Some of the state's most scenic areas, such as the Hocking Hills region in the southeast, are especially enjoyable in winter. It is a quiet time, when frozen waterfalls and snow-covered branches provide a picturesque backdrop in black and white. Many hope for a fresh dusting of snow before their winter visits.

Activities are at their peak from Memorial Day through Labor Day. Holidays and weekends are the most congested travel times in Ohio, as elsewhere. If you are able to plan weekday travel, particularly during summer months, you will avoid many of the lines and crowds.

The shops and main streets in the Amish counties are less traveled on weekdays, but even Saturday will be peaceful on the back roads and throughout tiny communities off the beaten track. Most of the shops and restaurants are closed on Sunday. Many bed-and-breakfasts in Amish areas serve hearty, full breakfasts during the week but provide continental fare on Sunday because their Amish helpers are not working. A trip to the Amish communities is worthwhile year-round.

The Lake Erie Islands offer a slower, more relaxing pace during the week—a good time for bike riding. Other attractions, from theme parks to zoos and museums, are more fun during the week, when you can avoid crowds.

The best time to visit depends on your hobbies and tastes. If you enjoy the first signs of spring, then wildflower tours should top your list. If the solitude of winter scenery is what you are after, bundle up after a fresh snowfall and take to the woods on foot, cross-country skis, or snowshoes. An annual winter hike, scheduled in January, attracts thousands to the Hocking Hills State Park region. If you want to join the organized activities, planning even a year ahead for accommodations is best.

Winter is also the season for dogsled demonstrations at Punderson State Park and ice fishing on Lake Erie. You can rent cross-country skis or enjoy skiing on several downhill slopes. Many inns and B&Bs offer specials during the off-season. From just after Labor Day to Memorial Day, look for bargain rates, special programming, and combination packages. The major cities have seasonal shopping packages, cures for cabin fever in the state parks, and fall bargain weekends at theme parks. Ohio zoos offer winter activities that often surpass their in-season schedules.

Most major museums offer the same schedules year-round, but smaller ones, especially those that rely on volunteers, adopt shortened winter hours. If you are not sure, it is best to call ahead to check times and avoid disappointment. Visitors can call the Ohio Travel and Tourism Hotline, 800/BUCKEYE, for updates on fishing and skiing, monthly activities, and a wealth of other travel information. The hotline provides answers to travel questions, sends out OhioPass—a guide containing coupons for many venues—and furnishes callers with packets of information for specific regions and interests.

HOW MUCH WILL IT COST?

No matter what the bank account looks like, we all have the same desire to take a break from our everyday lives. Everyone asks the same questions: Where can we go? What can we do? How much will it cost?

This travel planner is chock-full of interesting places to visit and ways to spend your valuable time. For out-of-state travelers, the destinations are within easy drives of the major airports or short distances from the interstates. Except in metropolitan locations, you will need a car. Do not hesitate to ask innkeepers if they can help. Many inns, such as Glenlaurel: A Scottish Country Inn in the Hocking Hills, will provide airport pickups for a reasonable fee.

If you are an Ohio resident, many sights are just a few hours away by car, and some may be practically at your back door. Residents who plan vacations within the state save on airfare and car expenses. You may be able to afford a more luxurious vacation if you stay closer to home.

By following my suggestions, you can choose the sightseeing options that best fit your style and budget. Some selections, including parks and recreational areas, are free; most others charge moderate admission fees. For example, zoo admissions range from $6 for adults and $4 for children in Columbus, Toledo, and Akron to $10 for adults, $7 seniors 62 and over, and $4.75 for children 2 to 12 in Cincinnati—all bargains for a day's worth of entertainment and education. Food costs can be minimized if you pack a picnic or take your own snacks and drinks. Even for those not concerned by high-priced refreshments, a picnic lunch can turn the day into a romantic getaway or a special family outing.

Ticket prices top out at the theme parks, where a family of four will spend well over $100 for admission alone. By purchasing tickets through travel clubs and with discount coupons offered by Ohio-based supermarkets like Kroger's, customers can save several dollars per ticket. Late-day admission tickets, such as Cedar Point's "Starlight" passes, can save you $10 off full-day tickets.

Based on per-person statistics, Ohio tourists spend $74 per day, nearly $11 less than the national average for travelers. Researchers cite Ohio's northeast, central, and southwest areas as the most frequently visited regions and Columbus as the city that received the most travelers in 1998. During the same year, more than 63.7 million people spent some leisure travel in Ohio, maintaining its ranking at sixth in volume of visits in the nation, behind only California, Florida, Texas, Pennsylvania, and New York.

Ask about discount packages as you plan your vacation. For example, birdwatchers can call 800/255-ERIE for a list of hotels along Lake Erie's shore that offer "birders' rates." By asking, you will find promotions at the Ritz Carlton in downtown Cleveland that compare with motels offering far fewer amenities. If you are celebrating a special occasion, you can choose a bed-and-breakfast or inn, such as the Inn at Honey Run, that provides appropriate extras.

ORIENTATION AND TRANSPORTATION

Major airlines provide commercial passenger service throughout the state, with frequent service at Cleveland's Hopkins International and Burke Lakefront, Akron/Canton, Greater Cincinnati/Northern Kentucky International (which is in Kentucky), Port Columbus International, Dayton International, and Toledo Airports. Hopkins is a hub for Continental Airlines, as is Cincinnati for Delta, and Port Columbus is a minihub for America West Airlines.

Once you are in the state, major cities and nearby recreational activities are most easily reached by car. Interstates 71 and 75 provide transportation north and south, while I-70 and the Ohio Turnpike (I-80 and I-90) cross the state east and west. Belts around Columbus, Cincinnati, and Cleveland, as well as other interstate connections, make traveling through the major cities efficient. The speed limit is generally 65 miles per hour on the interstates. Several historical highways, such as the National Road and the Lincoln Highway, cross through Ohio, and "Heritage Corridors" link places important in Ohio history. The Simon Kenton Historic Corridor, the Ohio & Erie Canal Corridor, the Land of Grant Corridor, the Maumee Valley Heritage Corridor, and the Toledo Metroparks Corridor are described in later chapters. Ohio has eight state scenic byways as well as one national scenic byway, the Ohio River National Scenic Byway. The Ohio River Towns chapter leads drivers along much of this newly designated route, stopping at many historic riverfront communities on the way.

Although many other scenic drives are available, along roads that served as major thoroughfares just a few decades ago you may discover a spectacular view or the best slice of apple pie. On a leisurely drive along the Ohio River, for instance, the scenery is great and the stories you will hear in the down-home restaurants recall an earlier way of life. Every so often you can catch a view of the river and the sound of a calliope aboard a passing steamboat that is too good to pass up.

CAMPING, LODGING, AND DINING

Perhaps the most memorable portion of any trip is the cuisine—part of the travel experience is opening the doors to new tastes. By sampling ethnic cuisine and heartland favorites as well as the old standbys, you will venture to far more exotic places than you ever dreamed of finding in the Midwest.

If you are ready for gourmet picnics at a winery, fresh vegetables and herbs from the garden, Spanish tapas, or platters of Italian pastas—not to mention hearty Amish fare and menus featuring early American cuisine and homemade desserts—then plan your trip and let the fun begin.

Accommodations run from national motel and hotel chains to B&Bs with historical connections, great breakfasts, and interesting, hospitable innkeepers. The Ohio Hotel & Lodging Association offers a new online reservation service, www.ohla.worldres.com, that allows visitors to book rooms via the Internet. You can also make reservations by calling 800/BUCKEYE, the state travel and tourism hotline. In the destination chapters that follow, you will find bed-and-breakfasts, small inns, and larger accommodations that offer unique characteristics. The national or regional chains mentioned also provide something special, be it a romantic getaway, excellent facilities for children and families, or the best location or price. I have shared my preferences—spots I look forward to revisiting.

Ohio offers thousands of possibilities for campers, with every type of campsite preference available. The state park service alone offers 73 parks, 57 with camping accommodations. Some are rugged, primitive sites nestled in wooded settings, while others include electrical hookups. All campsites, except the rent-a-camps, are first come, first served. If you wish to ensure a site or select one adjacent to friends, arrive earlier in the week and pay in advance for each night.

All campgrounds provide pet camp facilities for $1 extra per day. For those wishing to camp but lacking any or all the essentials, tent rent-a-camps range from $23 to $35 per day. Campers need only bring their food; even the dining canopy is ready and awaiting your arrival. If your style is still more genteel, you can opt for a fully furnished cabin. The queen and newest of the state resorts is Maumee Bay State Resort & Conference Center, where the cabins have fireplaces. A central listing, 800/AT-A-PARK (282-7275), makes reservations at all eight lodges as well as the cabins.

CAMPING OPTIONS

Ohio state parks offer a number of unusual styles of camping. You'll find Rent-A-Tepee at Indian Lake, Jackson Lake, and Mohican State Park ($27–$30) and Rent-A-Yurt at Pymatuning or Maumee Bay State Park ($40). Fully equipped RVs are available at Alum Creek, Caesar Creek, East Fork, East Harbor, Geneva, and Punderson Lake ($50–$65, depending upon site and length of stay). Houseboats may be rented at Paint Creek and Alum Creek State Parks (about $700 per week, $400 midweek) and *cabents* at South Bass Island ($425 per week). Constructed of wood, *cabents* have fabric roofs and small kitchens, and they sleep six. More than a dozen locations offer horsemen's camps.

Many private grounds offer a full range of amenities, from horseback riding to Amish cooking. Major attractions, including Cedar Point Amusement Park and Sauder Farm and Craft Village, offer camping facilities in addition to other on-site lodging. National camping chains dot the state as well.

RECOMMENDED READING

During the last decade especially, many nonfiction works about Ohio have been published. If you enjoy trivia, *Awesome Almanac Ohio, Ohio Trivia*, and *The 1997–1998 Ohio Almanac: An Encyclopedia of Indispensable Information about the Buckeye Universe* should be on your bookshelf. They will tell you more about Ohio than you probably want to know. Speaking of more than you want to know, *A History of Ohio*, edited by James Rodabaugh, is in its eighth printing. It sheds light on Ohio's early years and, by its weight alone, is the best over-the-counter cure for insomnia. In addition, several regional presses specialize in publications about specific areas; Gray & Co., for example, publishes titles about Cleveland.

Lehman's, in Kidron and Mount Hope, stocks many helpful reference works on the Amish community. *A Quiet Moment in Time* (Carlisle Press, 1997), written by George Kreps, Joseph Donnermeyer, and Marty Kreps, provides a contemporary look at Amish society and offers tips on making the most of your visit. The same authors have another book out, *Lessons for Living*, suggesting a method of simplifying hectic lifestyles. Wayne Weaver recently wrote his autobiography, *Dust Between My Toes*, telling readers of his experiences growing up in Ohio's Old Amish Order. His story follows unusual turns of events and captivates readers of all ages. For general information, try *20 Most Asked Questions about the Amish and Mennonites*, by Merle and Phyllis Good, or *Our People: The Amish and Mennonites of Ohio* by Levi Miller. *Back Roads & Buggy Trails*, by Lorraine A. Moore, is a visitor's guide to Ohio sights.

Notable cookbooks include the Country Inn Cooking series (Rutledge Hill Press) by Gail Greco. Several innkeepers in the state have authored cookbooks detailing the preparation of many of their most-requested dishes. You will find enjoyable collections at the Inn at Honey Run and the Inn at Cedar Falls, but do not hesitate to ask for a recipe at your favorite B&Bs even if a cookbook is not available. Usually innkeepers are eager to share their favorites with guests.

Readers who enjoy historical novels should pick up *Follow the River*, one of James Alexander Thom's best-sellers, based on the story of Mary Ingles in Ohio during the 1700s, and Allan Eckert's *The Frontiersmen*, an epic story that follows pioneers into the Northwest Territory.

1
CLEVELAND

Imagining Cleveland's Public Square full of farm animals ready for market, with horse-drawn carriages lining the same streets that today are bustling with skyscrapers and traffic jams, may be difficult. However, that is the way it was in Cleveland's early heyday.

The city has been a popular place since its beginning, when Moses Cleaveland arrived in 1796 and plotted a town square like the ones he had left in New England. By the early 1900s, according to population statistics, more than 500,000 people lived here, and by the 1930s some 900,000 lived throughout the city.

The population soon shifted toward the suburbs. Travelers will want to explore some of the charming communities, such as Shaker Heights, that blossomed during this peak. Today, growth continues. There are now more than 500,000 residents who live within the city, while there are 2.9 million in Greater Cleveland.

Cleveland's earliest settlers included British and Scottish New Englanders. These were soon followed by Irish, Germans, Bohemians, Hungarians, and Poles, eager to farm or build canals, as well as Italian and Eastern European craftspeople. Today's rich ethnic diversity also includes African Americans, Greeks, Asians, Puerto Ricans, Czechs, Slovaks, Slovenes, Croats, and Serbs, providing a variety of cultural festivals and a wide choice of delicious and authentic cuisine.

CLEVELAND

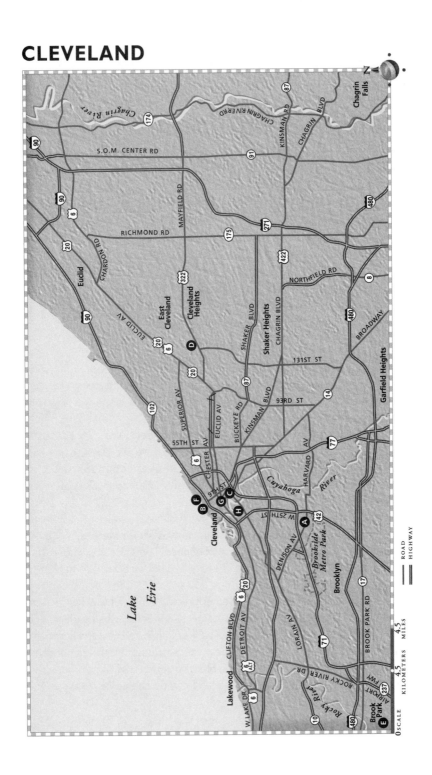

A PERFECT DAY IN CLEVELAND

Ride Lolly the Trolley for an overview of the city before visiting the museum of your choice, perhaps at the North Coast Harbor, where you will find the Rock and Roll Hall of Fame and Museum, Great Lakes Science Center, USS *Cod*, the Steamship *William G. Mather* Museum, and the new Browns stadium. In University Circle you can choose among a dozen or more museums. Have lunch in Little Italy if you opt for University Circle or in Ohio City or adjacent Tremont after a morning downtown. Enjoy neighborhood shops and galleries before an evening dinner cruise aboard the *Nautica Queen*. You will get magnificent skyline views and a peek at the Flats, Cleveland's bustling riverfront entertainment district, where you can stop for some live music or a nightcap at one of the riverside eateries.

TOURS

Spending an hour or two aboard **Lolly the Trolley** is the easiest and quickest way to get acquainted with Cleveland. The narrated sightseeing tour by well-trained docents offers local color. The trolley departs from the powerhouse on the West Bank of the Flats. Call 216/771-4484 or 800/848-0173 for details. A wheelchair-accessible trolley is available.

If you are looking for a unique vantage point from which to catch Cleveland's skyline, sights, and scenery, book a cruise. Buffet dining choices and entertainment are plenty aboard the **Nautica Queen**, 216/696-8888, anchored on the West Bank of the Flats next to the powerhouse facility. Meals are served on the enclosed, air-conditioned decks, and guests can stroll the outdoor observation decks. Luncheon cruises ($21.95 adults, $11.95 children) and sunset dinner cruises ($38.95 adults, $15.95 children weekdays, higher on weekends) are among the many options available. On the **Goodtime III**, North Coast Harbor, 216/861-5110, tourists can choose from various schedules, including a relaxing two-hour sightseeing cruise ($12.50 adults, $11.50 seniors, $7.50 children) that runs, rain or shine, at noon and 3:00, June 15 through Labor Day. The

---

SIGHTS

- Ⓐ Cleveland Metroparks Zoo
- Ⓑ Great Lakes Science Center
- Ⓒ Jacobs Field
- Ⓓ Lake View Cemetery/Garfield Monument
- Ⓔ NASA John Glenn Research Center at Lewis Field
- Ⓕ Rock and Roll Hall of Fame and Museum
- Ⓖ Terminal Tower Observation Deck
- Ⓗ West Side Market

---

triple-deck cruise ship is anchored at the East Ninth Street Pier next to the Rock and Roll Hall of Fame and Museum. Depending on the cruise, you may hear a running commentary about as many as six bridges you will pass under, as well as about the historical development of the area—the old powerhouse and early Ohio settlers. You will also get a great view of the bustling Flats, with its board-walk and the many area restaurants offering waterfront dining. North toward Lake Erie, you will glimpse Whiskey Island and freighters.

UNIVERSITY CIRCLE SIGHTSEEING HIGHLIGHTS

Even if you have only a few hours to spend sightseeing, you will fill them wisely in University Circle, an area four miles east of downtown. The curving streets intersecting Euclid Avenue encompass more museums and educational insti-tutions in a square mile than anywhere else in the country. Other attractions include shopping, galleries, restaurants, lodging, Severance Hall (home of the Cleveland Orchestra), and beautiful architecture and sculpture.

An easy way to get to these museums is by hopping aboard the green-and-white Circle-Link buses that stop throughout the museum area every 15 minutes or so (contact University Circle, Inc., 10831 Magnolia Dr., 216/791-3900). If you are seeking the ultimate walking tour, request the Thinking Person's Walking Tour Guide & Map.

★★★★ CLEVELAND MUSEUM OF ART
11150 East Blvd., 216/421-7340, www.clemusart.com

The Cleveland Museum of Art not only offers a comprehensive art collection but also attracts major traveling exhibitions as well as smaller shows and special events. Children especially love the re-cently renovated Medieval Armor Court, which features swords, hel-mets, and more.. The museum store is well stocked, and the Museum Cafe offers light cafeteria-style fare.

Details: *Tue, Thu, Sat, Sun 10–5, Wed and Fri 10–9. Free.* (2–4 hours)

★★★★ CLEVELAND MUSEUM OF NATURAL HISTORY
1 Wade Oval Dr., 216/231-4600

A trip to the area would not be complete without stopping at the Cleveland Museum of Natural History. It is the place to go if anyone in your family is interested in dinosaurs, volcanoes, animals, outer space, gems and jewels, or anything else in or out of this world.

HONORING CLEVELAND'S STAR ATHLETES

For easy, fast access between the Flats, the North Coast Harbor area, and Tower City, ride the RTA Waterfront Line, 216/621-9500. You might also want to check out the **Cleveland Sports Star Hall of Fame**, in the planning stages as of this writing, but to be located in the Regional Transit Authority passageway connecting Tower City to Jacobs Field and Gund Arena. That is where you will be able to learn more about such Cleveland favorites as Jim Brown, Paul Brown, and Jesse Owens when it is completed in 2000.

Details: Mon–Sat 10–5, Sun noon–5. $6.50 adults, $4.50 seniors, ages 5–17, and students with ID. Planetarium admission $1, free Tue and Thu 3–5. (2–4 hours)

★★★★ WESTERN RESERVE HISTORICAL SOCIETY MUSEUM
10825 East Blvd., 216/721-5722

To understand the history of the Western Reserve, take a walk through the **Crossroads** exhibit, where you'll learn about northeastern Ohio's early settlements. Artifacts, including Moses Cleaveland's surveying tools and maps, recall the area's history through the canal days and the railroad era of the 1850s. **The Frederick C. Crawford Auto-Aviation Museum**, on the lower level, relates the city's prominent role in the auto industry with an exhibit that includes more than 150 vintage automobiles. You can learn everything you need to know about genealogy in the **Archive Research Library**. Connected to the museum is the **Hay-McKinney Mansion**, designed by President Garfield's son. Stop here for a look into the lives of Cleveland's early movers and shakers, when high style and opulence prevailed in homes like this along Millionaire's Row.

Details: Mon–Sat 10–5, Sun noon–5. $6.50 adults, $5.50 seniors, $4.50 children 6–12. (2 hours)

★★ AFRICAN AMERICAN MUSEUM
1765 Crawford Rd., 216/791-1700

UNIVERSITY CIRCLE

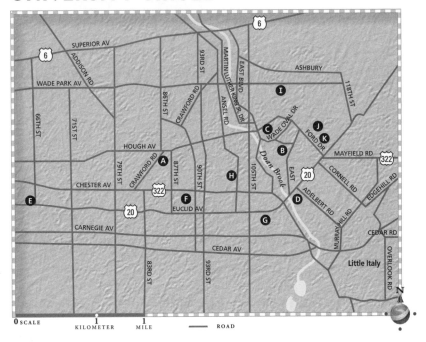

SIGHTS

- Ⓐ African American Museum
- Ⓑ Cleveland Museum of Art
- Ⓒ Cleveland Museum of Natural History
- Ⓓ Dittrick Museum of Medical History

SIGHTS (continued)

- Ⓔ Dunham Tavern Museum
- Ⓕ Health Museum of Cleveland
- Ⓖ Rainbow Children's Museum and TRW Early Learning Center
- Ⓗ Temple Museum of Religious Art

SIGHTS (continued)

- Ⓘ Western Reserve Historical Society Museum

FOOD

- Ⓙ Sergio's

LODGING

- Ⓚ Glidden House

Not only can you trace the history of Cleveland's African American population, but at this museum, you can also learn about Africans around the globe. The original stoplight, invented by Garrett Morgan of Cleveland, is on display, and an area is devoted to the Underground Railroad.

Details: *Usually open Fri–Sat 11–3. (1–2 hours)*

★★ RAINBOW CHILDREN'S MUSEUM AND TRW EARLY LEARNING CENTER
10730 Euclid Ave., 216/791-KIDS

This children's center offers special opportunities for toddlers, older kids, families, and caregivers. Changing exhibits bring fresh hands-on activities, but the permanent ones include a water sculpture area complete with rain gear, an over-and-under space for exploring the many types of bridges found in Cleveland, a weather studio for would-be TV broadcasters, and the little nest area, where toddlers can play in a "squirrel's den" and "bird's nest."

Details: Tue–Fri 10–3, Sat 11–3. $5 ages 16 and over, $4.50 seniors, $4 ages 18 mos–15. Free parking. (1–3 hours)

★ DITTRICK MUSEUM OF MEDICAL HISTORY
11000 Euclid Ave., 216/368-3648

Touted as one of the largest collections relating to medical history in the United States, this small but extensive museum emphasizes Cleveland's contributions and practices from early settlement days through the mid-19th century. Replicas of doctors' offices from 1880 and 1930 and an 1880 pharmacy are displayed.

Details: Mon–Fri 10–5. Free. (1 hour)

★ DUNHAM TAVERN MUSEUM
6709 Euclid Ave., 216/431-1060, www.logan.com/dunham

Just the spot to relive a bit of Cleveland's history. The museum building is the oldest building still standing on its original site in Cleveland. It was the home of Rufus and Jane Pratt Dunham, who came to the Western Reserve from Massachusetts in 1819. Rooms are furnished with period antiques. The Heritage Trail, a 900-foot path through the grounds, depicts the landscape as it might have been during the Dunham's era.

Details: Wed, Sun 1–4, $2 adults, $1 children. (1 hour)

★ HEALTH MUSEUM OF CLEVELAND
8911 Euclid Ave., 216/231-5010, www.healthmuseum.org

More than 150 exhibits help both children and adults discover how the human body works and the reasons behind making positive health choicesin their lives. Juno, the talking transparent woman, is a highlight.

Details: Mon–Fri 9–5, Sat 10–5, Sun noon–5. Closed major holidays. $4.50 adults, $3 students and seniors. (2 hours)

© Marcia Schonberg

★ TEMPLE MUSEUM OF RELIGIOUS ART
University Circle at Silver Park, 1855 Ansel Rd., 216/791-7755
The Temple, one of the earliest Reform Jewish congregations in the United States, houses the Temple Museum of Religious Art, the Abba Hillel Siver Archives, and the Temple Library. Included in the collection are antiquities from the Holy Land region, folk art objects from many countries and time periods, and historic documents. There is also an exhibit of Torah ornaments and antique hangings.

Details: Mon–Fri 9–4. Free. (1–2 hours)

GREATER CLEVELAND SIGHTSEEING HIGHLIGHTS

★★★★ CLEVELAND METROPARKS ZOO
3900 Wildlife Way, 216/661-6500
The wolves are back at the Cleveland Metroparks Zoo, in a setting similar to their natural habitat. *Wolf Wilderness: Wildlife of the Great Lakes* is the newest exhibit, but the Rainforest, with its orangutans, waterfalls, and tropical storms, is still a major attraction. The public greenhouse and the *Birds of the World* display are two other favorites. The park has a lot to see in its 165 acres, so plan wisely and dress comfortably.

Details: Zoo grounds open daily 9–5. Rainforest and zoo buildings open at 10. Rainforest open until 9 p.m. Wed. Extended weekend hours during summer. Zoo and Rainforest $7 ages 12 and older, $4 children 2–11. (half–full day)

★★★★ GREAT LAKES SCIENCE CENTER
610 Erieside Ave., 216/694-2000
Nestled between the Rock and Roll Hall of Fame and Museum and the new Cleveland Browns stadium, this shiny-domed, hands-on museum is the latest attraction in downtown Cleveland's North Coast Harbor area. Currently, more than 350 "edu-tainment" exhibits are on display. They are as entertaining and informal as they are educational. The center offers an unusual spin by focusing on the scientific environment of the Great Lakes region. Adventure areas stress the center's primary mission of stimulating interest, increasing understanding, and promoting greater science literacy. Adults and children can raise and lower a lift bridge similar to one in

the nearby Flats, and a *Pilot-a-Blimp* exhibit is included as well. You can compare your batting skills to those of the big leaguers before visiting the "sick Earth" in a hospital bed in the *Great Lakes Environmental Exhibition.* The **Polymer Funhouse** is designed for children seven and younger who are under 50 inches tall. A must-see (and for some a must-touch) is the real twist and twirl of a tornado. A 12-foot-high exhibit simulates an actual tornado while visitors encircle it. As you can tell, this place is not just for kids. Also see the current film at the **Cleveland Clinic Omnimax Theater**—whatever they are showing will appeal to adults and youngsters alike.

> **Details:** *Daily 9:30–5:30, to 9 Wed–Thu in summer. Daily Omnimax showings hourly 10–6. $6.75 adults for museum or theater, $9.95 for both, $6/$9 seniors, $4.50/$7 ages 3–17. (half–full day)*

★★★★ LAKE VIEW CEMETERY/GARFIELD MONUMENT
Entrances at 12316 Euclid Ave. and Mayfield Rd. at Kenilworth, 216/421-2665

Approximately 94,000 people have found their final resting place at Lake View Cemetery, amid the rolling gardens in Cleveland's University Circle area. For the living, the grounds are a popular spot for enjoying nature, flowers, art and architecture, and spectacular views of the city. Monuments include those to President James Garfield and many other history-making Clevelanders.

Begin at the Garfield Monument, where guides provide information about the 20th president and details about the architecture of the monument. Walk up 154 steps to the entrance of the hilltop structure, where both the president and his wife are buried. Visitors can view the flag-draped casket of the former president—unusual for presidential monuments.

Stop at the nearby picnic area for one of the best views of the city and of Lake Erie, which is six miles north, before heading through the well-manicured, arboretum-like surroundings toward Wade Chapel. Hundreds of trees are identified, and flower tours are arranged seasonally. Four trees—two tulip trees, an American beech, and a white oak—are dubbed "Moses Cleaveland Trees," meaning they were here when Moses Cleaveland surveyed the land more than 200 years ago.

Wade Chapel, constructed in 1900 to honor Jeptha H. Wade, founder of Western Union Telegraph, is one of three Tiffany interiors in the world. The chapel contains magnificent Tiffany mosaics, a Tiffany chandelier hanging overhead, and—the focal point—a luminous, leaded stained-glass window.

Details: Grounds open daily 7:30–5:30. Garfield Monument and Wade Chapel open seasonally with guides 9–4. Walking and bus tours offered seasonally. Free. (1 hour per tour)

★★★★ ROCK AND ROLL HALL OF FAME AND MUSEUM
1 Key Plaza, 800/493-ROLL, 216/781-7625

If you are not sure whether rock and roll is here to stay, you have not visited the Rock Hall. Film, video, interactive exhibits, and the latest technology take you back to the beginning of the rock-and-roll era. Most displays lead you down memory lane, if you are a baby boomer or older. You will see handwritten lyrics, signatures of the inductees to the Hall of Fame, costumes, guitars, and "originals" of many other sorts in the permanent and temporary exhibit areas.

Details: Daily 10–5:30, until 9 Wed. $14.95 adults, $11.50 seniors and children 4–11. Calling ahead for reservations is advisable, especially during summer and holidays. (2–4 hours)

★★★★ WEST SIDE MARKET
1995 W. 25th St., 216/664-3386

For the best selection, try to visit this historic market near downtown soon after it opens. Located just over the Hope Memorial Bridge in Ohio City, this indoor-outdoor, Old World–style area provides a gastronomic smorgasbord, with more than 100 vendors representing 21 nationalities (at last count). You can find many obscure ingredients, and nowhere else offers a greater selection of ready-to-eat delicacies. On the streets surrounding the massive yellow brick landmark, you will find ethnic restaurants and shops. **Farkas**, a Hungarian pastry shop, 2718 Lorain Ave., 216/281-6200, is open only on Friday and Saturday. **Athens Pastries and Imported Foods**, 2545 Lorain Ave., 216/861-8149, is a Greek general store that carries both foods and import items.

Details: Mon–Wed 7–4, Fri–Sat 7–6. Vendors take cash only. (2 hours)

★★★ JACOBS FIELD
2401 Ontario St., 216/420-4385

If you or your kids are baseball fans but you are not in town when the Tribe is, the next best thing to attending an Indians game may be a behind-the-scenes tour of the ballpark. You can visit the batting cages, press boxes, and dugout while you yearn for a hard-to-come-by ticket for an Indians game.

Details: May–Sept, when the team is on the road, tours depart 10–2 every half hour from the Indians Team Shop. $5 adults, $3 seniors and children. Purchase tickets at main box office, any Indians Team Shop, TicketMaster, or by phone, 216/241-8888, 11 days in advance. (1 hour)

★★★ NASA JOHN GLENN RESEARCH CENTER AT LEWIS FIELD
21000 Brookpark Rd., across from Cleveland Hopkins Airport, 216/433-2001

A visit to this facility, one of the most advanced research labs in the country, will give you an insider's peek at some of NASA's equipment and technology. You will see the zero-gravity drop tower, wind tunnels, and chambers used for jet-engine testing. Guides try to accommodate guests' interests and backgrounds.

Details: Visitors center open Mon–Fri 9–4, Sat and holidays 10–3, Sun 1–5. For small adult groups or individuals, tours of two research facilities begin at 2 on Wed. Call ahead for weekday tour reservations. Free. (1–2 hours)

★★★ TERMINAL TOWER OBSERVATION DECK
50 Public Square, 216/621-7981

While you are downtown, take a ride up to the 42nd floor of the 52-story Terminal Tower building for a 360-degree view of Cleveland. On a clear day, your view will be about 32 miles.

Details: Deck open May–Sept 11–4:30, Oct–Apr 11–3:30. $2 adults, $1 ages 6–16. (30 minutes)

FITNESS AND RECREATION

In Independence, 15 minutes south of Cleveland, you can pick up the **Ohio & Erie Canal Towpath Trail** through the **Cuyahoga Valley National Recreation Area** for a scenic 20 miles to Bath, just north of Akron. Eventually, the multiuse path will extend seven miles north to the **Cleveland Metroparks Zoo** for an even shorter freeway drive. Those who do not want to pedal or hike the entire trail can hop aboard the **Cuyahoga Valley**

Scenic Railroad, 800/468-4070, for the return trip. Call the park's **Happy Days Visitors Center**, 330/650-4636, for details.

The **Cleveland Metroparks** provide warm-weather recreation, as well as cross-country skiing, ice-skating, sledding, and ice fishing for winter enthusiasts. It also includes six public golf courses, with **Manakiki Golf Course**, 35501 Eddy Rd., Willoughby Hills, and **Sleepy Hollow Golf Course**, 9445 Brecksville Rd., Brecksville, designated as premier sites.

At the **Mill Stream Run Reservation**, 216/572-9990, you will find twin toboggan chutes that operate Thursday from 6 to 10, Friday from 6 to 10:30, Saturday from noon to 10:30, and Sunday from noon to 9:00, late November to February, weather permitting, even if snow is not on the ground.

Eight physical fitness trails are in the Metroparks at Bedford, Big Creek, Brecksville, Euclid Creek, Mill Stream Run, North Chagrin, Rocky River, and South Chagrin reservations. The Buckeye Trail connects with the hiking paths in **Brecksville Reservation**, but scenic hikes can be found in each of the 14 parks. Call the 24-hour park information line at 216/351-6300.

For sports fans, Cleveland has champions like the American Baseball League **Indians**, NBA **Cavaliers**, IHL **Lumberjacks**, WNBA **Rockers**, and professional indoor soccer with the **Crunch**. The **Cleveland Browns**, in the American Football Conference Central Division, are playing in their new stadium overlooking the North Coast Harbor. Collegiate play can be enjoyed at Cleveland State University.

FOOD

If you are willing to drive a few miles, you can find whatever makes your mouth water. For ethnic entrées, eclectic choices include upscale and authentic Brazilian fare at **Sergio's** in University Circle, 1903 Ford St., 216/231-1234; **Corky and Lenny's**, 27091 Chagrin Blvd., 216/464-3838, for corned beef, knishes, or blintzes; and **Tommy's**, 1824 Coventry Rd., Cleveland Heights, 216/321-7757, for veggies and Middle Eastern delights. **Li Wah**, 2999 Payne St., in the Asia Plaza, 216/696-6556, serves dim sum selections from 10 to 3 and is also open for dinner. You will discover wonderful Spanish and Portuguese flavors in the Warehouse District at **Mallorca Restaurant**, 1390 W. 9th St., 216/687-9494, and a wide menu including black-bean burritos and an extensive juice bar in Ohio City at **Johnny Mango**, 3120 Bridge Ave., 216/575-1919. For delicious sautéed pierogi, among other Polish specialties, visit **Sokolowski's University Inn**, 1201 University Rd., Cleveland (Tremont), 216/771-9236, Monday through Friday from 11 to 3 and Friday from 5 to 9, or try **Ewa's Family**

GREATER CLEVELAND

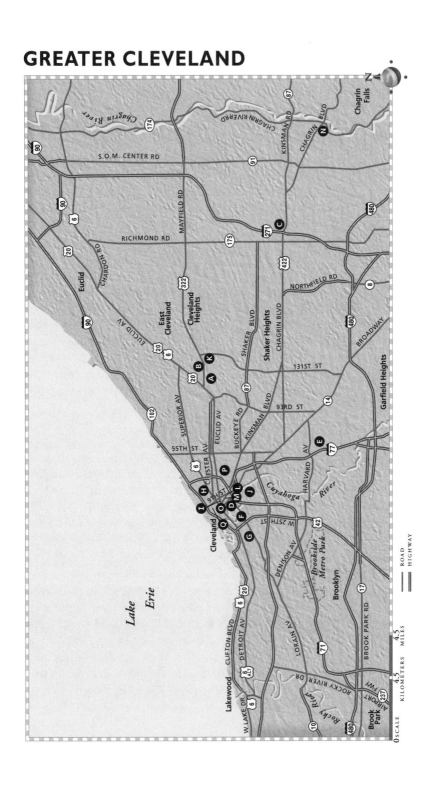

Restaurant, on the edge of Slavic Village, 4069 E. 71st St., 216/441-7040, is a favorite among neighborhood locals.

In Little Italy you will not go wrong anywhere, but try **Mamma Santa's**, 12305 Mayfield Rd., 216/231-9567, for pizza; **Trattoria Roman Gardens**, 12207 Mayfield Rd., 216/421-2700, for al fresco dining; **Guarino's**, 12309 Mayfield Rd., 216/231-3100; or stop at **Corbo's Dolceria**, 12200 Mayfield Rd., 216/421-8181, for biscotti (both lemon and hazelnut are great) and creamy cannoli.

Personal micropub favorites are **Great Lakes Brewing Company**, 2516 Market St., 216/771-4404, where brewery tours are available, and **Diamondback Brewery**, 728 Prospect (in the Gateway complex), 216/771-1988, where a pub menu and an upscale eclectic menu complement handcrafted brew and where you'll find the only champagne bar in town. When you visit the Rock Hall, stop for a burger at the **Hard Rock Café**, located downtown, 230 W. Huron Rd., 216/830-ROCK.

If your budget permits, choose French fare at the **Sans Souci Restaurant** at the Renaissance Cleveland Hotel, 24 Public Square, 216/696-5600, or the creative menu at the **Baricelli Inn**, 2203 Cornell Rd. in Little Italy, 216/791-6500. Enjoy tea at the **Ritz-Carlton**, 1515 W. Third St., 216/623-1300, as you like it: light, high, or the Royal Tea, which includes champagne; call ahead for reservations. The service is elegant, but dress need not be, so you can go on your way to a ball game, if you wish.

FOOD

- **Ⓐ** Barcicelli Inn
- **Ⓑ** Corbo's Dolceria
- **Ⓒ** Corky and Lenny's
- **Ⓓ** Diamondback Brewery
- **Ⓔ** Ewa's Family Restaurant
- **Ⓕ** Great Lakes Brewing Company
- **Ⓑ** Guarino's
- **Ⓓ** Hard Rock Café
- **Ⓖ** Johnny Mango
- **Ⓗ** Li Wah
- **Ⓘ** Mallorca Restaurant
- **Ⓑ** Mamma Santa's
- **Ⓓ** Ritz-Carlton

FOOD (continued)

- **Ⓓ** Sans Souci Restaurant
- **Ⓙ** Sokolowski's University Inn
- **Ⓚ** Tommy's
- **Ⓑ** Trattoria Roman Gardens

LODGING

- **Ⓐ** Baricelli Inn
- **Ⓛ** Embassy Suites
- **Ⓛ** Hampton Inn
- **Ⓜ** Holiday Inn & Express Suites
- **Ⓝ** Inn of Chagrin Falls

LODGING (continued)

- **Ⓞ** Marriott Downtown at Key Center
- **Ⓟ** Marriott Residence Inn
- **Ⓓ** Renaissance Cleveland Hotel
- **Ⓓ** Ritz-Carlton Cleveland
- **Ⓠ** Sheraton Cleveland City Center

Note: Items with the same letter are located in the same area.

LODGING

Cleveland offers quality over quantity in the B&B category, with each of these inns providing a luxurious and comfortable ambiance for your Cleveland getaway: the **Inn of Chagrin Falls**, 87 West St., Chagrin Falls, 216/247-1200; **Baricelli Inn**, 2203 Cornell Rd. in Little Italy, 216/791-6500; and the **Glidden House**, 1901 Ford Dr. in University Circle, 216/231-8900.

The **Ritz-Carlton Cleveland**, 1515 W. Third St., 216/623-1300 or 800/241-3333, and the **Renaissance Cleveland Hotel**, 24 Public Square, 216/696-5600 or 800/HOTELS-1, are attached to City Center and Gateway. Ask for weekend specials, particularly if your plans include the Rock and Roll Hall of Fame and Museum. Other downtown locations include the **Marriott Downtown at Key Center**, 127 Public Square, 216/696-9200 or 800/228-9290; the **Sheraton Cleveland City Center**, 777 St. Clair Ave., 216/771-7600 or 800/321-1090; and **Embassy Suites**, 1701 E. 12th St., 216/523-8000 or 800/EMBASSY. Try the **Hampton Inn**, at Ninth St. and Superior in the Gateway Complex, 800/HAMPTON, for more moderate rates. Special weekend rates at the Renaissance Cleveland, Marriott Downtown, and Hampton Inn run under $100 per night.

By this book's publication, several new properties, like the **Marriott Residence Inn** and **Holiday Inn & Express Suites**, should be open along with more urban sites on the near horizon. Travelers heading west, south, or east will find highways lined with national chains suited for every budget.

SHOPPING

Even if you do not want to buy anything, a must-see is the **Arcade**, 401 Euclid Ave., 216/621-8500, for the wonderful architecture of this polished-brass 1890 antique. **The Avenue** at Tower City, 50 Public Square, 216/771-0033, has many upscale stores and the best **Dillard's** around. It also has interesting "leapfrog" water displays. On the east side, **Beachwood Place**, 26300 Cedar Rd., Beachwood, 216/464-9460, features Nordstrom and the Galleries of Neiman Marcus (the first of its kind, specializing in jewelry, gifts, and decorative home accessories). **The Galleria** at Erieview, 1301 E. Ninth St., 216/861-4343, is convenient for parking, shopping, and eating if you are also heading down the street to the Rock and Roll Hall of Fame, Great Lakes Science Center, Steamship *William G. Mather* Museum, or USS *Cod*. Do not overlook neighborhood choices, including **Shaker Square**, **Larchmere Boulevard** for antiques, the art galleries in **Little Italy**, and an artsy mix of retail shops in the **Coventry** area, just beyond Little Italy at Mayfield and Coventry Roads.

NIGHTLIFE

For live theater, such as a Broadway series production, choose among the shows at the **Ohio, Palace, Allen,** and **State Theaters** in the renovated Playhouse Square district, 1501 Euclid Ave., 216/241-6000. The world-renowned **Cleveland Orchestra** performs at Severance Hall, 11001 Euclid Ave., 216/231-7300, and at Blossom Music Center, 1145 W. Steels Corner Rd., Cuyahoga Falls, 330/920-8040, during summer. For regional theater, choose a performance at the **Cleveland Play House**, 8500 Euclid Ave., 216/795-7000. The performing arts scene also includes African American theater at **Karamu House**, the **Cleveland Opera**, top names at the **Gund Arena**, jazz and comedy in the **Warehouse** and **Gateway Districts**, plus entertainment in the **Flats**. Pick up the *Plain Dealer's Friday Magazine* or free copies of the *Weekly Scene* or *Free Press* for a schedule of performances.

Scenic Route: Chagrin Falls

Part of the enjoyment of visiting Chagrin Falls from Cleveland is the scenic drive along the way, especially if you are coming from the eastern suburbs (Shaker Heights, perhaps).

Shaker Square is a good starting point. Drive east on Shaker Boulevard (Ohio 87) and marvel at the beautiful homes lining the street. After making a left turn onto Gates Mills Boulevard, the deep lawns of this residential community will catch your eye. Turn right onto Old Mill Road East, then right onto Chagrin River Road. The Chagrin River, with wildflowers and cottontails bordering its banks, is on the left. This route is not the quickest, but you will enjoy a longer span of the river.

Notice the manicured grounds as you drive through Hunting Valley and keep an eye peeled for a polo match. Pass Moreland Hills, birthplace of James Garfield. Turn right onto Woodland Road and right again onto Falls Road, driving the brick-lined road to North Main Street. With another right turn you will see the Village of Chagrin Falls, with its quaint shopping area and historic neighborhood homes, many in the Western Reserve style.

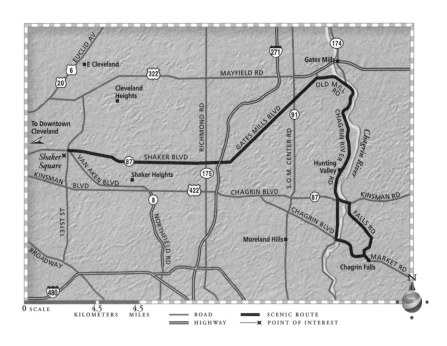

2
THE WESTERN RESERVE

The northeastern portion of Ohio will remind you of New England. When the United States was formed, each state claimed vast, uncharted territory to the west—as much land as it wanted. After realizing the continent's size, the federal government asked individual states to relinquish some of their property to make smaller, more manageable portions.

Connecticut abided by relinquishing its western holdings, but it "reserved" 500,000 acres for its Revolutionary War veterans and victims of the Firelands, whose homesteads had been destroyed by Tory raids. The Connecticut emigrants rebuilt their lives in Ohio towns such as Norwalk and New London, named for their former homes.

In 1796, a year after the Connecticut Land Company acquired the "Western Reserve" from Connecticut, Moses Cleaveland arrived in Conneaut, or Port Independence, to survey the land investment. Equipped with maps and 66-foot chains (which are now part of the Western Reserve Historical Society's collection), he measured the reserved tract—a 120-mile area west of Pennsylvania with the same northern and southern latitudinal borders as Connecticut. When he came upon the crooked riverbed of the Cuyahoga, he created a town with a 10-acre public square and gave it his name.

Some early settlements, such as Cleveland, have sprawled into major cities. However, many smaller communities still bear strong resemblance to their pioneer beginnings. They will take you back to another time and place.

THE WESTERN RESERVE

PENNSYLVANIA

OHIO

Lake Erie

Shenango River Reservoir

Pymatuning Reservoir

Pymatuning State Park

Andover

Mosquito Creek Lake

Lake Milton

Youngstown

Ashtabula

Geneva

Jefferson

Hartgrove

Mesopotamia

Warren

Niles

Leavittsburg

Canfield

Geneva-on-the-Lake

Geneva State Park

Madison

Montville

Middlefield

Newbury

Garrettsville

Hiram

Painesville

Fairport Harbor

Grand River

Mentor

Kirtland

Chardon

Punderson State Park

Aurora

Kent

Ravenna

Cuyahoga Falls

Chagrin Falls

Geauga Lake Park

Euclid

Shaker Heights

Bath

Akron

Cleveland

Lorain

Elyria

Wellington

Huron

Oberlin

STATE BOUNDARY

POINT OF INTEREST

ROAD

HIGHWAY

SCALE   KILOMETERS   18   18   MILES

A PERFECT DAY IN THE WESTERN RESERVE

Start out early to sample a few of the area's many attractions. Stop at Lake Farmpark first and then continue on to Holden Arboretum, followed by an easy hike at Penitentiary Glen Natural Area, perhaps along the Gorge Rim Loop. Head out for a fresh-catch lunch along Lake Erie at either Pickle Bill's or Brennan's Fish House in Grand River. After lunch, drive along U.S. 20 (Ohio 2), which is part of the Lake Erie Circle tour, en route to one of the wineries near Geneva and the Harperfield Covered Bridge, the longest in the state. In late afternoon, head west toward Chagrin Falls, arriving in time for window-shopping and dinner at a local eatery. End the day with an ice-cream cone while taking in the rushing falls.

SIGHTSEEING HIGHLIGHTS

★★★★ ASHTABULA COUNTY COVERED BRIDGES
Covered Bridge Festival, 25 W. Jefferson St., Jefferson, 440/576-3769

With 16 covered bridges still in use (once more than 50), Ashtabula County is the covered-bridge capital of the state. Thirteen bridges have been strengthened or rehabilitated to meet modern needs. Some bridges are 130 years old; the newest is the 1999 Netcher Road Covered Bridge. The Covered Bridge Festival is held the second full weekend in October, but you can tour the bridges year-round.

Details: Maps are available, and markers are posted along the way. Contact Ashtabula County Convention and Visitors Bureau, 800/878-9767, for additional assistance. (4 hours)

SIGHTS

- Ⓐ Ashtabula County Covered Bridges
- Ⓑ Ashtabula's Historic Bridge District
- Ⓒ Butler Institute of American Art
- Ⓓ Chagrin Falls
- Ⓔ Geauga Lake
- Ⓕ Geneva-on-the-Lake
- Ⓖ Hale Farm and Village
- Ⓗ Hiram
- Ⓘ Holden Arboretum
- Ⓙ James A. Garfield National Historic Site and Lawnfield
- Ⓚ Lake Farmpark
- Ⓛ Loghurst
- Ⓜ Mesopotamia and Middlefield
- Ⓝ National McKinley Birthplace Memorial
- Ⓞ Sea World of Ohio
- Ⓟ Shandy Hall
- Ⓠ Western Reserve Historical Society Museum

★★★★ ASHTABULA'S HISTORIC BRIDGE DISTRICT
Ashtabula Harbor area along Bridge St. between Lake St. and the lift bridge

Ashtabula County is well known for its many covered bridges. However, the Bascule Bridge, a lift bridge pointing skyward over Ashtabula Harbor, also attracts its share of onlookers and has led to the redevelopment of the quaint harbor area. No one seems to mind when traffic comes to a standstill while the bridge lifts.

The unusual bridge, from the French word for seesaw, *bascule*, is counterbalanced so that when one end is lowered, the other end is raised. The original 1889 swing-type bridge was replaced in 1925 and restored in 1986. Views of the bridge and the rest of the Ashtabula Harbor are best from Point Park, located just above the historic district on Walnut Boulevard. It is a pretty spot in which to enjoy a picnic or watch the activity below. Across the street is **Great Lakes Marine & U.S. Coast Guard Memorial Museum**, 1071 Walnut Blvd., Ashtabula, 440/964-6847, where nautical memorabilia and hundreds of artifacts are displayed in what was originally the lightkeeper's home. The museum is open Memorial Day to Labor Day Friday to Sunday from noon to 6 and during September from 1 to 5. Shops and eateries have rejuvenated the century-old buildings along Bridge Street.

History buffs will want to stop at the **Hubbard House Underground Railroad Museum**, Lake Ave. and Walnut Blvd., Ashtabula, 440/964-8168. The 1834 home was one of the last stops for slaves traveling the Underground Railroad to Canada. Tours are led by Tim Hubbard, a descendant of original owners William and Catherine Hubbard, pioneers in Ohio's antislavery society. Tours of Hubbard House, which is listed on the National Register of Historical Places, are given from Memorial Day through the end of September. An annual Underground Railroad pilgrimage takes place at the home during the second weekend in October.

Details: *Contact Ashtabula County Convention and Visitors Bureau, 800/3-DROP-IN. (half day)*

★★★★ BUTLER INSTITUTE OF AMERICAN ART
524 Wick Ave. (adjacent to Youngstown State University), Youngstown, 330/743-1711

The institute provides a retrospective of American art from colonial days through the contemporary period. In addition to a vast permanent collection, ongoing changing exhibitions drawn from a montage of international collections intrigue viewers. You will find a hands-on children's gallery, a sports art gallery, and works by America's most famous artists.

Details: *Tue, Thu, Fri, Sat 11–4; Wed 11–8; Sun noon–4. Free.* (2 hours)

★★★★ CHAGRIN FALLS
Chagrin Valley Chamber of Commerce, 440/247-6607

Upscale shops and restaurants, an old-fashioned ice-cream parlor, scenic river views, and Victorian homes give this prestigious area 18 miles southeast of Cleveland a relaxing ambiance. Its roots as an 1800s milling village are still apparent. The river and falls that once provided water power now offer scenic beauty.

The Chagrin Falls Historical Society, 440/247-4695, offers a "Village Victorian" walking tour to show off many fine examples of Gothic Revival, Italian, Federal, Greek Revival, Queen Anne, and Victorian styles. The typical Western Reserve style is an adaptation of Greek Revival. The society, run by volunteers, also displays a collection of local artifacts in its museum at 21 Walnut Street. Although regular hours are on Thursday from 2 to 4, volunteers will open the museum by special appointment.

Music, sometimes barbershop, sometimes big band, wafts through the air during the free summer concerts at Triangle Park, and the **Chagrin Valley Little Theatre**, 440/247-8955, around the corner from the falls, has been hosting amateur theater productions for over half a century.

Details: *Located on OH 87, east of Cleveland. (2–3 hours)*

★★★★ GEAUGA LAKE
1060 N. Aurora Rd., Aurora, 330/562-7131
www.geaugalake.com

Families have been enjoying the rides at this classic amusement park for over a century. Today there are more than 100 rides, magic shows, water rides, and roller coasters. There are roller coasters for enthusiasts, a skydive ride aboard the Geronimo Skyswing, and 15 children's rides. Admission includes the water area, where Hook's Lagoon and Turtle Beach await.

Details: *Memorial Day through Labor Day daily; May and Sept–Oct Sat–Sun. Summer hours usually Mon–Fri 11 a.m.–10 p.m. and*

Sat–Sun 10 a.m.–10 p.m. $25.99 for those over 48 inches tall, $12.99 for those under 48 inches, 14.99 seniors. (4 hours)

★★★★ HALE FARM AND VILLAGE
2686 Oak Hill Rd., Bath, 330/666-3711 or 800/589-9703
At this living history homestead in Bath, guests learn how difficult life was for early settlers in the mid-1800s in the 21 buildings on the original homestead of Connecticut farmer Jonathan Hale. His home, built in 1827, is under restoration until 2001. Interpreters describe the furnishings, times, and activities as they interact with guests. Craftspeople create candles, soap, hand-blown glass objects, and more. A blacksmith shop, carriage museum, and pottery shop are on-site along with the working barn and a log cabin depicting the early settlement in 1815. Visitors can purchase items made here at the Gatehouse's Museum Shop. Light refreshments are available, and visitors are welcome to picnic at the site. Public programs and workshops are held throughout the year.
   Details: *Tue–Sat 10–5, Sun noon–5. $9 adults, $7.50 seniors, $5.50 children 6–12. (half day)*

★★★★ HOLDEN ARBORETUM
9500 Sperry Rd., Kirkland, 440/946-4400
A visit to this 3,100-acre natural wonderland, the largest arboretum in the United States, offers something for everyone during each season. The arboretum has 20 miles of trails, gardens, and ponds, and usually a slate of planned activities.
   Details: *Tue–Sun 10–5. $4 adults, $3 seniors, $2 ages 6–16, children under 6 are free. (2 hours)*

★★★★ JAMES A. GARFIELD NATIONAL HISTORIC SITE AND LAWNFIELD
8095 Mentor Ave., Mentor, 440/255-8722
Lawnfield, Garfield's Mentor home, reopened recently after undergoing a complete restoration. Filled with mostly original furnishings and decorated with replica Anglo-Japanese wall coverings, the 30-room mansion is a showplace. Guided tours are available.
   Also stop at the visitors center in the original carriage house. You can view an award-winning video, narrated from the detailed pages of Garfield's diary, and explore interactive exhibits depicting important phases in the 20th president's life. His bronze death mask

and historical artifacts are on display throughout the stall area of the carriage house, where the original brick flooring contrasts strikingly with the modern portion of the gallery.

Details: *Mon–Sat 10–5, Sun noon–5. $6 adults, $5 seniors, $4 children 6–12. Wheelchair accessible. (1–2 hours)*

★★★★ LAKE FARMPARK
8800 Chardon Rd. (OH 6), Kirkland, 800/366-FARM

This open-air science and cultural center advertises "a little science and a lot of fun" and offers family-oriented activities centered around Midwest farming. More than 50 breeds of livestock, including some rare and endangered breeds, as well as Lake Farmpark's six-horse hitch of Percherons, Belgians, and Clydesdales, live at the center. The Plant Science Center explains hydroponic farming and features the Great Tomato Works, a 100-foot tomato vine with huge tomatoes that are used to teach children the "inner workings of plant life." Vintage Ohio, Ohio's winefest celebrating regional wines, is held at the park each August. For information about the winefest, contact the Ohio Wine Producers Association, 800/227-6972.

Details: *Park, gift and book shop, and Farmpark Cafe open daily 9–5. $6 ages 12–64, $5 ages 65 and over, $4.50 ages 2–11. (2–3 hours)*

★★★★ SEA WORLD OF OHIO
1100 Sea World Dr., Aurora, 800/63-SHAMU

This popular summer destination features such treats as Magellanic penguins and Commerson's dolphins at Patagonia Passage, a moving walkway through Shark Encounter, a 4-D high-tech special effects pirate adventure, and an interactive experience with a bottlenose dolphin at Dolphin Cove. These are all before you visit Carnivore Park or find a seat for Shamu's famous show. The amazingly well-trained killer whale befriends even the tiniest members of the audience. Well-kept grounds, an abundance of flowers, and friendly staff are added bonuses at this Anheuser-Busch theme park.

The food is not cheap, and the park somehow makes kids hungry as soon as they pass through the gate, so packing snacks and drinks is a good idea (although coolers are not permitted in the park), especially in the heat of summer. Public picnic areas are adjacent to the parking lot. For the most memorable Sea World experience of all, join the dolphin or sea lion interaction program, which runs $50

© Marcia Schonberg

to $150, depending on whether you observe or swim with the animals. Prior reservations are a must (330/562-8101, ext. 2034) and participants must be at least 48 inches tall.

Details: *Generally open daily 10 a.m.–11 p.m.; call for exact times. One-day passes $30.95 ages 12 and older, $22.95 ages 3–11. Parking $5. Strollers, wagons, and wheelchairs are available for rent. (half–full day)*

★★★★ **SHANDY HALL**
633 South Ridge, Geneva, 440/466-3680
Built in 1815, Shandy Hall is one of the oldest dwellings in the Western Reserve. The Harper family lived in the 17-room home for three generations and saved everything from diaries and letters to receipts for their furniture. "Originals," from American Empire furnishings to the shrubbery outside, are pointed out during the tour.

Details: *May–Oct Tue–Sat 10–5, Sun noon–5. $3 adults, $2 seniors and children. (1 hour)*

★★★ **GENEVA-ON-THE-LAKE**
OH 531, a few miles north of I-90 on Lake Rd.

If you want to take a trip down memory lane—say, back to the '50s and '60s or before—then visit this lakeside community, known nostalgically as "Ohio's first summer resort." Here, except for beach erosion, summer days remain bustling and unchanged. The food stands along the "strip" provide the same lakeside fare—foot-long hot dogs, hamburgers, ice cream, and French fries, along with more modern homemade potato chips. No California cuisine can be found for the health-conscious along this mile-long festival of eateries, amusements, and nightspots. **Eddie's Grill** has served as a gathering spot for over 40 years, but it has expanded and now includes a Dairy Queen, the only franchise in town.

Overlooking the lake, the **Erieview Amusement Park** offers rides that have greeted vacationers for more than 100 years. One childhood favorite, the tiny metal boats that follow each other in a circle, is still afloat. These boats have dual "steering wheels," so siblings can captain at the same time. The miniature cars and fire engines have the rounded fender designs of those built in the 1940s and '50s.

The Casino and Pier Ball Room, which once lured couples with the big-band sound, is gone. These days live entertainment is on the outdoor patio of the **Old Firehouse Winery**. Waterslides are also available, as are an assortment of electronic amusements, antique games of skill, and the oldest miniature golf course in continuous play in the United States. You can still rent a black inner tube to take down to the beach.

Details: Call Geneva-on-the-Lake Convention and Visitors Bureau, 440/466-8600. (1 hour–full day/overnight)

★★★ **NATIONAL MCKINLEY BIRTHPLACE MEMORIAL**
40 N. Main St. (OH 46), Niles, 330/652-1704
The 25th president, William McKinley, has two monuments in his honor, one here in Niles, commemorating his birthplace, and one in Canton, where he married and practiced law. Located on the corner opposite his boyhood home, this memorial houses a public library in one wing and a museum and auditorium in the other. You will find artifacts from his presidency, personal life, and assassination, as well as bronze plaques detailing accomplishments of regional movers and shakers of the time.

Details: Mon–Thu 9–8, Fri–Sat 9–5:30. Also open Sun 1–5 Sept–May. Free. (1 hour)

★★ HIRAM

Garrettsville-Hiram Chamber of Commerce
8309 Center, Garrettsville, 330/527-2411

Presidential history buffs will want to stop at the James A. Garfield Historical Society, 8115 High St., 330/527-5367, and drive by Hiram College, which Garfield attended when it was the Western Reserve Eclectic Institute and where he later served as president. The first home he owned is now a private residence. The **John Johnson Farm House**, 6203 Pioneer Trail, outside Hiram, 330/569-3170, offers free guided tours of a pioneer home filled with period furnishings.

Details: East of Cleveland on OH 82 and 305. (1–2 hours)

★★ MESOPOTAMIA AND MIDDLEFIELD

Geauga County Tourism Council, Inc.
8228 Mayfield Rd., Chesterland, 440/729-6002

These Amish communities in northern Ohio have not yet been discovered by most tourists, so the atmosphere is quiet and laid-back. You can shop at local cottage industries for Amish furniture, leather goods, and baked treats. In the tiny community of Mesopotamia, where more than half the residents are Amish, you will find a quiet way of life reminiscent of the early Western Reserve. About 30 nineteenth-century homes, some dating to 1816 and marked with National Record of Historic Places placards, circle the village square.

You can probably guess where the **End of the Commons General Store**, 8719 State Rt. 534, 440/693-4295, is located. Catering to the everyday needs of the town's Amish community, the original 1840 establishment carries the area's largest supply of bulk foods and convenience items, as well as hand-dipped ice cream, old-fashioned root beer, penny candy, and Amish souvenirs. It is located at the intersection of OH 534 and OH 87, about six miles east of Middlefield.

For ample Amish fare, try **Mary Yoder's Amish Kitchen**, 14743 N. State Ave. (OH 608), Middlefield, 440/632-1939. Stop at the **Middlefield Cheese House**, just north of OH 87 on OH 608, 440/632-5228 or 800/32-SWISS, to sample the Swiss cheese manufactured with milk from Amish dairy farms. A 20-minute movie explains how Swiss cheese developed in the Amish communities. Down the road, you can purchase locally produced items at the **Middlefield Original Cheese Cooperative**.

Details: *East of Cleveland on OH 87 in Geauga County. (1–2 hours)*

★ **LOGHURST**
3967 Boardman–Canfield Rd., Canfield, 330/533-4330
The log home you will tour at this Western Reserve Historical Society property was not built by pioneers as temporary housing. Constructed of local poplar and walnut in 1805, it is a three-story permanent home and the oldest log dwelling of its size in the Western Reserve. A few years after it was built, the home became an inn. Its owners, Jacob and Nancy Barnes, were staunch abolitionists who aided runaway slaves.

Details: *Tours May–Oct Tue–Sat 10–5, Sun noon–5. $3 adults, $2 seniors and children. (1 hour)*

FITNESS AND RECREATION

One of the most scenic areas in the state, **Nelson-Kennedy Ledges**, 11755 Kinsman Rd., Newbury, 440/564-2279, is a favorite spot for hiking. The small park has three miles of color-coded trails that take visitors to spectacular exposed sandstone rock formations, such as the Old Maid's Kitchen and Dwarf's Pass, and to Cascade Falls at one end and Minnehaha Falls at the other. Kennedy Ledges is undeveloped and access is by permit only. Contact Punderson State Park, 11755 Kinsman Rd., Newbury, 440/564-2279. **Mosquito Lake State Park**, 1439 OH 305, Cortland, 440/637-2856, has one of the largest lakes in the state (7,850 acres) and offers fishing, hunting, boating, primitive camping, swimming, hiking, and picnicking, along with 10 miles of bridle trails and nearly 30 miles of shoreline and wooded trails for snowmobilers. The park provides one wheelchair-accessible fishing dock and holds an abundance of wildflowers and wildlife species. **Geneva State Park**, 429 Padanarum Rd., Geneva, 440/466-8400; **Punderson State Park**, 11755 Kinsman Rd., Newbury, 440/564-2279; and **Pymatuning State Park**, U.S. Rt. 6, Andover, 440/293-6030, offer year-round recreational activities. Hiking trails, a nature center, and a wildlife center provide many activities at **Penitentiary Glen Reservation**, 8668 Kirkland–Chardon Rd., Kirkland.

Many public golf courses dot this section of the state. Contact Lake County Metroparks to make arrangements at **Pine Ridge Country Club**, 30601 Ridge Rd., Wickliffe, 800/254-7275, or call the Cleveland Metroparks for details about **Manakiki Golf Course**, 35501 Eddy Rd., Willoughby Hills, 440/942-2500. For more options, check with the Lake County Visitors Bureau, 800/368-5253.

THE WESTERN RESERVE

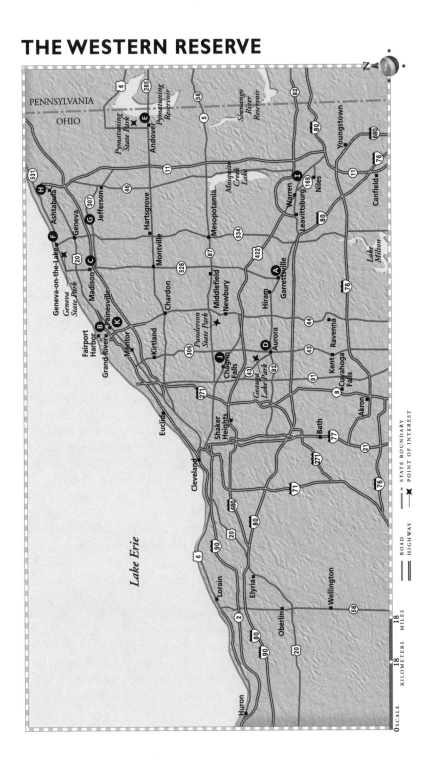

FOOD

Strolling the "strip" at Geneva-on-the-Lake, you will come to several local landmarks, such as **Eddie's Grill**, 440/466-1569, famous for their chili dogs, and **Old Firehouse Winery**, 440/466-9300. Down the street a little farther is **Madsen Donuts**, the place for hot doughnuts since 1938. In Geneva-on-the-Lake, most eateries close from fall to late spring. Along the lake, you can sample the catch of the day at **Brennan's Fish House**, 102 River St., Grand River, 440/354-9785, or at **Pickle Bill's**, 101 River Street, Grand River, 440/352-6343. In the same general area, you will find the "Napa Valley of Ohio," where many wineries flourish. Eleven wineries are in Ashtabula County at last count. At **Ferrante Winery and Ristorante**, 5585 OH 307, Geneva, 440/466-8466, you can enjoy authentic Italian cuisine along with winery tours and tastings. **Chalet Debonne Vineyards, Inc.**, 7743 Doty Rd., Madison, 440/466-3485, adds weekend steak cookouts and musical entertainment to the wine-making festivities. They operate year-round.

In the Niles–Warren area, stop for a gourmet coffee drink, wonderfully high-calorie pastries, and reasonably priced soups, sandwiches, and entrée specials at the **Mocha House**, 467 High St., Warren, 330/392-3020, housed in the town's former American Legion Hall.

When you are out hunting covered bridges, the obvious spot for dinner is the **Covered Bridge Pizza Parlor and Eatery**. Originally called the Forman Road Bridge, the 1862 Town Truss Bridge was replaced and sold to the highest bidder by the county. Five dollars bought it. The bridge was split in half and ultimately became two pizzerias at opposite ends of the county: One is in the south at 380 East Main Street in Andover, 440/293-6776; the other is on the northern edge, at OH 193 in North Kingsville, 440/224-0497 or

---

FOOD

- **A** Alessi's Ristorante
- **B** Brennan's Fish House
- **C** Chalet Debonne Vineyards
- **D** Coach Room Tavern
- **E** Covered Bridge Pizza Parlor and Eatery
- **F** Eddie's Grill

FOOD (continued)

- **G** Ferrante Winery and Ristorante
- **G** Madsen Donuts
- **A** Mill's Ice Cream Parlour
- **I** Mocha House
- **G** Old Firehouse Winery
- **D** Olde Stagehouse
- **B** Pickle Bill's

LODGING

- **D** Aurora Inn
- **I** Avalon Inn and Resort
- **G** Grapevine at Duckhill
- **J** Holiday Inn Express
- **J** Inn of Chagrin Falls
- **J** Lake House Inn
- **K** Quail Hollow Hotel and Conference Center
- **K** Rider's Inn

Note: Items with the same letter are located in the same area.

440/224-2252. A third restaurant is at 4861 North Ridge West, Ashtabula, 440/992-8155. Expect delicious pizzas, salads, and sandwiches in a rustic setting.

Lace curtains and Amish-made quilts provide a relaxing atmosphere in the **Olde Stagehouse** and the **Coach Room Tavern**, the two restaurants at the Aurora Inn, 30 E. Garfield Rd., Aurora, 800/444-6121, where New England flavors are specialties and children's menus are available; entertainment is often provided on weekends. In nearby Garrettsville, Silver Creek has provided the power for John Garrett's mill since 1804. Now Garrett's Mill grinds specialty flours on Saturday while guests watch through a glass window. Upstairs, **Alessi's Ristorante**, 8148 Main St., Garrettsville, 330/527-5849, serves Italian and American cuisine and brews from Garrett's Mill Brewing Company (located one more level up). Homemade ice cream is served with fine views of the creek and grist mill at **Mill's Ice Cream Parlour**, which features a three-tiered observation deck.

LODGING

Golfers especially enjoy the accommodations at the **Avalon Inn and Resort**, 9519 E. Market St., Warren, 800/828-2566, where three suites ($130), many smaller standard rooms ($80), and a patio restaurant overlook Avalon Lakes public golf course. The Avalon South course is across the street. An indoor Olympic-size pool, sauna, tennis and racquetball courts, and several other dining facilities are among the amenities. **Quail Hollow Hotel and Conference Center**, 11080 Concord Hambden Rd., Painesville, 440/352-6201, also caters to golfers, offering overnight guests two championship courses as well as swimming, hiking facilities, and dining choices. A new indoor pool and fitness center are among the renovations nearing completion. Depending on season, weekend rates begin at $109 for two adults, including breakfast.

Catering to families on their way to nearby Geauga Lake Park and Sea World of Ohio, the **Aurora Inn**, 30 E. Garfield Rd., Aurora, 800/444-6121, offers nineteenth-century New England ambiance. Antiques furnish the lobby, as do reproductions in the guest rooms. Dining facilities, indoor and outdoor pools with lifeguards, tennis courts, bocce, and croquet are among the amenities. Various packages are available year-round. The winter B&B package runs $85 per night; honeymoon pagckages are $119 in winter and $189 in summer and include champagne, chocolates, cheese, and fruit.

For surroundings overlooking grape country, opt for a stay at the **Grapevine at Duckhill** at Chalet Debonne Vineyards, 6790 S. River Rd., Geneva, 440/466-7300. The three-guestroom B&B was once a hunting lodge and retains some of its rustic character while providing gourmet breakfasts and seasonal activities, such as hayrides and sleigh rides. Rates range between $75 and $95 a night.

The **Inn of Chagrin Falls**, 87 West St., Chagrin Falls, 440/247-1200, offers Victorian charm in Western Reserve style, with 15 rooms plus a gathering room and the Gamekeeper's Taverne. A Sunday evening special, dubbed "And on the Seventh Day," offers substantial rate reductions and includes a two-for-one dinner special.

Rider's Inn, 792 Mentor Ave., Painesville, 440/942-2742, an 11-room B&B, opened to its first guests in 1812. Each room shares memories from the past, antiques perhaps belonging to the first owners or items left behind by slaves hiding in basement tunnels during their flight to freedom. Traditional colonial fare is served in the dining room; you'll get darts, games, and pub food in the English-style pub. Breakfast can be enjoyed in bed if you wish.

The **Lake House Inn**, 5653 Lake Rd., Geneva-on-the-Lake, 440/466-8668, originally built in the '50s during the community's heyday, offers eight economically priced cottages and a dozen rooms, some with private baths and all newly refurbished. The inn is popular for retreats, reunions, and fishing excursions and rents nightly and weekly. The new kid on the block, the **Holiday Inn Express**, OH 45 and I-90, 440/275-2020, is not your usual motel; international-themed suites (29 of them) give it a unique edge.

CAMPING

Geneva-on-the-Lake lacks the Victorian charm of other lakeside resorts, but it compensates with an abundance of campgrounds, cabins, and cottages for summer rental. Boating and fishing charters, golf courses, and public beaches provide outdoor activities at many of the sites. **Geneva State Park**, 429 Padanarum Rd., Geneva, 440/466-8400, rents 12 waterfront cabins and 91 pull-through sites. It offers a summer rent-a-camp program as well as snowmobiling, ice fishing, and cross-country skiing in winter. **Punderson State Park**, 11755 Kinsman Rd., Newbury, 440/564-2279 or 440/564-1195, provides all the amenities you could ask for at a state facility. Overnight accommodations are available at the lodge, in cabins, or at campgrounds, with activities including swimming, boating, fishing, golfing, hiking, cross-country skiing, snowmobiling, ice fishing, tobogganing, and dogsledding. **Pymatuning State Park**, U.S. Rt. 6, Andover, 440/293-6030, has over 300 campsites and more than 50 cabins. Many of the cabins have cable TV and whirlpool tubs. Ice fishing, ice-skating, and cross-country skiing are the winter sports, while hiking, fishing, and boating are summer highlights.

3
AKRON

Once you visit a few of Akron's main sightseeing attractions, you'll know the who, what, how, and why behind its development. For part of that story you will need to pedal or hike along the Ohio & Erie Canal Towpath as it winds through the Cuyahoga Valley National Recreation Area. You may notice the many references to the word "portage," as in Portage Path, one of Akron's popular arteries. The name reminds us of Native Americans—Wyandot, Ottawa, Chippewa, and Delaware—who "portaged" (or carried) their dugouts between the Cuyahoga and Tuscarawas Rivers.

A tour through Stan Hywet Hall and Gardens not only provides a glimpse into the lifestyle and opulence of Akron's elite in the early 1900s but also relates the success of its owner, Frank A. Seiberling. He, along with B. F. Goodrich, developed vulcanized rubber, which led to Akron's moniker, "the Rubber Capital of the World." You can learn more about their contributions at the World of Rubber Museum in the Goodyear complex. Although tires are no longer manufactured in Akron, Goodyear's national headquarters and testing tracks keep Akron in the rubber limelight.

"Polymer" is the newest buzzword in Akron, one you will learn when you visit Inventure Place and the National Inventors Hall of Fame. Next door, you can book a room in the former Quaker Oats Company silos. The former grain-storage facility has been turned into the Akron Quaker Hilton, and memorabilia from that earlier era rests in the adjacent Quaker Square Complex.

AKRON

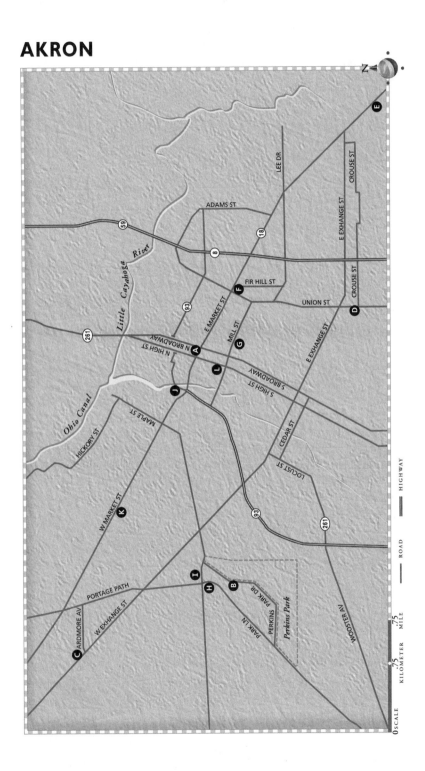

A PERFECT DAY IN AKRON

Start the day with a bike ride or walk along the Ohio & Erie Canal Towpath in the Cuyahoga Valley National Recreation Area, and stop at Hale Farm and Village before touring Stan Hywet Hall and Gardens. Have lunch in the café, then head to Kent State University for a tour of the fashion museum. Pick up a picnic dinner at the West Point Market or the Mustard Seed Market, and enjoy an outdoor evening at Blossom Music Center.

SIGHTSEEING HIGHLIGHTS

★★★★ AKRON MUSEUM OF ART
70 E. Market St., 330/376-9185

Even if you have only a short time to spend in Akron, relax in the sculpture courtyard or stroll through the well-lit exhibition galleries inside the museum. Architecture buffs won't want to miss the chance to view the transformation of an 1899 Italian Renaissance–style post office into a modern, world-class facility. Changing exhibitions as well as permanent galleries focus on art from 1850 to the present.

Details: Daily 11–5. Summer concerts held Thu evenings in the Myers Sculpture Garden. Free. (1–2 hours)

★★★★ DR. BOB'S HOME
885 Ardmore Ave., 330/864-1935

This home, where Alcoholics Anonymous was founded on June 10, 1935, is a must-see museum for those who follow the 12-step program. Memorabilia and a library, along with the simple furnishings of

---

SIGHTS

- Ⓐ Akron Museum of Art
- Ⓑ Akron Zoological Park
- Ⓒ Dr. Bob's home
- Ⓓ Don Drumm Studios and Gallery
- Ⓔ Goodyear World of Rubber
- Ⓕ Hower House

SIGHTS (continued)

- Ⓖ Inventure Place and the National Inventors Hall of Fame
- Ⓗ John Brown House
- Ⓘ Perkins Stone Mansion

FOOD

- Ⓙ Diamond Grille
- Ⓖ Goshen's Mill Street Tavern

FOOD (continued)

- Ⓚ Tangier
- Ⓖ Trackside Grill

LODGING

- Ⓚ Akron Quaker Hilton
- Ⓛ Radisson Hotel Akron City Centre

Note: Items with the same letter are located in the same area.

"Dr. Bob" Smith and his wife, Anne, are housed here. Restorations to the 1935 home where Dr. Bob and his friend Bill Wilson developed the tenets of the worldwide organization are ongoing. A Founder's Day celebration is held each summer.

Details: *Daily noon–3, other times by arrangement. Free, but donations are welcomed. (1 hour)*

★★★★ **INVENTURE PLACE AND THE NATIONAL INVENTORS HALL OF FAME**
Broadway at University Ave., 800/968-4332
More than 125 inventors and their contributions highlight the tiered levels in this high-tech exhibit hall. Motion-activated kiosks add personal anecdotes as visitors weave along the balconies leading to the workshop, where the interactive fun and discovery begin. You can tell that this is not just another look-but-don't-touch museum by the sign that reads "This is a place to mess around. No rights. No wrongs. Just experiments and surprises." You can be an artist, musician, filmmaker, and creative genius as you peruse some 45 science centers and workstations that offer children and adults a place to build their own inventions. Best of all, visitors can take their masterpieces home. It may be the most user-friendly exhibit hall you will ever visit, so allow yourself and your family enough time to really experiment.

Details: *Memorial Day–Labor Day Mon–Sat 9–5, Sun noon–5. Other seasons, closed Mon, except President's Day and Martin Luther King Jr. Day. $7.50 adults, $6 seniors and children. $5.50 per person for groups of 25 or more. (3 hours)*

★★★★ **KENT STATE UNIVERSITY MUSEUM**
Rockwell Hall, E. Main and S. Lincoln Sts., Kent, 330/672-3450
This unusual museum, with an immeasurably vast collection of fashion designs, costumes and accessories, textiles, paintings, and glass, receives worldwide recognition as a premier facility yet seems to be one of Ohio's best-kept secrets. Depending on the themes of the changing exhibits, you may find coronation gowns and Oriental imperial robes or psychedelic prints from the 1960s. Whatever you enjoy during your first visit is only a small portion of the fashion collection, donated by Ohio native Shannon Rodgers and his partner, Jerry Silverman, who also developed KSU's prestigious School of Fashion Design and

Merchandising. You will be equally awed by the china, porcelain, and glassware collection, which exceeds 200,000 pieces.

Details: *Wed, Fri, Sat 10–4:45; Thu 10–8:45; Sun noon–4:45. $5 adults, $4 seniors, $3 students 7–18. Wheelchair accessible. (1–2 hours)*

★★★★ MAY FOURTH SITE AND MEMORIAL
Kent State University, Kent, 800/988-KENT

This plaza on the Kent State campus honors four students killed by the Ohio National Guard during an antiwar protest in 1970. Benches within the wooded, two-and-a-half-acre plaza provide a retreatlike atmosphere for contemplating the inscription "Inquire, Learn, Reflect." Directions to the sight, overlooking Kent State University's commons, are available at campus buildings.

Details: *Free. (30 minutes)*

★★★★ STAN HYWET HALL AND GARDENS
714 N. Portage Path, 330/836-5533

Don't ask, "Who was Stan Hywet?" (although guides at this home and garden showplace frequently hear the question). The name of this magnificent Tudor Revival mansion, built for Goodyear Tire and Rubber Company cofounder Frank A. Seiberling, comes from the Middle English term for "stone quarry", after the sandstone quarry at the northern end of the 70-acre site.

Visitors to the castlelike edifice are first greeted by the motto *Non Nobis Solum* ("Not for Us Alone") carved above the entry of Stan Hywet Hall. The welcoming message is the first of several carvings that offer guests insight into the lives of the former owners.

The 65-room manor, built between 1912 and 1915, provides a glimpse of such modern conveniences of the early twentieth century as a central vacuuming system, central heating, steel-beam construction, and even an automatic card-shuffling machine. Fancy grillwork hides the modern heat registers, although 23 fireplaces can also be counted. Telephones (37 of them) link the 18 bedrooms, public rooms, and adjoining buildings.

Originally the estate spread across 3,000 acres, but now 70 acres of manicured lawns and gardens await visitors. The varied grounds include three formal gardens—the English Garden, the West Terrace, and the Japanese Garden—as well as a conservatory, a greenhouse, and waterfalls. Something wonderful is always in bloom from April through October, but the English Garden is at its best

AKRON REGION

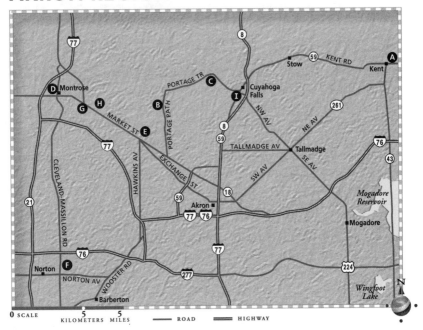

SIGHTS
- 🅐 Kent State University Museum
- 🅐 May Fourth Site and Memorial
- 🅑 Stan Hywet Hall and Gardens

FOOD
- 🅒 Cathedral Buffet
- 🅓 Ken Stewart's Grille
- 🅔 Mustard Seed Market
- 🅓 West Point Market
- 🅕 Winery at Wolf Creek

LODGING
- 🅖 Four Points by Sheraton
- 🅗 Holiday Inn Akron/Fairlawn
- 🅘 Inn at Brandywine Falls
- 🅘 Sheraton Suites

Note: Items with the same letter are located in the same area.

---

from mid-May through mid-June and again in August and September. Special seasonal events are planned each month. At Carriage House Café, you can enjoy light fare, beer, and wine indoors—and outside on the grounds during summer. The museum also has its own shop.

Details: *Daily 10–4:30; Feb–Mar Tue–Sat 10–4; Sun 1-4. Admission to mansion and gardens: $8 adults, $7 seniors, $4 children*

6–12. Admission to gardens only: $4 adults and seniors, $2 children. (1–2 hours; tour about 1 hour)

★★★ AKRON ZOOLOGICAL PARK
500 Edgewood Ave., 330/375-2525 information line 330/375-2550

This zoo experience combines learning about endangered species and picnicking in Perkins Woods with walks to meet the 300 animal, bird, and reptile residents. The Ohio Farmyard, filled with lambs, goats, cows, and such, is a child's highlight, as are annual Halloween and winter activities.

Details: *Mid-Apr–mid-Oct Mon–Sat 10–5, Sun and holidays 10–6. Some extended evening hours during summer. $7.50 adults, $6 seniors, $5 children. $1.50 parking. (2–3 hours)*

★★★ HOWER HOUSE
60 Fir Hill, University of Akron, 330/972-6909

If you do not know what the Akron Sunday School Plan is, then you need to visit this 28-room Victorian mansion on the University of Akron campus. Built in 1871 by Akron industrialist John Henry Hower, the Second Empire Italianate house features eight rooms radiating from a center hall on each floor, from the basement to the third story. The wall coverings and fireplaces painted to resemble marble are of special note, as is the unique telephone booth added in the 1920s. The Cellar Door is a six-room gift shop in the basement. A video of areas inaccessible to wheelchairs is available.

Details: *Guided tours Wed–Sat noon–3:30, Sun 1–4. Closed January and holidays. $5 adults, $4 seniors, $2 students. (1 hour)*

★★★ PERKINS STONE MANSION AND JOHN BROWN HOUSE
550 Copley Rd., 330/535-1120

Both of these home museums are Summit County Historical Society sites. The Perkins Stone Mansion, a prime example of Greek Revival architecture, tells of Akron's history and industrial growth. The permanent exhibit is mixed in with canal history. Abolitionist John Brown lived across the street from 1844 to 1854, during the time he spent in the sheep-raising business with Simon Perkins. His recently renovated home, also open for tours, concentrates on his march to Harper's Ferry and his simple lifestyle.

Details: Tours Tue–Sun 1–4. $5 adults, $4 seniors and children 12 and under. (1–2 hours)

★ GOODYEAR WORLD OF RUBBER
1144 E. Market St., 330/796-6546

Guided tours are available, but seeing this museum on your own is easy. A self-guided tour begins in a make-believe rubber-tree forest. Items made from Goodyear rubber are sold in the gift shop.

Details: Mon–Fri 9–4:30. Free. (1 hour)

FITNESS AND RECREATION

One of Ohio's most scenic spots for bicycling, hiking, cross-country skiing, and myriad nature activities is the **Cuyahoga Valley National Recreation Area**, 15610 Vaughn Rd., Brecksville, 800/433-1986. It stretches over 33,000 acres between Cleveland and Akron along the Cuyahoga River, whose name is derived from an Indian word meaning "crooked." Native Americans followed the crooked river from Lake Erie to the Ohio River, as did the Ohio & Erie Canal in later years. Outdoor enthusiasts list the **Ohio & Erie Canal Towpath Trail** among the most scenic in Ohio. Beaver dams, Brandywine Falls, and other points along the trail mark Mother Nature's diversity. Hiking and biking, cross-country skiing, nearby downhill slopes, sledding, and fishing are available. Other trails, including some horse trails and the **Buckeye Trail**, connect with the park. The **Cuyahoga Valley Scenic Railroad** in Peninsula, 216/526-5256 or 800/468-4070, offers a variety of rides through the park, including a combination that gives tired bikers a ride back to their starting point. You can hop off the train or trail near Hale Farm and Village for a leisurely stroll around the restored 1850s farm, village, and carriage museum.

Summit County Metroparks manages a wonderful park system and offers interesting seasonal programs. Maps and descriptions of 11 parks are available by calling the park office, 330/867-5511. For those more interested in watching than playing, catch the **Akron Aeros**, the Cleveland Indians' Class AA affiliate, at **Canal Stadium** in downtown Akron, 330/253-5151.

FOOD

While planning your Akron adventures, you may want to include some portable picnic fare, in which case I heartily recommend **Mustard Seed Market**, 3885 W. Market St., 330/666-7333, and **West Point Market**, 1711 W. Market St., 330/864-2151. Both of these gourmet superstores will fill

LOCAL COLOR

If you examine the Akron Hilton at Quaker Square, you will get a preview of artist Don Drumm's creative style. His massive sunbursts and fanciful creatures transformed the Quaker Oats silos here, and his public sculpture in downtown Akron reflects his international following. At the **Don Drumm Studios & Gallery**, 437 Crouse St., 330/253-6268, you will find two galleries chock-full of his sculpture, jewelry, and cookware, along with works by 500 other contemporary artists. A catalog of Drumm's distinctive pewter and cast-aluminum art is available.

your needs, no matter how plain or fancy your tastes. You can also dine at both establishments. One of the nicest spots for a picnic may be on the deck or grounds of the **Winery at Wolf Creek**, 2637 S. Cleveland–Massillon Rd., Norton, 330/666-9285. The winery is open Tuesday through Sunday year-round. Tours and tastings are available, and children are welcome.

Akron landmarks include **Tangier**, 532 W. Market St., 330/376-7171, for Mediterranean specialties; the **Diamond Grille**, 77 W. Market St., 330/253-0041, for steaks (the restaurant does not accept plastic, only cash or a business card with an address where they can send a bill); and the **Cathedral Buffet**, 2690 State Rd., Cuyahoga Falls, 330/922-0467, for an abundant home-style buffet priced very reasonably. (Note: The buffet is closed Monday.) Call the Quaker Hilton, 330/253-5970, for information about the **Trackside Grill**, 135 S. Broadway, in the Quaker Square complex, which features pizza and spaghetti, or dine in the converted barnstone cellar of the old Quaker Oats cereal factory at **Goshen's Mill Street Tavern**, 330/762-9333. You will enjoy one of the best meals in all of Ohio at **Ken Stewart's Grille**, 1970 W. Market St., 330/867-2555. The dinner menu changes every evening, but you can be assured of huge portions (live Maine lobsters weighing in at eight pounds), exciting fare, and reasonable prices.

LODGING

Akron's overnight accommodations are generally moderately priced, with some national budget chains to choose from. The **Holiday Inn Akron/**

Fairlawn, 4073 Medina Rd., 330/660-4131, boasts a chop house eatery and is accessible from I-77. Another choice in a good location for dining and shopping opportunities is the **Four Points by Sheraton**, 3150 W. Market St., 330/869-9000.

The **Sheraton Suites**, 1989 Front St., Cuyahoga Falls, 330/929-3000, offers some wheelchair-accessible suites as well as over 200 standard suites, many of which overlook the falls. The restaurant juts out over the water, so ask for a table near a window. Hikers and bikers who enjoy the Cuyahoga Valley National Recreation Area and the nearby ski area will surely enjoy a stay at the **Inn at Brandywine Falls**, 8320 Brandywine Rd., Sagamore Hills, 330/467-1812, just a short walk from the breathtaking falls. The **Akron Quaker Hilton**, 135 S. Broadway, 330/253-5970, has rooms converted from the grain-storage silos of the Quaker Oats Company, which was originally located on this site. Shops at Quaker Square are adjacent, and Inventure Place (see Sightseeing Highlights) is next door. **Radisson Hotel Akron City Centre**, 20 W. Mill St., 330/384-1500, also provides access to the university, museums, the convention center, and Quaker Square downtown.

NIGHTLIFE

The **E. J. Thomas Performing Arts Hall**, 198 Hill St., 330/972-7595, on the University of Akron campus, hosts a Broadway series, big-name entertainers, the **Akron Symphony Orchestra**, 330/535-8131, and the **Ohio Ballet**, 330/972-7900. During summer the **Cleveland Orchestra** and others perform at **Blossom Music Center**, 1145 W. Steels Corners Rd., Cuyahoga Falls, 330/920-8040. Lawn and pavilion seating are available.

Akron has many stages for live performances, including the **Porthouse Theatre Company**, 1145 W. Steels Corners Rd., Cuyahoga Falls, 330/672-2889; for tickets during summer in their open-air theater on Blossom Music Center grounds, call 800/262-9444. The **Carousel Dinner Theatre**, 1275 E. Waterloo Rd., 800/362-4100, serves up more prime rib than anyplace else in Ohio, so they say, to accompany their Broadway-type performances in the 1,133-seat dinner theater. Matinees and show-only seats are available. Try the **Coach House Theatre**, 732 W. Exchange St., 330/434-7741, and **Weathervane Community Playhouse**, 1301 Weathervane Ln., 330/836-2626, for more live theater. For lively entertainment, also check out **Hilarities Comedy Club**, 1546 State Rd., Cuyahoga Falls, 330/923-4700.

4
CANTON

Settlers came to Canton and the small communities around it in the 1830s, forming the backbone of the already-established canal system. With industrialization, Canton's population began growing. It is now the ninth-largest city in the state, with a population around 84,000.

For a few days each summer, Canton draws national attention as new Pro Football Hall of Fame inductees and a half-million fans converge for "Football's Greatest Weekend." Every nearby hotel and motel fills for the enshrinement, preseason play-off, and over a dozen other lavish events. Even spots for watching the nationally televised parade (one that rivals Macy's) are at a premium during this weekend of family activities.

The rest of the year the pace is low-key, but you'll discover a variety of interesting local attractions in the surrounding communities. Just a few blocks from the Hall of Fame, you'll find the McKinley Museum complex, which includes a children's science center, planetarium, and historical museum. Travel a little farther to enjoy a taste of the nearby Amish communities or to bite into a hamburger created from the original 1904 recipe.

A PERFECT DAY IN CANTON

With kids in tow, begin with a stroll through the Pro Football Hall of Fame. Make sure to take in the show at the Game Day Stadium and get a close-up

CANTON

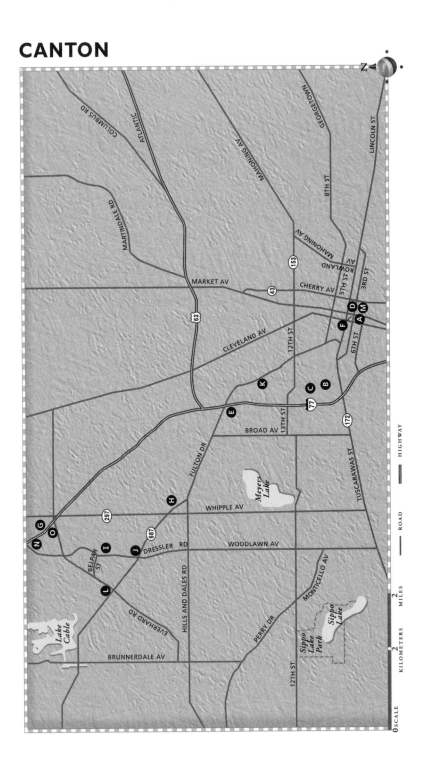

look at the array of diamond-studded Super Bowl rings. Next, stop at McKinley Museum's Discover World, a science center especially suited for the younger set. Climb all 108 steps of the McKinley National Monument, then walk the one-mile cushioned walking loop that encircles the adjacent portion of the city's park system. Pack a picnic lunch during the warm seasons. During winter, bring your ice skates for wonderful outdoor skating at Monument or Stadium Park.

SIGHTSEEING HIGHLIGHTS

★★★★ MASSILLON MUSEUM
121 Lincoln Way E, Massillon, 330/833-4061
One of the state's tucked-away treasures lies behind the facade of a renovated 1931 art deco building on the historic Lincoln Highway. The museum of contemporary art's first-floor gallery features frequently changing exhibits from its collection—over 50,000 works representing a cross-section of local and Native American culture. The artwork is off-limits to fingers, but visitors can open modernistic display cases to reveal additional pieces. Photography, textiles, and local glass are featured, as is a permanent display of the miniature Immel Circus, a 100-square-foot hand-carved replica of a complete circus. Some 2,620 pieces make up the exhibit. A museum café features luncheon fare, and the museum shop offers one-of-a-kind gift items.
Details: Tue–Sat 9:30–5, Sun 2–5. Free. (1–2 hours)

★★★★ MCKINLEY MUSEUM
800 McKinley Monument Dr. NW, 330/455-7043

SIGHTS	FOOD	LODGING
Ⓐ Canton Classic Car Museum	**Ⓕ** Bender's Tavern	**Ⓛ** Best Suites of America
Ⓑ McKinley Museum	**Ⓖ** Cité Grille	**Ⓜ** Canton Hilton
Ⓒ McKinley National Monument	**Ⓗ** Grinders Above and Beyond	**Ⓝ** Fourpoints Hotel Sheraton
Ⓓ National First Ladies' Library	**Ⓘ** Papa Bear's Italian Restaurant	**Ⓞ** Residence Inn by Marriott
Ⓔ Pro Football Hall of Fame	**Ⓙ** Ricky Ly's Chinese Gourmet	
	Ⓚ Taggart's	

Located at the edge of McKinley Park, this educational complex includes the McKinley National Monument; the McKinley Museum of History, Science and Industry; the Hoover-Price Planetarium; and Discover World, a hands-on interactive science center. There, a life-size allosaurus teaches youngsters how the large dinosaurs moved about. Other hands-on activities fill the Natural History Island, the Ecology Island, and Spacestation Earth. Exhibits and activities are just the right height for preschoolers and elementary school children. The Hoover Price Planetarium hosts ongoing and seasonal programs such as the Season of Light, Star of Bethlehem, and Autumn Skies. (Be aware that children under five are not admitted to programs.) The world's largest collection of William McKinley memorabilia is displayed in the McKinley Room, and a walk through the Street of Shops transports passersby to the 1800s before they leave.

Details: Mon–Sat 9–5, Sun noon–5, open until 6 in summer. $6 adults, $5 seniors, $4 ages 3–18. (2 hours)

★★★★ **MCKINLEY NATIONAL MONUMENT**
800 McKinley Monument Dr. NW, 330/455-7043
Owned by the Stark County Historical Society, this memorial to the 25th president of the United States was erected in the city the assassinated president called home. Canton is where he met his wife, practiced law, and raised his family. Climb 108 steps to reach the top of the dome-shaped monument surrounded by city parkland.

Details: Mon–Sat 9–5, Sun noon–5; open until 6 June–Aug. Free. (1 hour)

★★★★ **PRO FOOTBALL HALL OF FAME**
2121 George Halas Dr. NW, 330/456-8207
A seven-foot statue of Jim Thorpe, the Native American who was pro football's first big-name star, greets visitors as they enter the domed structure. The informative and historical journey through 100 years of professional football includes the early days when Thorpe played for the Canton Bulldogs. The self-guided tour curves into the *Pro Football Today* exhibit, where you'll see autographs of the Jacksonville Jaguars' first draft class and shiny helmets from all the teams. The original enshrinement gallery has grown into two large halls that honor all 199 Pro Football Hall of Fame inductees and display their personal mementos. You can see Y. A. Tittle's cracked helmet and a license plate, pipes, and warm-ups formerly belonging to

OHIO'S STATE SWEET

Ohioans enjoy a sweet confection—a rich peanut butter and chocolate candy shaped like a buckeye. Although created in home kitchens and candy shops around the state, the most perfectly shaped ones are professionally produced at **Harry London Candies**, 5353 Lauby Rd., North Canton, 800/321-0444. They run $12.95 per pound or 25 cents each. Factory tours are provided Monday through Saturday from 9 to 4 and Sunday from noon to 3:30. Admission is $2 for adults and $1 for ages 6 to 18.

other Hall-of-Famers. One of the most glittery displays is the Super Bowl Rings showcase. The diamonds are impressive—and the huge ring sizes of these gem-studded beauties are equally awesome.

The museum highlight takes place behind doors marked "Positively No Admittance." That's where, in *Championship Chase*, the museum's feature film attraction, state-of-the-art Panavision and Surround- Sound go behind the scenes at the Game Day Stadium for training camp followed by a complete season of action before a Super Bowl sampling.

Details: *Memorial Day–Labor Day daily 9–8; rest of year daily 9–5. $10 adults, $6.50 seniors, $5 ages 6–14. $25 family (parents and all dependent children). The Hall of Fame Festival usually occurs the last weekend in July. Call for festival information, assistance with accommodations, and tickets for events, 800/533-4302. (2 hours)*

★★★ CANTON CLASSIC CAR MUSEUM
555 Market Ave. S, 330/455-3603

This museum, where over 40 models from 1904 through 1981 are tucked between an eclectic collection of nostalgia items, fashions, and antiques, ranks among the area's highlights. Among the relics is the 1937 Studebaker "Bandit Car." It was purchased by the Canton Police Department to retaliate against mobsters and has gun ports in the windows, bulletproof tires, and trunk and rear-seat arsenals.

Details: *Daily 10–5. $5 adults, $3 seniors, $2.50 ages 6–17. (1–2 hours)*

SIDE TRIP: ZOAR

Enjoying a good German meal might be one reason for a visit to Zoar—about 20 minutes south of Canton, three miles southeast of Exit 93 off I-77 on OH 212. However, you should also spend some time walking through the community to learn about the unusual lifestyle of the German separatists who developed a communal settlement here in 1817.

Within a 12-block historic district, 10 buildings contain living history exhibits managed by the Ohio Historical Society, 800/262-6195. Demonstrations include German culinary practices around the "kettle-oven," a brick firebox with a cast-iron top. Interpreters are stationed in four of the buildings. Guided tours of the other restorations and the community garden are available. Allow two to three hours for your visit; tours take place on weekends during April, May, September, and October, and Wednesday through Sunday from Memorial Day through Labor Day. Admission is $5 for adults and $1.25 for children.

Merchants throughout the village offer shoppers an array of gifts, including primitive furnishings, candles crafted in Zoar, and antiques and collectibles. The Zoar Tavern and Inn, 1 Main St., 888/874-2170, built in 1831, is a good choice for German cuisine as well as enjoyable American fare. Spaetzle and cabbage accompany many of the German schnitzels and sausages, and bread pudding tops the list of homemade desserts. Overnight guests can choose from five small yet quaint guest rooms, each with a private bath, ranging from $70 to $95 per night.

About a half-dozen B&Bs are in the tiny village, each with Zoar ambiance. One particularly unique spot is the **Cowger House #9**, 197 Fourth St., 330/874-3542, owned by onetime village mayor Ed Cowger and his wife, Mary. They also serve candlelight dinners by reservation in their 1817 log cabin. Dinners cost around $25 and are available to the public by reservation. Guests can opt for lodging in their 1833 post-and-beam home or their Amish Oak Cottage, the most modern of the accommodations. Rates range from $70 to $159 and include a full country breakfast. Contact the Tuscarawas County Convention and Visitors Bureau, 800/527-3387, for additional B&B recommendations and assistance.

★★★ HARTVILLE
North of Canton on OH 43

At the turn of the century, the first Amish settlers moved into this village north of Canton. Now, less than a half hour's drive on OH 43 from Canton, you can sample Amish-style cooking, pick up bargains at the **Hartville Flea Market** on OH 619 and Market St., and purchase produce at stands along Swamp Road, where muck farming in the region's rich, black soil is still much the same as it was in the late 1800s. Browsing unique shops, antiquing, and stopping for homemade candy and ice cream round out the activities. While in Hartville, visit the **Pantry Restaurant**, 101 N. Prospect St., 330/877-9661. It was originally the Hartville Hotel, a station along Ohio's Underground Railroad.

Details: Contact the Lake Township Chamber of Commerce, 330/877-5500, or the Canton/Stark County Convention and Visitors Bureau, 330/454-1439 or 800/533-4302. (2–4 hours)

★★★ NATIONAL FIRST LADIES' LIBRARY
331 Market Ave. S, 330/452-0876, www.firstladies.org

Let a docent, attired as one of the nation's first ladies, take you on a tour through this elegant Victorian restoration of Ida Saxton McKinley's home. Rooms are filled with artifacts of William McKinley, 25th president of the United States, and his spouse. The significance of the newly established first ladies' library and its computerized databases are explained.

Details: Reservations required for tours Wed, Sat 10–2. $5 adults, $4 seniors and students. (1–2 hours)

FITNESS AND RECREATION

Attention golfers: Bring your clubs when visiting Canton—it's touted as the golf capital of Ohio because it boasts more than 40 golf courses in a 50-mile radius. A 32-page guide that lists accommodations and golfing packages, as well as detailed information about specific courses, is available by calling the Canton/Stark County Convention and Visitors Bureau, 800/552-6051.

Hikers and walkers will enjoy the city's park system, which includes a one-mile, soft-surface fitness path at **Stadium Park**. Interpretive hiking trails provide natural outdoor scenery and exercise for visitors at **Quail Hollow State Park**, 13340 Congress Lake Ave., Hartville, 330/877-6652. Cross-country skiers can enjoy 10 miles of trails during winter, and a four-mile bridle trail is

CANTON REGION

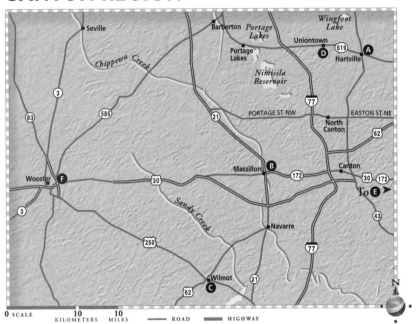

SIGHTS

Ⓐ Hartville
Ⓑ Massillon Museum

FOOD

Ⓒ Amish Door
    Restaurant and Village

FOOD (continued)

Ⓑ Copper's Bar and
    Grille
Ⓐ Hartville Kitchen
Ⓓ Menches Brothers
Ⓔ Spread Eagle Tavern
    & Inn
Ⓕ Wooster Inn

LODGING

Ⓒ Hasseman House Inn
Ⓒ Inn at Amish Door
Ⓔ Overholt House B & B
Ⓕ Wooster Inn

Note: Items with the same letter are located in the same area.

---

available for daytime use. The **Buckeye Trail** passes through Tuscarawas County near **Atwood Lake and Park**, 330/343-6780, between New Cumberland and Dellroy. Atwood also offers swimming, boating, fishing, camping, hunting, and seven miles of trails.

For a leisurely walk or ride amid interesting scenery, hop on the towpath of the Ohio & Erie Canal, especially around Lock 4 in Canal Fulton. Part of the

87-mile Heritage Corridor linking Cleveland to Zoar, this portion is suitable for jogging, biking, and horseback riding. Canoe trips along the Tuscarawas River in Canal Fulton leave from Indiana Bob's Indian River Canoe, 215 Market St. W, Canal Fulton, 800/CANOE-4-YOU, or you can entertain the kids at **Sluggers & Putters Family Fun Center and Sports Park**, 333 Lafayette Rd., Canal Fulton, 330/854-6999. Miniature golf, bumper boats, and batting cages are among the options.

FOOD

Most of the national chains are lined up door-to-door on the streets encircling Belden Village Shopping Mall and surrounding strip shopping centers off I-77 north of town. However, a variety of local establishments offer more unique recipes for family dining. **Papa Bear's Italian Restaurant**, 4990 Dressler Rd. NW, 330/493-0090, is a family-owned spot—transplanted Cantonians get their "pizza fix" here when they return for a visit. Considered the area's oldest restaurant, dating from 1902, **Bender's Tavern**, touted for its seafood and atmosphere, is a downtown landmark located at Second and Courts Sts., 330/453-8424. **Taggart's**, 1401 Fulton Rd., 330/452-6844, another Canton landmark (since 1926), has changed ownership through the years but still serves the same rich homemade ice cream and sauces, soups, and salad dressings. Save room for a Bittner Special, three-fourths of a pound of homemade vanilla ice cream laced with homemade chocolate sauce and sprinkled with roasted pecans (a large is $2.95, and the slightly smaller size is $2.40).

Drive north to Uniontown to sample hamburgers the way they were invented by the **Menches Brothers** in 1885. Today's Menches brothers are the great-grandchildren, but they serve up burgers from the vintage recipe—as well as homemade bread and the waffle cones invented by their forefathers at the 1904 St. Louis World's Fair—in a modern establishment at 3700 Massillon Rd., Uniontown, 330/896-2288. The **Hartville Kitchen**, 1015 Edison St. NW, Hartville, 330/877-9353, dishes out hearty portions of Amish-style pot roast, chicken, mashed potatoes, and dressing, along with a long list of homemade pies and other dishes. The Kitchen's salad dressings are sold in grocery stores throughout the state. (Note: The restaurant is closed on Wednesday and Sunday.)

South of Canton you can sample more Amish fare at the **Amish Door Restaurant and Village**, 1210 Winesburg St., Wilmot, 330/359-5464, billed as the "Gateway to the Amish Country." Its well-stocked shop features apple butter and peanut-butter whip (a peanut butter, maple, and marshmallow topping traditionally served at Amish weddings). The restaurant is closed on Sunday and on the Amish holiday of Old Christmas in early January.

East of Canton, in the small town of Hanoverton, you'll be pleasantly surprised when you discover the **Spread Eagle Tavern & Inn**, 10150 Plymouth St., 330/223-1583. Restored to the days when it served as a stop along the canal, the inn has fireplaces and nuances of earlier days that meld with an interesting American menu, making this out-of-the-way restaurant on a quiet brick road well worth the drive.

Stop at **Grinders Above and Beyond**, 3114 Whipple Ave., Canton, 330/477-5411 (and other nearby locations in Massillon, Minerva, Alliance, North Canton, and Orrville), for New England–style sandwiches, homemade soups, and desserts. Try **Copper's Bar and Grille**, 31 First St. SW, Massillon, 330/832-2232, a casual, moderately priced local spot with a varied menu, when you're near the Massillon Museum. **Ricky Ly's Chinese Gourmet**, 4696 Dressler Rd. NW, Canton, 330/492-5905, offers Mandarin, Szechuan, and Thai entrées in a pleasant atmosphere, and you'll find innovative items on the contemporary American menu at **Cité Grille**, 6041 Whipple Ave., North Canton, 330/494-6758. In Wooster, dining possibilities include the **Wooster Inn** (see Lodging); try the Ohio farm-raised trout.

LODGING

Local accommodations in Canton include many of the popular national chains—**Best Suites of America**, 4914 Everhard Rd., 800/237-8466 or 330/499-1011; the recently renovated **Fourpoints Hotel Sheraton**, 4375 Metro Circle NW, 330/494-6494 or 800/325-3535; and the **Canton Hilton,** 320 Market Avenue S, 330/454-5000 or 800/445-8667. The **Residence Inn by Marriott**, 5280 Broadmoor Circle NW, near Belden Village, 330/493-0004, includes complimentary breakfast and evening social hour in their reasonable rates for suites.

The **Inn at Amish Door**, 1210 Winesburg Rd., Wilmot, 888/AMISH-DOOR, uses locally made, handcrafted furniture in its 50 rooms, some of which are suites, and features Amish baked goods for breakfast, which can be enjoyed outside on broad porches. A swimming pool and other modern amenities enhance the Amish-style ambiance. Just beyond this inn is the **Hasseman House Inn**, 925 U.S. 62, Wilmot, 330/359-7904. Guests at this Victorian inn are served their complimentary breakfast at the Amish Door Restaurant. **Wooster Inn**, 801 E. Wayne Ave., Wooster, 330/264-2341, on the College of Wooster campus, is within an easy walk of the Freedlander Theatre and offers a full-service dining room featuring seasonal favorites. The historic **Overholt House B&B**, 1473 Beall Ave., Wooster, 800/992-0643, is well known for its "flying staircase." The innkeepers furnish one of the common rooms as a Victorian Christmas parlor year-round. Contact the Wayne County Convention & Visitors Bureau, 800/36-AMISH, for more B&B suggestions in the Wooster area.

NIGHTLIFE

Canton's performing and fine arts are housed in one modern complex at the **Canton Civic Center**, 1001 Market Ave. N. There you'll find a full schedule of events for the **Canton Ballet**, 330/455-7220; the **Canton Museum of Art**, 330/453-7666; the **Players Guild** for community theater, 330/453-7619; and the **Canton Civic Opera**, 330/455-1000; along with the ticket office for the **Canton Symphony Orchestra**, 330/452-2094.

Summer matinee and evening productions of the **Ohio Light Opera**, the resident professional company of the College of Wooster, are held at the college's **Freedlander Theatre**. Its $26 tickets can be ordered at the box office, 330/263-2345. The epic outdoor drama *Trumpet in the Land* portrays the Gnadenhutten Massacre of 1782, which led to the slaying of 96 neutral Christian Indians by American militia. Other performances, including *The White Savage*, are also held in the 1,400-seat **Schoenbrunn Amphitheater**, 330/339-1132. Reserved tickets are $13 for adults and $6 for children. The dramas begin at 8:30 nightly, except Sunday, from mid-June through August.

5
AMISH COUNTRY

Each year tourists crowd the narrow roads leading to "Amish country"—
Ohio's northeastern counties of Holmes, Wayne, and Tuscarawas, home to
the world's largest community of "plain people."

Hilly roads leading to Berlin, the heart of the area, provide the pictorial
preface for the rest of your visit. You'll pass Amish schools, with dozens of
youngsters enjoying a recess together outdoors. Their attire, like that of their
Amish teachers, hasn't changed in the 100 years since their forefathers settled here to escape religious persecution in Europe.

As you travel along, carefully sharing the asphalt with horse-drawn buggies, scenic views include farmers plowing the fields behind their draft horses
and clotheslines carefully pinned with stark attire. Occasionally, a couple will
unhitch the horse from their buggy at a rural intersection and offer fresh bakery items for sale. Straight painted fences, farm animals, and cemeteries complete the pastoral scene.

When you reach Berlin, you'll likely notice some tourist congestion.
Somehow, though, everybody finds room, and a day of enjoying hearty Amish
cooking and baking, shopping for handmade crafts, and soaking up the atmosphere begins.

Start at the Mennonite Information Center near Berlin at 5798 County
Road 77. There you'll find "Behalt," a 265-foot cyclorama illustrating the history of the Amish and Mennonites, from their 1525 Anabaptist roots in

AMISH COUNTRY

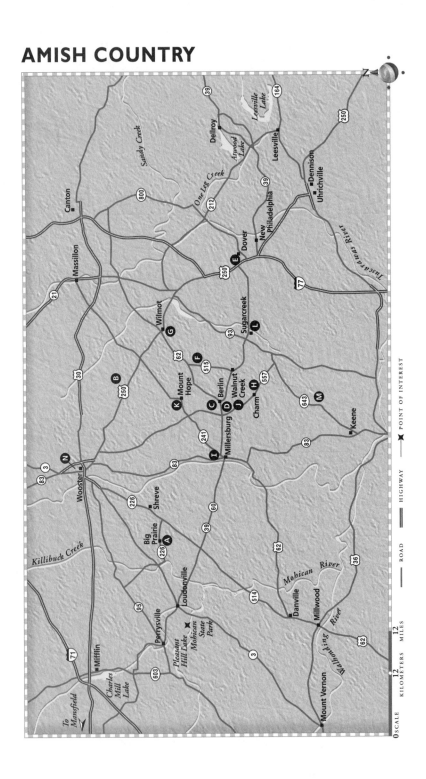

Zurich, Switzerland, to their present-day lifestyle. I suggest that you do some reading before your trip, (see Recommended Reading page 14) then visit an Amish farm and take a back-roads tour once you arrive.

A PERFECT DAY IN AMISH COUNTRY

To enjoy the area's relaxing and peaceful qualities, spend the night in one of the many communities. The bed-and-breakfasts and larger inns go to extra lengths to add Amish touches while retaining the modern amenities tourists enjoy. Make sure to get off the main state routes and drive through the small crossroads villages for a more authentic, less crowded experience. Stop in Mt. Hope for lunch at Mrs. Yoder's Kitchen, and continue on to Winesburg to visit local furniture and quilt shops. Take in one of the weekly auctions, the public marketplace for the Amish. After you've enjoyed enough heavy, Amish-style cooking, opt for dinner (if not an overnight stay) at the Inn at Honey Run, where the fresh fare is often grown on the premises and the surroundings are delightfully quiet and secluded.

SIGHTSEEING HIGHLIGHTS

★★★★ SCHROCK'S AMISH FARM & HOME
1 mile east of Berlin on OH 39, 330/893-3232

Tours through a 150-year-old home provide a glimpse into the

SIGHTS
- Ⓐ Holmes County Pottery
- Ⓑ Kidron-Sonnenberg Heritage Center
- Ⓒ Mennonite Information Center
- Ⓓ Shrock's Amish Farm & Home
- Ⓔ Warther Carvings and Gardens
- Ⓕ Yoder's Amish Home

FOOD
- Ⓖ Amish Door Restaurant and Village
- Ⓓ Boyd and Wurthmann Restaurant
- Ⓓ Der Bake Oven
- Ⓐ Der Dutchman
- Ⓓ Dutch Harvest Restaurant
- Ⓗ Homestead Restaurant
- Ⓘ Inn at Honey Run
- Ⓙ Miller's Bakery
- Ⓚ Mrs. Yoder's Kitchen
- Ⓛ Swiss Hat

LODGING
- Ⓖ 1881 Antique Barn
- Ⓘ Bigham House
- Ⓐ Carlisle Village Inn of Walnut Creek
- Ⓗ Charm Countryview Inn B&B
- Ⓖ Hasseman House B & B
- Ⓖ Inn at the Amish Door
- Ⓘ Inn at Honey Run
- Ⓐ Oak Ridge
- Ⓝ Overholt House B&B
- Ⓘ Swan Lake Cottage
- Ⓝ Wooster Inn

Note: Items with the same letter are located in the same area.

SUNDAYS IN AMISH COUNTRY

Along with the rural ambiance and pristine scenery of Amish country come the hazards of sharing the road with Amish buggies and slow-moving farm machinery. Ohio statistics point to more than 120 buggy accidents a year, and over half of Ohio's traffic fatalities occur on country roads. Please remember that our rural roads are less easily maneuvered than city streets and that the normal speed for horse-drawn carriages is five to eight miles per hour. Look for the orange caution symbol posted on Amish buggies, then slow down, keep a safe distance, and take a relaxing drive through the countryside.

---

lifestyle of the Amish. You'll learn about Amish dress, chores, and religious customs. The complex also houses a furniture shop and a quilt shop; bakery items are for sale in the home's kitchen. After a tour, short buggy rides around the property provide another opportunity for guests to experience the simple lifestyle found among the Amish and Mennonites.

Details: Mon–Fri 10–5, Sat 10–6, closed Sun. $3 house tour, $3 buggy ride. (1–2 hours)

★★★★ **WARTHER CARVINGS AND GARDENS**
331 Karl Rd., Dover, 330/343-7513
The arts of wood carving and knife making have been handed down from one generation to the next in the Warther family. The unique accomplishments of the eldest, Ernest, are displayed in the museum, which is set amid acres of Swiss gardens that were planted by his wife. Her collection of some 73,000 varieties of buttons is also open to the public. His intricate work includes an extensive collection of railroad models. Ernest's grandson, David Warther, carries on the carving craft in his own shop on Old Route 39 in Sugarcreek, 330/852-3455.

Details: Daily 9–5 except Christmas, New Year's Day, Easter, and Thanksgiving. The last tour begins at 4. $7 adults, $3 ages 6–17. (2 hours)

★★★★ YODER'S AMISH HOME

6050 State Rt. 515 between Trail and Walnut Creek, Millersburg, 330/893-2541

Enjoy a guided tour of an Amish farm, including the family kitchen (and bakery, where you can purchase goodies) and living and sleeping rooms, before ending with buggy rides and a visit to the petting barn. Part of the tour takes visitors through an 1800s Dawdy home, where the grandparents live. The main house is typical of current Amish lifestyle. In the fall, apple-butter stirring and old-fashioned butchering (including stuffing sausage and rendering lard) are among the activities you can view.

Details: Tours mid-Apr–Oct Mon–Sat, Memorial Day, July 4, Labor Day 10–5 tours. $3.50 adults, $2 children 12 and under. Buggy rides $2.50 adults, $2 children. (1–2 hours)

★★★ HOLMES COUNTY POTTERY

8500 County Rd. 373, Big Prairie, 330/496-2406

This studio is not owned by Amish farmers, nor is it on the beaten path of usual tourist attractions. However, it is well worth a stop if you like pottery and would like to see the largest wood-burning kiln in the state. Potter Cary Hulin and his wife, Elaine, settled in Holmes County for many of the same reasons people come to visit: the pastoral setting and the quiet lifestyle. They found soil rich in clay and Amish neighbors eager to assist in firing up the gigantic bank kiln each season. Hulin spends several months producing his wares, then stacks some two and a half tons of clay objects in the kiln after Amish draft horses deliver wood by the wagonload for fuel. The selection in Hulin's shop is best soon after one of those events.

Details: Mon–Sat 9–5, except Wed noon–5. Open houses are usually held after each firing. (1 hour)

★★ KIDRON-SONNENBERG HERITAGE CENTER

13153 Emerson Rd., Kidron, 330/857-9111

Here is another spot to learn about the history and ways of the Mennonite community. Furniture, Bibles and prayer books, and the crafts and textiles of early settlers are displayed. An extensive genealogy library is housed upstairs, along with exhibits by local artisans. The modern museum building is located across the street from Lehman's (see Shopping, below) and the livestock auction.

Less than an hour's drive from the Amish counties is the city of Mansfield, where a host of different activities await. Pick sights from my list of "must-sees" for an enjoyable day.

More than 40,000 tulips arranged in different patterns each season welcome spring at **Kingwood Center**, 900 Park Ave., 419/522-0211. Later in the year, thousands more annuals brighten some 47 acres, while lilies, roses, and other flowers invite you to sit for a spell on one of the many benches. You can also tour the mansion and greenhouses of early industrialist Charles King and walk the nature trails.

Downtown, in the Carrousel District, music from the band organ at the **Richland Carrousel Park**, corner of Fourth and Main Sts., 419/522-4223, wafts through streets during good weather. After a ride or two on the 1930s hand-carved merry-go-round, you can browse the restored area, where you'll find a bookstore, gallery, and gifts, and stopping spots for ice cream, coffee, lunch, and cigars.

Touring the castle-like **Ohio State Reformatory**, 100 Reformatory Rd., 419/522-2644, built in 1886 and used for nearly a century, takes visitors to the cell blocks, guard tower, and the "hole" made famous by many popular films, including Shawshank Redemption and Air Force One. Tours are $5 for 90 minutes, Sunday from 1 to 4. Proceeds benefit the Mansfield Reformatory Preservation Society. Children under seven and pregnant women cannot tour because of the peeling lead-based paint. Reservations are recommended.

The **Mansfield Art Center**, 700 Marion Ave., 419/756-1700, is an award-winning contemporary structure with an ongoing schedule of invitational, juried, and themed exhibitions. (Tuesday through Saturday 11 to 5, Sunday noon to 5, free.) **Oak Hill Cottage**, 300 Springmill St., 419/524-1765, an 1847 Gothic structure with seven gables and fireplaces and five double

Details: June–Sept Tue, Thu, Sat 11–3. Oct–May Thu, Sun 11–3; Free, but donation recommended: $4 adults, $2 students. (1 hour)

★★ **MENNONITE INFORMATION CENTER**
5798 County Rd. 77, Berlin, 330/893-3192
A 30-minute guided tour accompanies a walk past "Behalt," a 265-

chimneys, houses original period furnishings. (April through December Sunday 2 to 5; tours $5 for adults and $1 for children.)

A trip to this area would not be complete without visiting **Malabar Farm State Park**, 4050 Bromfield Rd., Lucas, 419/892-2784, and one of the state's most scenic spots, **Mohican State Park**, 3116 OH 3, Loudonville, 419/994-5125. Tours of the 32-room **Big House** at Malabar, built by Ohio author and conservationist Louis Bromfield, highlight the Pulitzer Prize winner's life and the fact that his friends Humphrey Bogart and Lauren Bacall were married here. The grounds include a working farm with wagon rides and seasonal events. Admission to the Big House is $3 for adults and $1 for children 6 to 18. Wagon rides are $1 for adults; children under 12 ride for free. Hours vary with the season.

If you follow a small sign marked "Mt. Jeez Overlook" on Pleasant Valley Road, midway between OH 603 and Bromfield Road, you can capture a view of the whole area and utter "Jeez!" for yourself. Mohican State Park combines a gorge and recess cave, waterfalls, a scenic bridge, and a river with camping, hiking, canoeing, and picnicking. An overnight lodge and camping facilities are available. The drive and park are especially beautiful during fall, when you can view the colorful foliage.

Area B&Bs include the **White Fence Inn**, 8842 Denman Rd., Lexington, 419/884-2356; **Heartland Country Resort and Riding Stables**, 2994 Township Rd. 190, Fredericktown, 800/230-7030; the **Blackfork Inn**, 303 N. Water St., Loudonville, 419/994-3252; **Winfield B&B**, 1568 OH 60, Ashland, 419/281-5587; **Angel Woods Hideaway**, 1983 Pleasant Valley Rd., 419/892-2929; and **Hide Away B&B**, 1601 OH 4, Bucyrus, 800/570-8233.

If you haven't had your fill, stop at **Der Dutchman Restaurant**, 419/886-7070, at 720 OH 97 and I-71. Remember: It is closed on Sunday.

foot cyclorama illustrating the history of the Amish and Mennonites, from their Swiss Anabaptist roots to the present day in rural Ohio. Along with a 15-minute video, the tour prepares visitors for their trip to Holmes County. A bookstore and gift shop are also on-site.

Details: Mon–Thu 9–5, Fri–Sat 9–8. $5.50 adults, $2.50 children 6–12. (1 hour)

© Marcia Schonberg

FITNESS AND RECREATION

A boardwalk takes you through the old-growth oak and hickory forest at **Johnson Woods State Nature Preserve**, four miles north of Orrville, off OH 57 on Fox Lake Rd. It is a good place to enjoy spring wildflowers, too.

Trails lead to a recess cave, gorge, and waterfalls at **Mohican State Park**, 3116 OH 3, Loudonville, 419/994-5125, and throughout the rolling farmland at **Malabar Farm State Park**, 4050 Bromfield Rd., Lucas, 419/892-2784. Bridle trails are found in the **Mohican State Forest**, adjacent to the park.

Canoe liveries dot the shore along the Mohican River and the Clearfork leading into it. The river can get crowded, so if you can canoe during the week—or opt for one of the special moonlight trips—your trip may be more relaxing. Try Pleasant Hill Canoe Livery, 914 OH 39, Perrysville, 800/442-2663, or Mohican Canoe Livery, 3045 OH 3 S, 800/MO-CANOE.

If you would like to fish where the catches are practically guaranteed, bring your pole (or borrow one from the owners) and head to the **Trout Ranch**, Township Rd. 457 off OH 3, Loudonville, 419/994-4605. The cold, spring-fed lake is full of trout just the right size for dinner—especially nice if you're camping nearby. The ranch is open Wednesday through Friday from noon to 7 and Saturday, Sunday, and holiday Mondays from 10 to 7. The cost is $3 per fish.

The **Richland B & O Bike Trail**, a paved, 18.4-mile multipurpose system, runs between Mansfield and Butler and is open year-round. For a map of parking and bike accesses, call the **Gorman Nature Center**, 419/884-3764. The nature center provides additional walking trails, picnic shelters, and natural experiences with special programming and events. Dogs are permitted on leashes. The **Holmes County Trail** is a Rails-to-Trails multiuse project in progress. Eventually a 29-mile path will cross Holmes county; but for now, take the five-and-a-half-mile leg along crushed limestone, sharing the stretch with Amish buggies, from Holmesville to Millersburg, and stop for ice cream or a sandwich at Skip's Trail Depot Stop at the trail head, where the parking lot offers a hitching post for Amish customers.

During the racing season, **Mid-Ohio Sports Car Course** in Lexington, 419/884-4000 or 800/MID-OHIO for tickets, hosts six national motor-sport events.

FOOD

Wayne, Holmes, and Tuscarawas Counties have more to offer than Amish-style cooking—mashed potatoes, noodles, pot roast, and chicken topped off with peanut-butter pie. But you may regret it if you don't indulge in at least one of these Amish feasts. If you're lucky enough to be visiting during one of the quilt auctions, flea markets, or livestock sales in Mount Hope (Wednesday), Farmerstown (Tuesday), Kidron (Thursday), or Sugarcreek (Monday and Friday), you may be in for an authentic taste treat. After looking over the sale items, you can indulge with the local Amish and Mennonite families and stand in line for fresh-roasted chicken with all the trimmings.

Amish patrons also frequent the tiny **Boyd and Wurthmann Restaurant**, 330/893-3287, a local landmark in Berlin on Main Street. It opens for breakfast at 6 and features home-style cooking and homemade desserts. For other bakery items, pies especially, **Der Bake Oven** has two locations, one on Main Street in Berlin, 330/893-3365, the other at County Roads 207 and 77 north of Berlin, 330/893-2114. If you can find **Miller's Bakery**, off OH 557 at 4280 Township Rd. 356, Millersburg, 330/893-3002, you won't be disappointed. Not only does it have a great assortment of baked goods, but the cheese tarts are unique; I haven't seen them anywhere else.

Another landmark is the **Homestead Restaurant** in Charm on OH 557, 330/893-2717. At **Der Dutchman**, on OH 515 in Walnut Creek, 330/893-2981, patrons wait in line or rock in the chairs on the wide, sweeping porch out front before getting a table. Six other locations around the state provide similar hearty and friendly Amish kitchen cooking and decor. The **Dutch Harvest Restaurant**, one mile west of Berlin at OH 39 and OH 62, 330/893-3333, serves up Amish-style fare; leave room for their original "Bag Apple Pie." **Mrs. Yoder's Kitchen**, 8101 OH 241, Mt. Hope, 330/674-0922, is also popular, as is the **Amish Door Restaurant and Village**, 1210 Winesburg St., Wilmot, 330/359-5464 (and a new location, 6655 E. Lincolnway [U.S. 30], Wooster, 330/263-0547). The **Swiss Hat**, 108 E. Main St., Sugarcreek, 330/852-2821, is one of the few area restaurants open on Sunday.

For a special lunch or dinner, make reservations at the **Inn at Honey Run**, 6920 County Rd. 203, Millersburg, 800/468-6639. You'll find fresh-cut flowers grown on the premises and a refreshing decor that blends Amish and Shaker styles.

LODGING

Staying overnight in one of the area's many inns or B&Bs provides a chance for leisurely enjoyment of the Amish nuances that many innkeepers incorporate into their lodgings. One of the newest and most child-friendly establishments is the **Oak Ridge Inn**, 4845 Milo Dr., Walnut Creek, 800/723-6300. Its large rooms can easily accommodate families traveling with children. Although cribs are currently unavailable, children under 12 stay free. Rates are $85 to $125,

SUNDAYS IN AMISH COUNTRY

Generally, B&Bs in Amish areas serve hearty breakfasts during the week but offer continental fare on Sunday mornings, when Amish helpers aren't working. When planning your trip, keep in mind that most shops and restaurants are closed on Sunday.

If you're visiting on the weekend, take in the Amish attractions on Saturday and stop at a few of the following sites, Amish and otherwise, that remain open on Sunday: **Amish Oak Furniture**, 268 W. Main St., Loudonville, 800/686-8855; **Killbuck Valley Museum**, Front St., Killbuck, 330/377-4572; **Victorian House Museum**, 484 Wooster Rd., Millersburg, 330/674-0022; **Winesburg Collectibles**, U.S. 62, Winesburg, 330/359-5343; **Pine Tree Barn & Farms**, north of Shreve on SR 226, 330/264-1014; **Guggisberg Cheese**, OH 557 near Charm, 330/893-2500; **Skip's Trail Depot Stop**, 7501 OH 83, 330/279-2200; **Swiss Hat Restaurant**, 108 E. Main St., Sugarcreek, 330/852-2821; **Warthers Carvings and Gardens**, 331 Karl Ave., Dover, 330/343-7513; **J. E. Reeves Victorian Home & Carriage House Museum**, 325 E. Iron Ave., Dover, 800/815-2794; **Wayne County Historical Society**, 546 E. Bowman St., Wooster, 330/264-8856; and many of the shops and restaurants in Wooster.

including a continental breakfast and complimentary snacks. Another new establishment, **Inn at the Amish Door**, 1210 Winesburg St., Wilmot, 888/AMISH-DOOR, offers Amish scenery, buggy rides, and breakfast, along with an indoor pool and fax and copy services. A gift shop, an Amish bulk-food pantry, and a shop with handmade wooden toys are also located within the complex. The **1881 Antique Barn**, 330/359-7957, and the four guest rooms at **Hasseman House B&B**, 330/359-7904, just down the road, offer more options.

Beautiful scenery, no matter what the season, is in store for guests at **Charm Countryview Inn B&B**, OH 557 east of Charm, 330/893-3003, where the views include Amish farmlands and rolling countryside. If you're looking for a quiet spot, try **Swan Lake Cottage**, 330/674-7029, a hidden getaway tucked behind an Amish farm a few miles west of Millersburg. The cottage accommodates four people and overlooks a lake. The **Carlisle Village Inn of Walnut Creek**, OH 515, Walnut Creek, 330/893-3636, next to Der Dutchman Restaurant, offers off-season specials and moderate prices other times on their 52 smoke-free rooms, some of which are wheelchair accessible.

The **Inn at Honey Run**, 6920 County Road 203, Millersburg, 800/468-6639, an award-winning contemporary inn amid orchards and hiking trails, is a popular spot for those celebrating a special occasion or just wanting to enjoy nature (bird feeders are in view of every window). Wheelchair-accessible rooms are available. Rates run $65–$240 depending upon season and room type, including breakfast. The **Bigham House**, 151 S. Washington St., Millersburg, 800/689-6950, has more of an English flavor, though it is just a few miles from the Amish communities. Breakfast is served in an authentic English tearoom, which can also be reserved for afternoon tea. The **Overholt House B&B**, 1473 Beall Ave., Wooster, 800/992-0643, features a "flying staircase" that appears to hang with no support and a year-round Christmas parlor. The **Wooster Inn**, 801 E. Wayne St., Wooster, 330/264-2341, offers 16 rooms and suites in a quiet, colonial atmosphere on the College of Wooster campus.

CAMPING

Thousands of campsites await you in this scenic portion of the state. **Charles Mill Lake and Park**, 1271 OH 430, Mansfield, 419/368-6885, has 500 sites, with and without electricity. **Atwood Lake and Park**, 4956 Shop Rd. NE, Mineral City, 330/343-6780, offers over 500 primitive, electric, and nonelectric lots. Leesville Lake provides camping at **Clow's Marina**, 4131 Deer Rd. SW, Bowerston, 614/269-5371 and at **Petersburg Boat Landing and Campground**, 2126 Azalea Rd. SW, Carrolton, 330/627-4270. **Pleasant Hill Lake and Park**, 3431 OH 95, Perrysburg, 419/938-7884, adds 380 more sites to the list, all of which are managed by the Muskingum Watershed Conservancy District, 330/343-6647.

Aditionally, over 300 sites are available at **Mohican State Park**, 3116 OH 3, Loudonville, 419/994-4290, and **Whispering Hills Recreation Area**, OH 514, Shreve, 800/992-2435.

SHOPPING

Shopping in Holmes and the surrounding counties for Amish-made furniture, gifts, and baked goods is a pastime in itself. Amish scenes appear on souvenirs throughout the region (and state, for that matter). Here are a few of the many shops that have sprung up in response to the area's thriving tourism, as well as several that cater primarily to locals.

One unique shop is **Wendell August Gift Shoppe and Forge**, off the main road at 7007 Dutch Country Lane on OH 62, Berlin, 330/893-3713. Craftspeople and a die engraver hammer and press a variety of metalware—decorative gift items and functional trays, coasters, and plates—from aluminum, bronze, and pewter. Visitors can tour the workshop area and watch as crafters demonstrate the 11-step process used to create their products, then visit a museum where forges and other objects are displayed (daily 9 to 6; closed Sunday).

Lehman's, 4779 Kidron Rd., Kidron, 330/857-5757 (with a branch in Mount Hope on OH 241, 330/674-7474, that opens at 7 a.m. to accommodate its Amish trade), stocks a complete selection of items used by the Amish, including nonelectric "sadirons," cookstoves, wood burners, gas refrigerators, cookie cutters, and other baking staples sold through their 70,000-item *Nonelectric Heritage Catalog*. A trip to this area would not be complete without a stop here. The 1890s general store made national headlines, catching the attention of those with Y2K worries. Ironically, you can check out their catalog on the Web (www.lehmans.com), but the real experience is better. Don't leave town without noticing the 155-foot-long hitching rail or peeking in at the famous Kidron livestock auction if you're here on a Thursday.

The **Lone Star Quilt Shop**, County Rd. 77, Mount Hope, is where Sara Yoder works on the quilts she sells from her store here. Many are original designs she and her daughter have created. Her son operates **Homestead Furniture**, located behind the quilt shop, 800/893-3702, ext. 0210.

Other quilt shops include **Miller's Dry Goods**, 4500 OH 557, Charm, the oldest in the county, and **Helping Hands Quilt Shop and Museum**, Main St., Berlin, 330/893-2233, where the profits are donated to charity. If you can't find what you're looking for among the large selection neatly folded over wooden pegs or stacked on the bed at **Swartzentruber Bakery and Quilts**, 7977 Township Road 654, Millersburg, the shop takes special orders—as do other stores.

Ruth's Amish Dolls, on U.S. 62 in Winesburg, is a good place to find original handmade cloth dolls in various sizes. Ruth also sells clothes and patterns. While in Winesburg, if you're in the mood to browse, stop at **Winesburg Collectibles**, U.S. 62 Main St., 330/359-5343, for new and old furniture and lots of "etceteras." If you're in the market for a hand-carved sandstone birdbath or a mantel carved from an Amish barn beam, stop at **Eagle Song Studio**, 2175 County Rd. 160, Winesburg, across from the village school on U.S. 62, 330/359-5786. You'll likely find the carver in his studio adjacent to the shop, where samples of his work and that of a few others are for sale. Antique shops dot the area, as do other shops with specialties that the Amish take great care in preserving. Handmade furniture, leather goods and tack, rockers, clocks, and quilts are among the most popular products of cottage industry. If you stop before noon, you'll catch the cheese makers busy producing baby Swiss using the secrets imported by Alfred Guggisberg at **Guggisberg Cheese, Inc.**, 5060 OH 557, just north of Charm.

You'll find an assortment of Amish-made folk art, country crafts, furniture, quilts, and edible gifts, along with other regional art, at the **Gallery in the Vault**, 105 E. Liberty St., downtown Wooster, 800/541-9202. A few doors away, **Everything Rubbermaid Retail Store**, 115 S. Market St., 330/264-7119, and the **Corning Revere Factory Store**, 140 S. Walnut St., 330/262-4200, stock large selections and are open on Sunday. The Granary & Gardens at the **Pine Tree Barn & Farms**, 4374 Shreve Rd., Wooster, 330/264-1014, open from 10 to 5 daily (closed Monday during winter), offers furniture and gifts and serves gourmet lunches along with picturesque views of Killbuck Valley.

Scenic Route: Mohican Valley

*Routes weaving through Ohio's rolling hills abound, but some of my favorites lead through Richland and Ashland Counties to Mohican State Park and Forest and to Amish farmland to the east. For a pastoral shortcut for I-71 travelers en route to Holmes County, take OH 97 east (exit 165 on I-71) toward Bellville. You'll cross the 18-mile Richland B&O Bike Route several times before coming to the Clearfork River. Continuing on, you'll reach Butler, passing canoe liveries as you follow the river. Soon you'll enter the Mohican State Forest and Park, where signs point out the **Memorial Shrine** and the fire tower for spectacular views. However, the best vistas are at **Clearfork Gorge**. If you're ready for a walk, leave your car near the covered bridge, where you can catch the two-mile **Lyons Falls Trail** and follow its curves through the park.*

Back on OH 97, continue east, turning north (left) onto OH 3 for a short distance to OH 39 in Loudonville. Drive east through Millersburg, and you're nearing the heart of Amish country and miles of back roads.

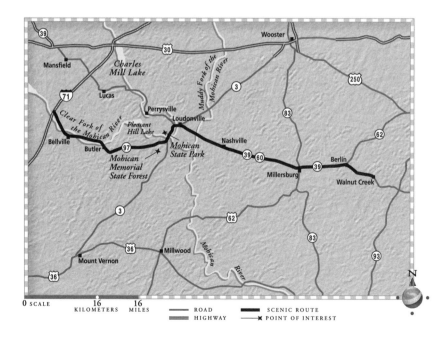

6
ZANESVILLE

As you plan your journeys through Ohio, you may wonder what Zanesville, a small community of 28,000, has to offer seasoned travelers. However, once you spend a little time in the area, you'll find many sightseeing attractions that may make this region one of your favorites.

After visiting North America's largest wildlife conservation facility for a safarilike experience, playing golf on one of Ohio's finest courses, touring the historic Putnam District—where "safe houses" hid fleeing slaves—or hunting for local pottery and good buys in the antique shops, you'll find several nearby state parks and excursions—enough for several more days of vacation. Roscoe Village, an 1830s restored canal town in Coshocton, and New Concord, birthplace of astronaut John Glenn, are among the favorite spots.

Rich in natural clay deposits and fine sand, Zanesville became known as "clay city" in its infancy and still boasts many working art potteries and several permanent exhibits dedicated to the craft.

Located on I-70, Zanesville is an hour east of Columbus. Long before interstate transportation, the National Road (U.S. 40) connected Zanesville to other destinations, from Cumberland, Maryland, to Vandalia, Illinois. Now the road offers a pleasant contrast to busy interstate traffic for travelers who like to slow down and visit the main streets in towns along the road. You can stop at the Ohio Historical Society's National Road/Zane Grey Museum to commemorate both the nation's first federal highway and locally born author Zane Grey.

ZANESVILLE REGION

A PERFECT DAY IN ZANESVILLE

First, take your group on a visit to the Wilds for an up-close-and-personal rendezvous with giraffes, zebras, rhinos, and scores of exotic and endangered species in natural-looking settings. After a few hours on a make-believe safari in the middle of Ohio, avid golfers should head to EagleSticks, an award-winning public course, while shoppers can continue on to nearby pottery factories for tours and discounts. Before the day ends, stop for some child's play at Kidzville in Riverside Park and dessert at Tom's Ice Cream Bowl.

SIGHTSEEING HIGHLIGHTS

★★★★ NATIONAL ROAD/ZANE GREY MUSEUM
8850 E. Pike, Norwich, about 10 miles east of Zanesville, 740/752-2602 or 800/752-2602

This museum commemorates the highway on which it sits—U.S. 40, also known as the National Road because it was America's first federal highway. Begun in 1806 in an effort to expand U.S. territory beyond the Appalachians, the road now parallels I-70, but its unique history remains along the area's many main streets. Noteworthy exhibits include a collection of area art pottery, a Conestoga wagon, and the Zane Grey Wing, in tribute to the Zanesville-born novelist whose stories about the Western frontier are better known than the ones about Ohio.

Details: Mar–Apr Wed–Sat 9:30–5, Sun noon–5; May–Sept

SIGHTS

- **A** Historic Putnam District
- **B** National Road/Zane Grey Museum
- **C** Ohio Ceramic Center

Pottery Factory Tours and Shops:
- **D** Alpine Pottery
- **C** Beaumont Pottery

Pottery Factory Tours and Shops (continued):
- **B** Bogart's Antiques
- **A** Fioriware
- **F** Hartstone Inc.
- **E** Ohio Pottery at Norwich
- **D** Robinson-Ransbottom Pottery
- **A** Zanesville Pottery & China

- **G** Roscoe Village
- **H** The Wilds
- **I** "World's Largest Basket"
- **A** Y Bridge
- **A** Zanesville Art Center

Note: Items with the same letter are located in the same area.

Mon–Sat 9:30–5, Sun and holidays noon–5; Oct–Nov Wed-Sat 9:30–5, closed holidays. $5 adults, $4 seniors, $1.25 children 6–12. (1-2 hours)

★★★★ OHIO CERAMIC CENTER

Ceramic Rd., OH 93 at County Rd. 98, between Roseville and Crooksville, 740/697-7021 or 800/752-2604

To understand how important ceramics were in the development of this area, visit this five-building complex to hear about the past and present industry. Exhibits tell an informative story of the 41 local potteries. You can watch a volunteer potter, on loan from Ohio University/Zanesville, at work in a studio. Hundreds of unique paving bricks from Ohio streets, antiques, and current pieces are displayed.

Details: Mid-May–mid-Oct Wed–Sat 9:30–5, Sun noon–5. $2 adults, $1 children over 12. Two picnic shelters; tables are scattered throughout the grounds. Overnight camping $15 per night. (1–2 hours minimum)

★★★★ POTTERY FACTORY TOURS AND SHOPS

The Zanesville area, once renowned as the ceramic capital of the United States, still boasts more than a dozen pottery manufacturers and even more retail shops. Not only will you discover the rich history of art pottery here, but you will also find bargains on items often seen in the pages of Gourmet and Country Living and in upscale retail shops. **Robinson-Ransbottom Pottery**, Ransbottom Rd., Roseville, 740/697-7355, offers free self-guided or guided tours of its plant, the largest stoneware facility in the United States. Makers of the distinctive natural spongeware patterns and the Williamsburg style of pottery, the company has been operating here since 1900. A large room in the retail shop features factory seconds at reduced prices. This pottery is the place to find birdbaths. **Alpine Pottery**, 7674 Ceramic Rd. NE, Roseville, 740/697-0075, a family-owned plant, utilizes local clay and adds hand decoration to the ware for a country look. Factory tours are offered Monday through Friday from 8 to 4 and Saturday from 10 to 4.

Nearby **Beaumont Pottery**, 315 E. Main St., Crooksville, 740/982-0065, uses salt glazes to create an early-American style of art pottery. The distinctive look has a gray background with blue hand-painted designs. The company produces dinnerware and figurines and offers short guided tours of the factory.

Two factory shops whose wares are much different from

Roseville and Crooksville crockery lines are must-sees: **Hartstone Inc.**, 1719 Dearborn St., South Zanesville, 740/452-9000, sells seconds and first-quality dinnerware and bakeware from its extensive line of hand-decorated American styles. Even more bargains are available on Saturday. You'll know you're at **Fioriware**, 333 Market St., downtown Zanesville, 740/454-7400, because of the brightly decorated mosaic benches and gates bordering the corner. Although the craftspeople utilize traditional nineteenth- and early twentieth-century pottery techniques, the signature colorful hand-painted patterns definitely add an upscale and sophisticated look. The prices are also upscale, but you'll find some bargains.

If your schedule is more hurried, many one-stop retail shops carry large selections of local pottery, including several on U.S. 40 east of Zanesville, such as **Zanesville Pottery & China**, 7395 E. Pike, Zanesville, 800/860-6456, and **Ohio Pottery** at Norwich, 740/872-3137. Antique pottery buffs will enjoy **Bogart's Antiques**, 7527 E. Pike, Norwich, 740/872-3514.

Most of the pottery companies are clustered in Roseville and Crooksville (to the south of Zanesville off OH 93) or near the downtown area. Tours last from 15 minutes to one hour, and videos are often shown in the sales shops. For a complete list of manufacturers and a map of the areas, contact the **Zanesville-Muskingum County Convention & Visitors Bureau**, 800/743-2303. Ask for antiquing information, too. If you want to tour, avoid visiting the pottery factories during lunch hour. (half day)

★★★★ **ROSCOE VILLAGE**
381 Hill St., Coshocton, 800/877-1830
A visit to the living history museum at Roscoe Village, Coshocton's restored nineteenth-century canal town, portrays a slice of life during the canal-boat port's heyday, from 1830 through the Civil War. The town, called Caldersburgh in 1816, was renamed Roscoe in 1831 to honor a famous English author and abolitionist. Because the town was a thriving stop on the Ohio & Erie Canal, its population grew to 500, similar to its current census. Although the short-lived canal routes ended with the great flood of 1913 and the chug of locomotives, local industrialist Edward E. Montgomery and the ensuing Roscoe Village Foundation rehabbed the deteriorating village. Now the village, a collection of 11 restored, 10 preserved, 2 reconstructed, and 5 new buildings, plus hundreds of hoopskirted and

SIDE TRIP: NEWARK

If your grandmother handed down her glass dishes and other dinnerware that she used every day, you may well own some Heisey glass, worth many, many times what Grandma paid for it. Collectors know that the pressed ware brings high prices in the secondary market—antique shops and flea markets. What they might not realize is that Heisey glass, as ornate as it is, used to be sold in local five-and-dime stores for low prices before the Newark glassworks closed shop in 1957.

*At the **National Heisey Glass Museum**, 169 Church St., Newark, in Veterans Park, 740/345-2932, you'll find hundreds of patterns and all the designs and colors produced since the company's beginning in 1896. The museum also shows one-of-a-kind pieces designed especially for the Heisey family. Museum hours are Tuesday through Saturday from 10 to 4 and Sunday from 1 to 4. Admission is $2 for adults; those 18 and under are admitted free with an adult.*

*The **Institute of Industrial Technology**, 55 S. First St., Newark, 740/349-9277, features artifacts of Newark's industrial heritage in a hands-on setting and a working glass studio operated by the Heisey Collectors of America. Hours are from noon to 4 Wednesday through Sunday. Admission is $2 for adults and $1 for children and seniors.*

*At **Flint Ridge State Memorial and Museum**, County Rd. 668, 740/787-2476 or 800/283-8707, you'll learn about the Paleo-Indians of 8,000 to 10,000 years ago. The site is open Memorial Day through Labor Day Wednesday through Saturday from 9:30 to 5, Sunday from noon to 5;*

suspendered workers, successfully brings the canal era back to life along Whitewoman Street, named after the Walhonding River, which flows through town.

The visitors center at the end of the street offers a good starting point with its founders' gallery, bookstore, wide-screen theater show about early transportation, exhibit hall displaying miniature dioramas, and ticket counter for guided tours through the living-history community. From there, costumed interpreters escort small groups to each building, where working craftspeople share their skills. Leisurely self-guided tours are free. Favorite stops include the **Johnson-Humrick House Museum**, the blacksmith shop for hand-forging

September through October Saturday from 9:30 to 5, Sunday from noon to 5. Admission is $3 for adults and $1.25 for children 6 to 12.

Moundbuilders State Memorial and Ohio Indian Art Museum, 50 W. Locust St., Newark, 740/344-1920 or 800/600-7174, with artifacts representing all the known prehistoric cultures in Ohio from 10,000 B.C. to A.D. 1600, provides another link to the prehistoric past. Admission is $3 for adults and $1 for children.

Something is always new at **Dawes Arboretum**, five miles south of Newark on Ohio 13, 800/44-DAWES, but my favorite spot is the Japanese Garden. A nine-and-a-half-mile driving tour and a four-mile walking tour change with the seasons. **Blackhand Gorge State Nature Preserve**, six miles east of Newark off OH 146, 740/763-4411, is another must-see for nature lovers. A four-mile bike trail and several hiking trails lead to beautiful views of the sandstone gorge, named Blackhand after a dark, hand-shaped petroglyph once engraved on its face. The petroglyph was destroyed during construction of the Ohio & Erie Canal Towpath in 1828. During spring the paths are lined with wildflowers and the woods are filled with blossoming dogwoods. Picnicking is not permitted in the preserve, but a grassy area between the parking lot and bike trail makes a good spot.

The New England–style town of Granville is home to Denison University and several interesting museums, shops, B&Bs, and eateries. Go farther north to **Ye Olde Mill** in Utica, 740/892-3921, for ice-cream concoctions created with the Velvet Ice Cream manufactured there.

demonstrations, and the **Montgomery Press**, where costumed guides demonstrate working presses and explain the art and skill of printing. A one-and-a-half-mile ride on the horse-drawn canal boat *Monticello III* demonstrates the kind of travel that led to the town's prosperity. The narrated boat ride departs hourly noon to 5.

Shops filled with antiques, candles, baskets, folk crafts, toys, food, and more round out the touring possibilities.

Details: Hours vary each season, but generally shops are open daily 10–5. Prices also vary, and tour packages, combined with the canal-boat ride and admission to the Johnson-Humrick House Museum are available. The basic "Villager" admission, which includes tours of *the living-history craft buildings, is $8.95 adults, $3.95 children 5–12. Senior and AAA discounts. No fee to enter the village to shop and/or dine. (full day)*

★★★★ **THE WILDS**
14000 International Rd., Cumberland, 740/638-5030
To take an African safari without a passport and an expensive plane ticket, just climb aboard a school bus–style vehicle at the Wilds, where guided tours depart for the "savanna" continuously. The park, developed from 14 square miles of reclaimed strip-mining area, is home to scores of endangered species and animals that are extinct in the wild. Visitors can see and hear the animals in habitats most like their native ones.

As you drive through the pastures, sharing the narrow gravel paths with the animals, you may have to yield to the southern white rhinos, who, at over 4,000 pounds, clearly have the right of way. If you don't see all that you'd like on your safari, you're welcome to try the tour again before leaving. Take your camera for close-up shots. An interactive computer program at the visitors center adds another educational component to the nonprofit preserve, the largest research and conservation center in North America. Picnic areas on the plateau near the visitors center offer views overlooking the lakes and woodlands. Picnic lunches, soups, salads, and sandwiches are available at the Overlook Café.

Details: May–Oct daily 9–5 for 1.5-hour, wheelchair-accessible tours. Call ahead during other seasons for hours. $10 adults, $9 seniors, $7 children 4–12, children 3 and younger free. (half day)

★★★★ **ZANESVILLE ART CENTER**
620 Military Rd., Zanesville, 740/452-0741
Stop here to continue your pottery excursion. In addition to 10 galleries exhibiting the permanent collection, you'll find the largest retail selection of the area's pottery, decorative arts, and glass, including world-renowned makers such as Steuben, Tiffany, Ming, and Wedgewood. The center also displays other regional and national exhibitions and holds annual events like a holiday open house and, in September, an outdoor arts festival featuring regional artists and entertainers.

Details: Tue, Wed, Fri 10–5, Thu 10–8:30, Sat–Sun 1–5; closed major holidays. Free admission and parking. Handicapped facilities. (1–2 hours)

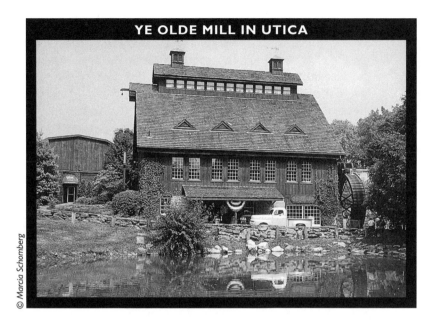

YE OLDE MILL IN UTICA

© Marcia Schomberg

★★★ HISTORIC PUTNAM DISTRICT

Turn onto Pine Street from the Y Bridge. Streets like Muskingum and Woodlawn lead into the area. This community was originally named Springfield but was renamed Putnam in 1841 in honor of Rufus Putnam, a Revolutionary War general and early settler in Ohio. Many of its founders were staunch abolitionists during the pre–Civil War years. Their homes, on the south side of the Muskingum River, were "safe houses" for fleeing slaves, and their churches were meeting places for "conductors" on the Underground Railroad. Little by little, homeowners are restoring properties within the 15-block area, which is listed on the National Register of Historic Places.

Harriet Beecher Stowe's brother, the Reverend Henry Ward Beecher, was the first pastor of the **Putnam Presbyterian Church**, 467 Woodlawn Ave., one of the community's oldest and most architecturally unique churches. Among its many stained-glass works is a Tiffany window. Listed in both the **Historic Putnam Walking Tour** and a new audio driving tour of the area is **Dr. Increase Mathews House**, a stone building at 304 Woodlawn Ave., 740/454-9500. Built in 1805 and now owned by the Pioneer and Historical Society of Muskingum County, it is the oldest house in Zanesville. Rooms are dedicated to various topics of local history.

Stone Academy, 115 Jefferson St., 740/454-9500, was constructed from locally quarried stone in 1809 in hopes of its becoming Ohio's first capitol. Instead, as a public building, it became a meeting place for the state abolition society and a safe house for those following the Underground Railroad. You can see the trap door and other evidence of its probable use.

Details: June 1–Labor Day Sat 10–4, Sun 1–4. General admission to both buildings is $3. A free audio tour is available at the Visitors Welcome Center, 205 N. Fifth St., downtown Zanesville, 800/743-2303, and at area libraries and motels. (2 hours)

★ "WORLD'S LARGEST BASKET"
Dresden Village Association, Dresden, 740/754-3401
Longaberger Homestead, OH 16, Frazeysburg
740/322-5588, www.longaberger.com

If you're a basket enthusiast, you may recognize Dresden as the home of Longaberger's World's Largest Basket. For others, a visit here reveals a storybook town from the pages of Americana—spotlessly tidy; flowers abloom; friendly, cheerful townspeople; and shops brimming with gifts and country crafts. The hallmark basket, a 48-foot-long hardwood maple basket on the corner of Fifth and Main Streets, remains in Dresden, although the Longaberger Homestead, a short distance away, now focuses on the family and the history of basket making in this region. A visit to the Homestead includes the manufacturing tour, shopping opportunities, and various forms of entertainment—perhaps you'll arrive during a festival or a how-to demonstration. There are seven different buildings and five eateries on 34 acres.

Details: Mar–Dec Mon–Sat 8–6, Sun 11–6; Jan–Feb Mon–Sat 9–5, Sun 11–5. Free parking and admission. (2–4 hours)

★ Y BRIDGE
Intersection of W. Main St., Linden Ave., and U.S. 40

For the best view of this interesting bridge, which crosses the confluence of the Muskingum and Licking Rivers, visit the **Putnam Hill Park Overlook** off Pine Street in Zanesville. Bridges have been constructed at the same location five times since the first one spanned both rivers in 1814. On this three-way overpass, it is possible to cross the bridge yet not cross the river. West Main Street, Linden Avenue, and U.S. 40 meet in the middle.

Details: (30 minutes)

FITNESS AND RECREATION

Little ones will enjoy **Kidzville**, an outdoor playground at **Riverside Park**. Soccer, volleyball, softball fields, and a boat ramp are also available. **Dillon State Park**, 5265 Dillon Hills Dr., Nashport, 740/453-4377; **Salt Fork State Park**, 14755 Cadiz Rd., Lore City, 740/439-3521; and **Blue Rock State Park**, 7924 Cutler Lake Rd., Blue Rock, 740/674-4794, provide hiking trails, fishing, hunting, and boating, as well as other winter recreational activities. Of the several public golf courses, **EagleSticks**, 2655 Maysville Pike, Zanesville, 740/454-4900, is among Ohio's top-ranked courses.

FOOD

Finding enjoyable eateries in the Zanesville environs is easy. If you're in the midst of the pottery junket, try **Peach's Place**, 121 E. Main St., Crooksville, 740/982-1213. It's a popular spot for a quick and inexpensive lunch.

If you're hungry for New Mexican choices, try **Zak's**, 32 N. Third St., 740/453-2227. The local pizzeria of choice is **Adornetto's**, 2224 Maple Ave., 740/453-4288, or 2440 Maysville Pike, 740/454-6261. For Italian dishes other than pizza, try **Maria Adornetto's Restaurant**, 953 Market St., 800/343-5026. **Old Market House Inn**, 424 Market St., 740/454-2555, has a pleasant pub-style atmosphere and an eclectic menu; and the **Inn at EagleSticks**, 2655 Maysville Pike, South Zanesville, 740/454-1032, features American cuisine with scenic golf-course views. If you're hungry for homemade ice cream any day but Monday, order one of the hefty sundaes at **Tom's Ice Cream Bowl**, 532 McIntire Ave., 740/452-5267.

In Coshocton, the **Roscoe Village Inn**, 200 N. Whitewoman St., Roscoe Village, 800/237-7397, has several restaurants. The **Centennial Room** features an outstanding changing menu of regional favorites served in upscale fashion but at reasonable prices, while **King Charley's Tavern** serves light meals in a rustic setting. Other dining options include **Captain Nye's Sweet Shop**, 365 N. Whitewoman St., Roscoe Village, 740/622-7732; **Roscoe Village Bakery**, 101 N. Whitewoman St., Roscoe Village, 740/623-6530; and the **Warehouse Restaurant and Lock 27 Pub**, 400 N. Whitewoman St., Roscoe Village, 740/622-4001, known for its ham and bean soup. Stop at the pub to hear live music provided by village shopkeepers.

LODGING

Many outstanding B&B choices are located in the outlying areas. The **Inn at Dresden**, 209 Ames Dr., Dresden, 800/DRESDEN, was originally the home

ZANESVILLE REGION

Clendening Lake
Piedmont Lake
70
Dennison
Uhrichsville
250
36
Senecaville Lake
Lore City
285
Salt Fork Lake
77
40
J
I
Cambridge
Cumberland
83
E
New Concord
Norwich
208
B Coshocton
60
Warsaw
83
Dresden
H
Zanesville
Philo
60
250
A
South Zanesville
C
Roseville
93
Crooksville
D
541
16
Dillon Lake
Dillon State Park
146
22
Somerset
Danville
K
Toboso
16
36
586
62
G Newark
13
Mount Vernon
Granville
F
40
70
229
Johnstown
256
161
37
16
Reynoldsburg

N

OSCALE   15   15   KILOMETERS   MILES

——— ROAD   ═══ HIGHWAY   ➤ POINT OF INTEREST

To New Philadelphia

of Longaberger company founder Dave Longaberger. Now it is a delightful B&B overlooking the town. You'll find **Bogart's B&B**, 62 W. Main St., New Concord, 740/826-7439, on the historic National Road just across from the entrance to Muskingum College. The innkeepers also own an antique shop, which gives them ample resources for furnishing the B&B. For a romantic getaway, try **Misty Meadows Farm**, 64878 Slaughter Hill Rd., Cambridge, 740/439-5135. The innkeepers specialize in a secluded gourmet "Picnic in the Meadow" ($60 per couple). The **White Oak Inn**, 29683 Walhonding Rd., Danville, 740/599-6107, adds delicious dinner menus to overnight options and offers themed weekends year-round. For accommodations in Roscoe Village, try the 51-room Shaker-style **Roscoe Village Inn**, 200 N. Whitewoman St., 800/237-7397, or the **Apple Butter Inn**, 455 Hill St., 740/622-1329.

Additionally, you'll find an assortment of motel chains located off I-70 at Exit 155 (running through Zanesville). Those that provide complimentary breakfast include **AmeriHost Inn**, 740/454-9332; **Fairfield Inn**, 740/453-8770; and **Hampton Inn**, 740/453-6511.

Family cabins that sleep six and the 148-room lodge at **Salt Fork State Park**, 14755 Cadiz Rd., Lore City, 740/439-3521, provide rustic but very scenic accommodations year-round.

CAMPING

In addition to **Blue Rock State Park**'s 101 nonelectric campsites, some of which are hike-in areas for tent camping, more than 200 electric spots (with 18

FOOD

- Ⓐ Adornetto's
- Ⓑ Captain Nye's Sweet Shop
- Ⓒ Inn at EagleSticks
- Ⓐ Maria Adornetto's Restaurant
- Ⓐ Old Market House Inn
- Ⓓ Peach's Place
- Ⓑ Roscoe Village Bakery

FOOD (continued)

- Ⓑ Roscoe Village Inn (Centennial Room and King Charley's Tavern)
- Ⓐ Tom's Ice Cream Bowl
- Ⓑ Warehouse Restaurant and Lock 27 Pub
- Ⓐ Zak's

LODGING

- Ⓐ AmeriHost Inn
- Ⓑ Apple Butter Inn
- Ⓔ Bogart's B & B

LODGING (continued)

- Ⓕ Buxton Inn
- Ⓖ Cherry Valley Lodge
- Ⓐ Fairfield Inn
- Ⓕ Granville Inn
- Ⓑ Apple Butter Inn
- Ⓐ Hampton Inn
- Ⓘ Misty Meadows Farm
- Ⓑ Roscoe Village Inn
- Ⓙ Salk Fork State Park
- Ⓚ White Oak Inn

Note: Items with the same letter are located in the same area.

wheelchair-accessible sites) are available at **Salt Fork State Park** and nearly 200 more at **Dillon Lake State Park**. Private campgrounds include the **Zanesville KOA**, 2850 S. Pleasant Grove Rd., Zanesville, 800/562-3390. After contacting American Electric Power, 800/672-2231, to obtain a complimentary permit, campers can enjoy camping, hiking, hunting, and fishing on thousands of acres of reclaimed mining land throughout the region.

7
COLUMBUS

Ohio's capital city provides a friendly, low-key atmosphere for travelers. The downtown area bustles with convention business, tourist attractions, shopping opportunities, and a refurbished state capitol on High and Broad Streets. Several distinct districts border downtown's skyline interjecting unique flavors and events in all directions. Once a test-market capital where businesses eager to survey potential success tried their products, the city is a microcosm of middle America. These days, Columbus moves forward with more than $2.5 billion worth of development projects planned or in progress to greet the 21st century.

The largest city in Ohio, Columbus has grown into a sophisticated community, where vacation and getaway possibilities include something for everyone. You'll find an amazing number of ethnic restaurants for a city with so few ethnic neighborhoods and a host of attractions tucked away in all corners and suburbs of the city. You can rev up your adrenaline in the annual Columbus Marathon or at one of the high-spirited spectator events, then relax at one of several botanical delights. Visitors can tour the state capitol, lunch in the Brewery District, shop in the Short North (home to North Market and dozens of galleries) or the upscale Columbus City Center, climb the rigs of the *Santa Maria*, moored on the Scioto River, and visit the new Center of Science and Industry for some hands-on experimenting before strolling the brick-lined streets of German Village—all without leaving greater downtown.

COLUMBUS

N

I D

Franklin
Park

FRANKLIN
PARK S

TAYLOR AV

MILLER AV

FRANKLIN
PARK W

BRYDEN RD

LIVINGSTON AV

CHAMPION AV

33

ATCHESON ST

MT VERNON AV

E BROAD ST

COLUMBUS ST

WHITTIER ST

ST. CLAIR AV

e

G

HAMILTON

PARSONS AV

K F

WASHINGTON AV

CLEVELAND AV

B

L

TOWN ST

MAIN ST

FULTON ST

MOHAWK ST

Schiller
Park

GRANT AV

C b

E

f

2ND AV

1ST AV

4TH ST

3RD ST

9

23 23

S

SUMMIT ST

G

A h

P

HIGH ST

V U

a H

R Q

NATIONWIDE BLVD

SPRING ST

LONG ST

X

J

FRONT ST

O

SHORT ST

70

71

40

McDOWELL ST

Scioto River

71

62

1ST AV

3RD AV

315

Olentangy River

DUBLIN AV

SONDER AV

62

OLENTANGY RIVER RD

TWIN RIVERS DR

RICH ST

M

N

To Ohio State
University

GOODALE BLVD

DUBLIN RD

Scioto River

McKINLEY AV

CENTRAL AV

TOWN ST

SULLIVANT ST

Y

To W

Z

GRANDVIEW AV

33

70

W BROAD ST

To d

670

0 SCALE   .75   .75
KILOMETER   MILE

ROAD   HIGHWAY

A PERFECT DAY IN COLUMBUS

Begin the day early with coffee and pastry in German Village and a stroll around Schiller Park, which is especially charming in summer's bloom. Then browse the 32-room Book Loft and the Golden Hobby Shop across the street before leaving the village for a statehouse tour. Afterward, head to the Short North for a quick gallery hop and lunch along North High Street, perhaps at Martini's Ristorante & Bar. Add a stop at Inniswood Metropark Gardens in Westerville, and end the day with a relaxing dinner at Fifty-Five on the Boulevard before an overnight at the Lofts downtown.

SIGHTSEEING HIGHLIGHTS

★★★★ BARBER MUSEUM AND THE BARBERING HALL OF FAME

SIGHTS

- **A** Capitol Square: Ohio Statehouse and Veterans' Plaza
- **B** Columbus Museum of Art
- **C** COSI Columbus
- **D** Franklin Park Conservatory and Botanical Garden
- **E** German Village
- **F** Kelton House Museum and Garden
- **G** Martin Luther King, Jr. Performing and Cultural Arts Center
- **H** North Market
- **I** Ohio Governor's Residence Tour
- **J** *Santa Maria* replica
- **K** Thurber House
- **L** Topiary Garden: "A Sunday Afternoon on the Island of La Grande Jatte"

FOOD

- **M** Buckeye Hall of Fame Cafe
- **N** Cap City Diner
- **O** Columbus Brewing Company
- **N** Columbus Fish Market
- **P** Cup O'Joe Coffee Dessert House
- **Q** Damon's
- **R** Frank's Diner
- **G** G. Michael's Italian-American Bistro & Bar
- **S** Handke's Cuisine
- **T** Hoster Brewing Company
- **U** Lemongrass: An Asian Bistro
- **E** Lindy's
- **V** Martini Ristorante & Bar
- **W** Red Door Tavern
- **X** Sammy's New York Bagels

FOOD *(continued)*

- **E** Schmidt's Sausage Haus and Restaurant
- **Y** Spain
- **Z** Stauf's Coffee Roasters
- **a** Tapatio Restuarant
- **b** Wendy's Original Restaurant

LODGING

- **c** 50 Lincoln Inn
- **d** Crowne Plaza
- **e** Henderson House
- **f** Inn on City Park
- **g** Lansing St. B&B
- **d** Lofts Hotel
- **d** Red Roof Inn
- **h** Westin Great Southern Hotel

Note: Items with the same letter are located in the same area.

2 S. High St., Canal Winchester, 614/833-9931

This unique museum isn't just for men who remember barber poles and shaves with straightedge razors. It's for anyone who wants to see collecting at its best. Ed Jeffers, the curator and a barber himself, has spent the last 40 years collecting over 541 shaving mugs, nearly 60 barber poles (including rare ones with clocks on top), barbering chairs from most of America's wars, and other memorabilia—tonic bottles, wooden chairs, and tools from the days when barbers also performed surgery and dentistry. Seven barbershops, along with other displays and artifacts, are painstakingly restored and arranged neatly and logically.

Details: *Year-round; hours by appointment. Free. Wheelchair accessible. (1–2 hours)*

★★★★ CAPITOL SQUARE: OHIO STATEHOUSE AND VETERANS' PLAZA
Bounded by High, State, Broad, and Third Streets
614/752-6350, 888/OHIO-123

A $114-million renovation of the statehouse transformed it into a stunning classic Greek Revival structure that includes modern safety features and technological advancements. The bright salmon shades of the rotunda are illuminated by a reproduction stained-glass skylight with a replica of the 1861 Seal of Ohio. This stunning feature was funded by schoolchildren throughout the state. Faux finishes, leaded ceilings, and reproduction furniture in the House and Senate chambers recall the mid-1800s, when President Lincoln addressed the assemblies here.

The Ohio Historical Society provides guided tours and displays historical artifacts in the Statehouse Education and Visitors Center. You can see Ohio's first flag, designed in 1901, and a facsimile of the calumet (peace pipe) shared by Major General "Mad Anthony" Wayne and American Indian leaders at the 1795 Treaty of Greenville. A Civil War–era stagecoach is the display's focal point. On the east side of the capitol, bordered by 88 Ohio flags representing each of the state's counties, is the newest part of the complex, Veterans Plaza. This moving outdoor marble monument comprises letters from Ohio veterans relating their personal war experiences.

Details: *Guided tours from Third St. entrance Mon–Fri 9:30–3:15 every 15 minutes; Sat–Sun 11:15, 12:30, 2, and 3. Free. Self-guided tours are also available Mon–Fri 9–5 and Sat–Sun 11–4. (1 1/2 hours)*

ANTIQUE SHOPPING TIPS

An antique treasure hunt is under way in central Ohio. You'll find shops in the Short North, German Village, and Grandview in Columbus, but you can venture to nearby communities for more pleasant surprises. Famous for their annual flea markets, the towns of Powell and Sunbury also offer antique shops. Delaware, Worthington, and Mount Vernon each boast historic downtown areas with shops and century-old facades. Contact the Delaware County Convention and Visitors Bureau, 888/DEL-OHIO, the Convention and Visitors Bureau of Worthington, 800/997-9935, and the Knox County Convention and Visitors Bureau, 800/837-5282, for shop directories.

★★★★ **CENTER OF SCIENCE AND INDUSTRY (COSI) COLUMBUS**
333 W. Broad St., 614/228-COSI, www.cosi.org
This new 300,000-square-foot center, with its "Learning Worlds" (the latest name for the high-tech exhibition areas) and four state-of-the-art theaters, is a must-see for children and adults alike. Nowhere else in Ohio will you find a 3-D space show like the one in the dome-shaped Space Theater or an IWERKS Theater with a screen towering more than six stories. COSI, with another location in Toledo, has been showing off the world of science since its original hands-on center opened here in 1964. The new space combines the same fun, learning, and science concepts but adds a host of new activities and topics—like "I/O," celebrating achievements in technology, and "Gadgets," where guests discover how gadgets change the way things are done. Old favorites, such as "High Wire Cycle," are still among the hands-on activities. "Little Kidspace" is designed for infants through preschoolers and even has a security entrance. "Life: Mind, Body, Spirit" explores issues of special interest to adults and teens.

Details: Daily 10–5. Fri–Sat theaters, Simulation Zone, retail shop, and restaurant 10–9. $12 adults, $10 seniors, $7 children 2–12; an "Exhibits + 1" ticket package saves visitors up to $2 for the combination to exhibits and a theater show. (4 hours–2 days)

SIDE TRIP: CHILLICOTHE

After you've visited Ohio's current capital, take a 46-mile drive south on U.S. 23 to Chillicothe, Ohio's first capital city. One of the first sights on your list should be the **Hopewell Culture National Historical Park**, 16062 OH 104, 740/774-1125. Self-guided tours of Mound City, with a stop at an excavation of a burial mound and a museum of archaeological findings, provide an in-depth look at a culture that prevailed throughout Ohio and the Scioto River Valley 2,000 years ago.

A visit to **Adena**, off OH 104 on Adena Rd., 800/319-7248, takes visitors to Ohio's early days as a state. The restored estate of Thomas Worthington, Ohio's sixth governor and "father of Ohio's statehood," was a meeting place for frontier politicians and Indian chiefs. Rooms are filled with artifacts and period furnishings, and guides add anecdotes about notable visitors and overnight guests. From his front lawn, Worthington and his friend William Creighton observed the sun rising over Mount Logan and the Appalachian foothills. That scene became the basis for the Great Seal of Ohio.

Architectural buffs will not want to miss the historic walking tour down **Caldwell Street** and adjacent streets. At the Ross-Chillicothe Convention & Visitors Bureau's red caboose at Yoctangee City Park, pick up a tour brochure detailing more than 35 restored, mid-nineteenth-century homes. If you can't walk the walk, at least drive through this historic section. There are few restored

★★★★ COLUMBUS MUSEUM OF ART
480 E. Broad St., 614/221-4848

This museum exhibits traveling works in addition to its own collections of American and European art from 1850 to 1950. *Eye Spy: Adventures in Art* (on exhibit through 2001) combines hands-on activities, art projects, interactive exhibits, and computer stations to inspire children and families. "First Thursday" (on the first Thursday of each month) is a special event featuring live music, food, and free admission from 5:30 to 8:30 p.m., and "First Saturday" is for children's workshops.

Details: *Tue–Sun 10–5:30, until 8:30 Thu. $3 adults, $2 students and seniors, children under 12 free. (2 hours)*

blocks like these around. You may also want to drive past the **Lucy Hayes Heritage Center**, 90 W. Sixth St., 740/775-5829, a simple white frame home where Lucy Webb Hayes, wife of the 19th U.S. president, Rutherford B. Hayes, was born.

Another restored building, saved from the wrecking ball in the nick of time, houses the **Pump House Center for the Arts** in Yoctangee Park, 740/773-2715. Changing exhibits in a modern gallery that utilizes the old brick of the original 1882 pump house often include the work of regional artists.

Before leaving Chillicothe, spend an evening outdoors as the story of the Shawnees unfolds in **Tecumseh!**, 740/775-0700, an epic drama by Allan Eckert about the Shawnee Indian leader. The season runs from June to September. Buffet dining and backstage tours are available before the show.

A few local eateries are available, including the **Harvester Restaurant**, 9 N. Paint St., 740/773-3354, as well as bed-and-breakfasts, such as the **Greenhouse B&B**, 740/775-5313, an 1894 Queen Anne Victorian classic on the walking tour at 47 E. Fifth St., and the **Victoria Manor B&B**, 30 Western Ave., 740/775-6424, an 1859 Italianate farmhouse on a hill overlooking Chillicothe. You'll also find national chains, including a **Hampton Inn & Suites**, 100 N. Plaza Blvd., 740/773-1616.

★★★★ **COLUMBUS ZOO**
9990 Riverside Dr., Powell, 800/MONKEYS
This zoo is just the right design and price for young families. Without being overwhelmed, youngsters can easily meander through the exhibits before tiring. They'll meet Colo, the first gorilla born in captivity (40 years ago), and 650 other species from all over the world, including those in the Petting Barn. They'll love the elephant and pony rides, the manatee exhibit, and the new African forest, too. Take along lunch or dinner to enjoy at the zoo's picnic grounds.

Details: Memorial Day–Labor Day daily 9–6; Labor Day–Memorial Day Sat–Sun 9–5. $6 adults, $5 seniors, $4 children 2–11, children under 2 free. $2 parking. Wheelchair accessible. (2–4 hours)

EASTON TOWN CENTER

Easton Town Center, located on Columbus's northeast side, off I-270 at the Easton exit, is the city's newest shopping and entertainment project, with development still under way at the time of this writing. It's a lively mix, dubbed a "Disney World for shoppers" by some. So if you're looking for entertainment, try the 30-screen complex of **Planet Movies**, the **All-Star Café** next to **Planet Hollywood** or **GameWorks** (which combines a high-tech video arcade with a restaurant). The younger crowd will set their sights on **Jeepers**, an indoor amusement park. The nation's largest **Barnes & Nobles** and scores of other specialty retailers and restaurants are also here. The **Columbus Hilton**, **Towers at Easton**, and a **Residence Inn** by Marriott, among others, will provide overnight accommodations in the area.

★★★★ **FRANKLIN PARK CONSERVATORY AND BOTANICAL GARDEN**
1777 E. Broad St., 800/214-PARK

No matter the season, something is always blooming at the conservatory. Changing exhibits can lead you to a more in-depth exploration of the seven climatic zones. You'll find butterflies in the tropical rain forest and bugs in the desert. Exhibits change each season. A café serves light lunches from 11 to 3.

> **Details:** *Tue–Sun 10–5, Wed 10–8. $5 adults, $3.50 seniors and students with ID, $2 children 2–12. (1–3 hours)*

★★★★ **GERMAN VILLAGE**
South of Downtown Columbus via Third Street

Visitors to this charming historic district, touted as the largest privately restored neighborhood in the United States, will discover an Old World ambiance. The brick-lined streets, slate roofs, ironwork, and flower boxes remind visitors of the 1800s, when German immigrants created this working-class neighborhood. You'll find a mixture of upscale dining, corner cafés and delis, and unique gift shops and galleries among the residences and businesses. Special events and festivals, like the annual German Village Octoberfest (September) and the **German Village Haus und Garten Tour** reflect the neighborhood's heritage and pride.

The **Golden Hobby Shop**, 630 S. Third St., 614/645-8329, has taken over the village's 125-year-old brick schoolhouse, where immigrants once learned English, and has filled each classroom with items hand-crafted by seniors living in Franklin County. You'll find a room with quilts made by a husband-wife team (at very reasonable prices), a toy room, an outdoor gallery, and spaces devoted to crocheted items, needlepoint, and handmade wooden items. The shop is open Monday through Saturday from 10 to 5 and Sunday from 1 to 5.

Browsers can, and do, get lost among the 32 rooms in the **Book Loft**, across the street at 631 S. Third St., 614/464-1774. The rooms are arranged in mazelike fashion, possibly because the shop, which features books, cards, and posters at discount prices, has grown through the years by expanding in every direction. It is open Sunday through Thursday from 10 a.m. to 11 p.m. and Friday and Saturday until midnight.

Outdoor summer theater performances at **Schiller Park** provide additional evening entertainment.

Details: *A video and tours of the area, listed on the National Register of Historic Places, begin at the Meeting Haus, 588 S. Third St., 614/221-8888. One-hour tour: $5 adults, $4.50 seniors, $2.50 students; two-hour tour: $15 adults, $12.50 seniors, $5 students. (2–4 hours)*

★★★★ **INNISWOOD METROPARK GARDENS**
940 Hempstead Rd., Westerville, 614/891-0700, TDD 614/895-6240

One of central Ohio's best-kept secrets lies behind the black wrought-iron gates of this 92-acre facility in Westerville. Visitors are told straight off that this park is different from other metroparks in Columbus and Franklin County. No picnicking, jogging, or biking are allowed here, not to mention pets or loud music. However, a peaceful and serene ambiance is created by running brooks, soft breezes, and paths under a wooded canopy next to a carefully planned rock garden. Nine cultivated garden areas, along with the natural woodland trails, provide ample room for visitors to refresh themselves year-round. Complimentary guided tours are available by appointment.

Details: *Daily 7 a.m. until dark. (1–2 hours)*

★★★★ MARTIN LUTHER KING, JR. PERFORMING AND CULTURAL ARTS COMPLEX
867 Mt. Vernon Ave., 614/252-5464, for box office and information

The King Arts Complex offers a wide range of activities and programs focusing on local, regional, national, and international talent. Two galleries house changing exhibitions, often featuring African American works, while the 440-seat theater offers plays, dance, and music. Lectures and symposiums are also held throughout the year. Try to visit during the annual Holiday Festival of Gifts in mid-November, especially if you're looking for great presents.

Details: *Tue–Sat 1–4; Tue, Thu until 7. Call TicketMaster for events. (1-2 hours)*

★★★★ NORTH MARKET
59 Spruce St., just west of the Columbus Convention Center, 614/463-9664

Whether you're looking for a hard-to-find ingredient, great carry-outs, or just browsing, you'll enjoy a visit to Columbus's old-fashioned marketplace in the Short North. Colorful sights and a

HARDING MEMORIAL IN MARION

© Marcia Schonberg

bustling combination of shoppers, some thirty merchants, and weekend entertainers bring a unique, energetic ambiance to the shopping and dining mecca that has attracted folks since 1876. (It was also the location of Columbus's first graveyard.)

Details: *Mon 9–5 (optional for merchants), Tue–Fri 9–7, Sat 8–5, Sun 12–5. (2 hours)*

★★★★ OHIO CRAFT MUSEUM
1665 W. Fifth Ave., 614/486-4402

This museum on the outskirts of the Grandview area offers changing themed art exhibitions and an annual juried show by members of the Ohio Designer Craftsmen. The organization has more than 2,000 members—artisans and patrons from all over the country, many of whom are invited to exhibit in the three upper galleries here. You'll see contemporary fine arts and crafts as well as one of the six to eight special exhibits planned each year. The gallery shop offers works by members and focuses on pieces by current exhibitors.

Details: *Mon–Fri 10–5, Sun 1–5. Free. (1 hour)*

★★★★ OHIO VILLAGE AND THE OHIO HISTORICAL CENTER
I-71 and 17th Ave., 614/297-2300 or 800/OLD-OHIO

You can visit Ohio during the Civil War era by strolling the streets of this re-created town, shopping at the general store where village crafters sell their wares, and eating an 1860s-style meal at the Colonel Crawford Inn. A wooden boardwalk connects Ohio Village buildings, including a town hall, print shop, pharmacy, lawyer's office, and several craft shops, where a tinsmith, harness maker, weaver, and others explain their trades. In the newest old building, a Gothic Revival–style church, you can attend Civil War–era living history lessons via the modern technology of cyberspace and fiber optics in an educational center on the lower level. A full calendar of family-oriented events occurs throughout the year, including special programs like the American Girls series featuring Addy, a child escaping from slavery in the 1860s. At the adjacent center, permanent and changing exhibits highlight Ohio's diverse history and ancient Indian cultures.

Details: *Historical Center: Mon–Sat 10–5, Sun and holidays 10–5; Ohio Village: Wed–Sat 9–5, Sun and holidays 10–5. Closed during the Ohio State Fair and Wed following a Mon holiday. Check for extended holiday hours. $4 adults, $1 children 6–12. Fees include admission to both the village and the historical center. (half–full day)*

NOW YOU'RE COOKING

With a few extra hours in Columbus, you can take home the recipes and enjoy a sampling of your favorites at cooking school. Classes, both the hands-on variety and demonstration-style options, are offered regularly at the **Culinary Academy at Columbus State Community College**, 550 E. Spring St., 614/287-COOK, **Handke's Cuisine**, 520 S. Front St., 614/621-2500, and **Columbus Fish Market Cooking Classes**, 1245 Olentangy River Rd.,

★★★★ **THURBER HOUSE**
77 Jefferson Ave., 614/464-1032
If you're looking for a cozy and comfortable place where you can take a book from the shelf and make yourself at home, or snoop around a bit if you wish, then stop by this interesting museum that commemorates James Thurber, one of this century's most famous humorists and cartoonists. Each room in the small, two-story, 1873 Victorian home, where "the budding young writer" spent his college years, is delightfully marked by a plaque in the literary style of the author. The house is a good place to shop for Thurber's works, many of which are set in this house, as well as autographed copies of books written by others.
   Details: *Daily noon–4. Narrated tours Sun on a drop-in basis. Guided tours $2 adults, $1.50 children 3–17. Self-guided tours free. (1–2 hours)*

★★★ **KELTON HOUSE MUSEUM AND GARDEN**
586 E. Town St., 614/464-2022
This restored Greek Revival home on the city's near east side was built in 1852 for a prominent abolitionist family whose relatives occupied the home for 123 years. Opulent Victorian furnishings reflect life in the late 1800s. Tour guides provide detailed anecdotes, complete with ghost stories, Civil War history, and Underground Railroad tales. The home is managed by the Junior League of Columbus and is available for private rentals.

Details: Sun 1–4. Group tours Mon–Fri by appointment. $1.50 adults, $1 children. (1 hour)

★★★ OHIO STATE UNIVERSITY
Student Visitor Center, 154 W. 12th Ave., 614/292-3980
Ohio State has the country's largest student population on a single campus. You can take a guided walking tour and a behind-the-scenes tour, and also visit **Ohio Stadium**, where all 93,000 seats are filled when the OSU Buckeyes take to the field on football Saturdays. Don't miss browsing the **Wexner Center for the Arts**, a contemporary museum at the main entrance to the campus at North High and 15th Streets. Then it's a ride over to Value City Arena at the **Jerome Schottenstein Center**, home of the Buckeyes' men's and women's basketball and men's ice hockey teams. When sports teams aren't on the courts, the center hosts big-name events and entertainers.

Details: Campus tours from the Student Visitor Center Mon–Fri 10–2. Reservations 2 weeks prior are needed. Call 3 weeks ahead for the free behind-the-scenes tour, 614/292-0418. Free tours of Wexner Center, 614/292-0330, Thu, Sat 1 p.m. Regular museum hours Tue–Sun 10–6, to 9 Thu. Suggested admission $3 adults, $2 seniors and students. Free Thu 5–9. (1–2 hours)

★★★ TOPIARY GARDEN: "A SUNDAY AFTERNOON ON THE ISLAND OF LA GRANDE JATTE"
Corner of E. Town and Washington Ave., one block south of the Columbus Museum of Art, 614/645-0197
Located on the grounds of the old Deaf School Park on Columbus's near east side, this exhibit is the only current topiary interpretation of a master's painting. The original hangs in the Art Institute of Chicago, but some 50 topiary people, along with eight boats, a monkey, and a cat, re-create a living scene of Georges Seurat's famous work. The effects are fullest from mid-July through November. It is operated by the Columbus Recreation and Parks Department.

Details: Daily sunrise–sunset. Free. Wheelchair accessible. For topiary information and gifts, visit Yewtopia on Town in the gatehouse. (1 hour)

★★ HANBY HOUSE STATE MEMORIAL
160 W. Main St., Westerville, 614/882-4291

SIDE TRIP: MARION

A short drive northwest of Columbus will lead you to this community that's known for its many unique museums.

Warren G. Harding was born in nearby Blooming Grove on November 2, 1865, but it was from the front porch of his Marion home that he launched his presidential campaign and issued his "back to normalcy" pleas following World War I. The home, at 380 Mount Vernon Avenue, was built in 1891 and was occupied by the Hardings until they moved to the capital. Today it's operated by the Ohio Historical Society and is open for tours Memorial Day weekend through Labor Day Wednesday through Saturday from 9:30 to 5 and on holidays and Sunday from noon to 5. During September and October, hours are Saturday from 9:30 to 5 and Sunday from noon to 5. November through May the house is open by appointment. Call 800/600-6894 for more information and to make an appointment. A short drive from the presidential home is the **Warren G. Harding Memorial**, at the corner of Delaware Avenue and Vernon Heights Boulevard, where the tombs of the former president and his wife are encircled by marble pillars. This largest presidential monument outside Washington, D.C., sits on 10 acres off U.S. 23 in Marion and is open year-round, sunrise to sunset.

While you're reminiscing, stop at the **Wyandot Popcorn Museum** on the lower level of Heritage Hall, 169 E. Church St., 614/387-4255, home of the Marion County Historical Society. The hall is open May through October Wednesday through Sunday from 1 to 4 and on weekends from 1 to 4 the remaining months. Donations only are requested.

The **Victoriana Bed-and-Breakfast**, 343 S. State St., 614/382-2430, offers four beautifully furnished and decorated guest rooms with private and shared baths, at very reasonable rates. One of the special treats of this distinctive B&B is the vast collection of musical machines the innkeepers display for guests and visitors to enjoy. A reproduction grand piano, old Victrolas, and a mechanical violin, not to mention an assortment of nickelodeons, music boxes, and antique arcade games, provide old-fashioned entertainment. Don't judge this B&B by its facade, which was in need of scraping and painting when I visited. The interior is nicely restored, and the innkeepers are eager to show you a good time. Nonguests are welcome to make an appointment for a free tour. Give them a call—I'm sure they'll drop a nickel in the nickelodeon for you.

This home museum, a station on the Underground Railroad, is the pre–Civil War home of composer Benjamin Hanby, who wrote many familiar tunes, including "Up on the Housetop."

Details: Tours May–Oct Sat–Sun 1–4, other times by appointment. $2 adults, $1.50 adult groups of 5 or more, 75¢ children 6–12. (1 hour)

★★ **MOTORCYCLE HALL OF FAME MUSEUM**
13515 Yarmouth Dr., Pickerington, 614/882-2782 or 614/856-1900, www.ama-cycle.org/
Cycles spanning more than a century, on loan from private owners, usually remain on exhibition here for two years alongside the special exhibits displayed in this museum dedicated to preserving America's motorcycling heritage. You'll admire vintage models and the shiny ones of later periods, and you can purchase memorabilia in the museum shop. The new museum is located on the same campus as the American Motorcyclist Association.

Details: Mar–Oct daily 9–5; other months Mon–Fri 9–5. $3 adults, $2 seniors, children 17 and under free. Wheelchair accessible. (1–2 hours)

★★ **OHIO GOVERNOR'S RESIDENCE TOUR**
358 N. Parkview Ave., 614/644-7644, resident manager
One of the city's little-known secrets is a tour of this lavish mansion. Guided tours of the garden, when weather permits, and first-floor public spaces give visitors a peek at some of the home's original furnishings as well as those on loan from the Ohio Historical Society and collected by Ohio's First Ladies.

Details: Tours currently available for groups of 10–50. Reservations required. Tue 1:30 and 2:30. Free. (1 hour)

★★ *SANTA MARIA* **REPLICA**
109 N. Front St., 614/645-8760
If you've ever wondered what it was like on Christopher Columbus's flagship during his exploratory voyage, then tour this museum-quality reproduction, docked downtown on the Scioto River in Battelle Riverfront Park. You'll visit the dark living quarters and perhaps help the onboard interpreter-sailors hoist the sails or tie a knot.

Details: Call ahead for hours, which vary by season. $3.50 adults, $3 seniors, $1.50 students. (1–2 hours)

FITNESS AND RECREATION

Outdoor enthusiasts do not have to travel far to find hiking trails, bike paths, and nature centers. Ten Columbus Metroparks, 614/891-0700, encircle the city and offer a year-round calendar of planned events as well as facilities for leisure activities. You'll find nature trails at nearly all parks and biking-jogging paths through **Blacklick Woods**, 6975 E. Livingston Ave., and **Sharon Woods**, 6911 Cleveland Ave. Five parks have cross-country-ski rentals, and others offer wildlife observation areas, fishing, and canoeing. Cyclists, in-line skaters, and walkers can enjoy the **Olentangy-Scioto Bikeway**, a Rails-to-Trails project. Especially scenic portions wind along the Olentangy River, around the lake at **Antrim Park**, and through the **Whetstone Park of Roses**, all on the north side of town. For additional information call the City of Columbus Recreation and Parks Department, 614/645-3300.

Golfers can obtain a detailed visitor's guide to 73 of the area's courses, both public and private. Call the Greater Columbus Convention & Visitors Bureau, 800/354-2657. Information about indoor exercise facilities and a wide variety of spectator sports, including games at the **Columbus Crew Stadium**, 614/221-CREW, the first professional soccer stadium built in the United States, and the new **Nationwide Arena**, home of Columbus's NHL franchise, the **Blue Jackets**, due to open September 2000.

FOOD

Columbus can boast about its dining possibilities. Although Columbus has few ethnic neighborhoods, the area's menu selections span the globe. Try **Tapatio Restaurant**, 491 N. Park St., 614/221-1085 (behind the North Market), for upscale dining and atmosphere with tastes of the Caribbean and Mexico. Don't miss **Spain**, 3777 Sullivan Ave., 614/272-6363, or 888 E. Granville–Dublin Rd., 614/840-9100, for northern Spanish favorites and delicious homemade sangria. New Mexican fare is at its best at **Chile Verde**, 4852 Sawmill Rd., 614/442-6630, and 375 Stoneridge Ln., 614/478-6525 and to the north, casual French fare is new at **Voilà**, 55 Hutchinson Dr., Columbus, 614/846-5555.

Irish pub food and music are only a short drive away, in Dublin, Ohio, at **The Brazenhead**, 56 N. High St., Dublin, 614/792-3738.

Children will enjoy **Bravo! Italian Kitchen**, 3000 Hayden Rd., in northwest Columbus, 614/791-1245, and 1470 Vantage Dr., in North Columbus, 614/888-3881, as will grown-ups who love wood-fired pizza and wood-grilled entrées of substantial portion and reasonable price. Great upscale Italian food with a martini bar to match are at Cameron Mitchell's **Martini Ristorante & Bar**, 455 N. High St., in the Short North, 614/22-ITALY.

While in the Short North, also try the seafood at **R. J. Snappers Bar and Grill**, 700 N. High St., 614/280-1070, the American and Mediterranean fare at **Rigsby's Cuisine Volatile**, 698 N. High St., 614/461-7888, and **Lemongrass: An Asian Bistro**, 641 N. High St., 614/224-1414. **Frank's Diner** in the North Market, 614/621-2233, is open for breakfast, lunch, and dinner, but breakfast is exceptional.

Another restaurant, in the Cameron Mitchell group of restaurants scattered about the city and suburban communities, is **Cap City Diner**, 1299 Olentangy River Rd., 614/291-FOOD, where you;ll find blue-plate specials served in up-scale style. At the **Columbus Fish Market**, you'll find not only uniquely prepared fresh catches on the menu but also a retail market selling delicacies in this upbest, lively restaurant. **Columbus Brewing Company**, 525 Short St., 614/464-2739, in the Brewery District, adjacent to German Village, offers small-batch beers, a unique and varied menu, and outdoor dining.

Try great house brews and lighter fare at **Hoster Brew Pub**, 550 S. High St., 614/228-6066, a spot for live entertainment, too. You'll find ribs at the lively **Damon's**, 89 E. Nationwide Blvd., 614/228-7421, located in the midst of the downtown convention area.

Many dining possibilities can be found in German Village, but one especially interesting ethnic landmark dating from 1886 is **Schmidt's Sausage Haus and Restaurant**, 240 E. Kossuth St., 614/444-6808. Stop in for a Bahama Mama (spicy sausage), a frosty mug of beer, cream puffs, and a German songfest. Other favorites in the neighborhood are **G. Michael's Italian-American Bistro & Bar**, 595 S. Third St., 614/464-0575, and **Lindy's**, 169 E. Beck St., 614/228-4343.

For spots with a neighborhood feeling, visit the **Drexel Radio Café**, 2256 E. Main St., 614/231-0498, which serves *panini* (sandwiches) and the like at reasonable prices, before or after a movie at the Drexel Art Theater next door. You'll also find Italian authenticity at **Giuseppe's Ritrovo**, 2268 Main St., Bexley, 614/235-4300, in the same block. The **Red Door Tavern**, 1736 W. Fifth Ave., 614/488-5433, has been a local hangout for Buckeye fans for years, and the **Buckeye Hall of Fame Café**, 1421 Olentangy River Rd., 614/291-2233, offers American dishes, a huge collection of football memorabilia, and a game room.

Handke's Cuisine, 520 S. Front St., in the Brewery District, 614/621-2500 and **Fifty-Five on the Boulevard**, 55 Nationwide Blvd., downtown, 614/228-5555 offer fancier options.

On the lighter side, coffeehouses such as **Stauf's Coffee Roasters**, 1277 Grandview Ave., 614/486-4861, and **Cup O'Joe Coffee Dessert House**, 627 S. Third St. in German Village, 614/221-1JOE, are fun people-watching

GREATER COLUMBUS

N

Whitehall

Gahanna

HAVENS CORNERS RD

MILLERSBURG RD (JOHNSTOWN RD)

DUBLIN-GRANVILLE RD

WALNUT ST

Westerville

D

C

E

PARK RD

161

71

WORTHINGTON RD

FLINT RD

O

P

N

Worthington

R

23

M

MORSE RD

CLEVELAND-COLUMBUS-WOOSTER RD

SUNBURY RD

AGLER RD

17TH AV

5TH AV

INDIANOLA AV

H

4TH ST

SUMMIT ST

23

HIGH ST

G

Olentangy River

315

F

KENNY RD

BETHEL RD

K

I

SAWMILL RD

Q

COLUMBUS-MARYSVILLE RD

Upper Arlington

33

(RIVERSIDE DR)

Scioto River

B

257

J

Dublin

HAYDEN RUN RD

270

33

70

BROAD ST

62

670

NELSON RD

Bexley

MAIN ST

L

40

40

16

SPRING ST

Columbus

HIGH ST

CENTRAL

BROAD ST

40

To A

ROAD   HIGHWAY

SCALE   KILOMETERS   MILES

0   4   4

spots with outdoor seating and outstanding coffees to linger over. Although the bagel business is booming all over the city, my favorite is **Sammy's New York Bagels** at City Center Mall, 614/228-8425, and also at 1583 W. Lane Ave., 614/487-1126. All 20 varieties are strictly kosher.

If you crave fast food, by all means stop where square burgers first hit the griddle back in 1969—**Wendy's Original Restaurant**, 257 E. Broad St., downtown, 614/464-4656. The museum/restaurant exhibits memorabilia (all the toys that ever came with the kids' meals), reruns of your favorite commercials (including the famous "Where's the beef?" one), and more of what made this Columbus-based chain unique.

LODGING

Bed-and-breakfasts near downtown put you close to sightseeing, shopping, and cultural activities. The only African American B&B in the state, **Henderson House**, 1544 Atcheson St., 614/258-3463, blends history, elegant antiques, and ties to former presidents and famous people. Good choices in German Village are the **Inn on City Park**, 1023 City Park Ave., 614/443-3048, and **Lansing St. B&B**, 180 Lansing St., 800/383-7839. Close to the bustle in the Short North is **50 Lincoln Inn**, 50 E. Lincoln, 888/299-5051, with an artsy atmosphere. The **Westin Great Southern Hotel**, 310 S. High St., 614/228-3800 or 800/228-3000, is a historic downtown landmark adjacent to the recently restored Southern Theatre. The historic **Worthington Inn**, 649 High St., Worthington, 614/885-2600, provides Victorian flavor in each of its uniquely decorated rooms and suites. You can find national hotels and motels within every price range throughout the

SIGHTS

- Ⓐ Barber Museum and the Barbering Hall of Fame
- Ⓑ Columbus Zoo
- Ⓒ Hanby House State Memorial
- Ⓓ Inniswood Metro Park Gardens
- Ⓔ Motorcycle Hall of Fame Museum
- Ⓕ Ohio Craft Museum
- Ⓖ Ohio State University

SIGHTS (continued)

- Ⓗ Ohio Village and the Ohio Historical Center

FOOD

- Ⓘ Bravo! Italian Kitchen
- Ⓙ The Brazenhead
- Ⓚ Chile Verde
- Ⓛ Drexel Radio Café
- Ⓜ Giuseppe's Ritrovo
- Ⓝ Spain
- Ⓞ Voilà

LODGING

- Ⓟ Sheraton Suites
- Ⓠ Woodfin Suites Hotel & Business Cneter
- Ⓡ Worthington Inn

Greater Columbus area, but a few, like the **Red Roof Inn**, 111 Nationwide Blvd., 614/224-6539 or 800-THE-ROOF, located downtown across from the convention center in what used to be a warehouse, have distinctive accommodations. The **Lofts Hotel**, 55 Nationwide Blvd., 614/461-2663 or 800/73-LOFTS, adjacent to the **Crowne Plaza**, 33 Nationwide Blvd., 614/461-4100 or 800/465-4329, in the same region, oozes with upscale New York style for a luxuriously sophisticated getaway; prices are New York style, too. The newly refurbished **Sheraton Suites**, 201 Hutchinson Ave., 614/436-0004, and **Woodfin Suites Hotel & Business Center**, 4130 Tuller Rd., Dublin, 800/237-8811, are great for families.

CAMPING

Scenic wooded sites, both electrical and primitive, are available at nearby state parks, including **Delaware State Park**, 614/369-2761, **Alum Creek State Park**, 614/548-4631, and **Deer Creek State Park**, 614/869-3124. Deer Creek also offers cabins and a full-service lodge. The historic **Harding Cabin**, used by the president and his staff as a retreat during the Teapot Dome scandal, is also available for rent and touring, 800/282-7275. Campsites are first come, first served; fees vary from $9 for nonelectric sites at Delaware to up to $15 for electric hookups at all three. Call 800/BUCKEYE for more details.

NIGHTLIFE AND THE PERFORMING ARTS

One of the most popular spots for an evening's worth of free entertainment is Short North during Gallery Hop, the first Saturday evening of each month, when galleries stay open late, crowds mill the sidewalks, and street performers entertain. The **Actors' Theatre**, 614/645-5415, performs several free productions at the Schiller Park amphitheater in German Village each summer, while community and college productions gear up elsewhere around town. An ample supply of live theater productions—professional, community, and touring varieties—are available. Call the Greater Columbus Arts Council, 614/224-2606, for a listing that includes opera, dance, and theater companies. The local daily newspaper, the *Columbus Dispatch*, will keep you abreast of the current area billings, including the **Columbus Symphony Orchestra** season, summer **Picnic with the Pops** performances, 614/228-9600, and the **Fifth Third Bank Broadway Series**, 614/224-7654.

8
HOCKING HILLS REGION

If you've ever wanted to escape to a cabin in the woods, you couldn't find a better Ohio spot than the Hocking Hills. Even if you can't move permanently, you can live out your fantasy at one of the many cabins for rent or choose from motel, B&B, and lovely country inn accommodations in every price range.

Many of Ohio's most scenic panoramas are found along the miles of trails within this southeastern region. During spring and early summer, waterfalls and wildflowers are both plentiful and breathtaking. Some of the adventure of spring hiking lies in listening for and finding unknown and unnamed waterfalls that will disappear after a summer dry spell, and in spotting the first wildflowers of the season. Trillium, lady's slipper orchids, and dogwoods cover the landscape with pastel shades, while ferns and moss are among the rich green hues of the woodland floor. Fall colors bring the largest crowds to the hills and gorges, while winter's snowfall and frozen waterfalls attract a hardy breed of hiker and thousands of day-trippers who appear on the third Saturday of January for the annual six-mile winter hike.

The 2,000 acres of Hocking Hills State Park and the surrounding 9,000 acres of Hocking State Forest have become some of the state's most popular attractions, with over one million visitors per year. Yet the parks continue to maintain their pristine character, truly reflecting their cultural and geological history.

A PERFECT DAY IN THE HOCKING HILLS REGION

Begin with breakfast outdoors on the deck of a cabin or at one of the area's B&Bs or country inns. If you're visiting in winter, opt for breakfast indoors, perhaps near a cozy fire, before getting ready for a morning hike. Arrange for a lesson in rappelling, unless you're experienced, in the Hocking State Forest. Take an afternoon hike at Conkle's Hollow State Nature Preserve. Return for a soak in the outdoor hot tub and enjoy a glass of wine before treating yourself to a romantic gourmet dinner at one of the unique local inns.

SIGHTSEEING HIGHLIGHTS

★★★★ ATHENS
Athens County Convention & Visitors Bureau, 800/878-9767 or 740/592-1819

This college community, home of **Ohio University** (the first college in the Northwest Territory), unfurls a wealth of creativity. Local artists, both performing and visual, enjoy the combination of peaceful and economical rural surroundings in Appalachian hill country and the intellectual energy of the educational community. The uptown area features galleries, gift and specialty shops, local college watering holes, and some upscale eateries as well. If you wander into **Blue Eagle Music**, 40 N. Court St., 740/592-5332, you'll find hand-crafted acoustic guitars and mandolins and likely meet those who perform at the **Casa Cantina**, down the street. The owners feature "organic, hand-prepared Mexican and eclectic cuisine" and walls of art in the **Casa Nueva** restaurant portion of their establishment. Galleries adding local flavor include **Court Street Collection**, 64 N. Court St., 740/593-8261; **Lamborn's**, 19 W. State St., 740/593-6744; and **Mountain Leather & General Store**, 25 S. Court St., 740/592-5478.

You'll want to visit the **Kennedy Museum of Art**, on the campus at Lin Hall, The Ridges, 740/593-1304. Amid the 1860s Victorian Italianate restoration of a hilltop building first known as the Athens Lunatic Asylum, you'll discover a wonderful collection of Native American art, other American pieces, and, of course, great architecture. Another must-see, **Dairy Barn Southeastern Ohio Cultural Arts Center**, adjacent to the university, 8000 Dairy Ln., 740/592-4981, began as a huge dairy barn and was spared from the

HOCKING HILLS REGION

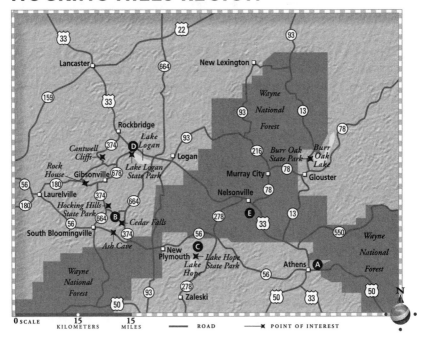

SIGHTS

- **A** Athens
- **B** Hocking Hills State Park
- **B** Hocking State Forest
- **C** Lake Hope State Park and Zaleski State Forest
- **D** Lake Logan State Park
- **E** Robbins' Crossing

Note: Items with the same letter are located in the same area.

wrecking ball just in time to create a state-of-the-art exhibition space that focuses on regional art.

Ohio University provides the music and live entertainment during your visit with events such as the **Performing Arts Series**, 740/593-1762, the **Athens International Film & Video Festival**, 740/593-1330, and the **Annual Spring Literary Festival**, 740/593-4181. Nearby, **Stuart's Opera House**, on the square in Nelsonville, 740/753-1924, combines live community per-

© Marcia Schonberg

formances and the ambiance of earlier times in yet another 1879 Victorian restoration.

Details: *At U.S. 33 and U.S. 50 in southeastern Ohio. (half day minimum)*

★★★★ HOCKING HILLS STATE PARK
20160 OH 664, Logan, 740/385-6841

The park's visitors center on OH 664 is a good spot to start. Trail maps explaining the geological timetable of the Blackhand sandstone and shale bedrock layers that form the park's spectacular scenery are available here, as well as picnic sites, restrooms, and a gift shop. Cedar Falls, Old Man's Cave, Ash Cave, Conkles Hollow, Rock House, and Cantwell Cliffs are among favorite sites. Hiking trails weave throughout the 11,000-acre park and forest.

Behind the visitors center, a short trail leads hikers to **Old Man's Cave**, the most popular spot in the park. The unique rock formations here may have interested visitors for thousands of years. Nomadic hunters might have found shelter here during the Ice Age. According to literature, the Adena culture, and then the Fort Ancient Indians, also found homes within these rocks. The area was named after a recluse, Richard Rowe, who lived in the caves during Civil War times. Legend has it that he is buried beneath the ledge of the main recess cave.

Trails lead hikers to the **Upper and Lower Falls**, the **Devil's Bathtub** (a pothole in the sandstone formed by a swirling stream carrying sand and gravel), and **Sphinx Head** (named for its resemblance to the Egyptian riddler). Some six miles of trails begin in this area and connect three of the six cave areas of the park: Ash Cave, Cedar Falls, and Old Man's Cave.

One of the most impressive sites in the park is **Ash Cave**. After walking through a narrow gorge lined with old-growth hemlocks, hikers come upon a 700-foot-wide expanse of sandstone with a 90-foot waterfall cascading to a plunge pool below. It's the largest recess cave in the state, but what's really noteworthy is that it's easy and totally wheelchair accessible. The rugged **Cantwell Cliffs**, the **Rock House**, and **Conkle's Hollow State Nature Preserve** each offer unique rock formations and diverse plant life. The **Upper Rim Trail**, considered by many to be the best trail in the state, encircles the gorge at Conkle's Hollow for spectacular views. Because of its height, it is dangerous and not appropriate for young children, according to park naturalists, who advise all hikers to be cautious and to remain on trails. It's one of the most scenic spots in the area, especially during spring and fall. Cliff faces reach heights of more than 200 feet.

Details: Year-round. Free. (1 day minimum)

★★★★ HOCKING STATE FOREST
19275 OH 374, Rockbridge, 740/385-4402

Managed for multiple use, this forest provides a blend of vegetation common in northern locations. Many of the marked trails are favorites among horseback riders, while parts of the **Buckeye Trail** weave through other sections. Rock climbing and rappelling in 99 acres of rocky terrain a mile east of Conkle's Hollow State Nature Preserve, and hunting and fishing in season, are permitted. One particularly scenic spot is **Airplane Rock**, accessible by hikers and horseback riders and a perfect spot for a picnic. From the parking lot on Hockman Road off Big Pine Road, be prepared for the three-mile hike to Airplane Rock. Berries, nuts, and mushrooms may be picked, except at nature preserves.

Details: Year-round, but because of seasonal hazards, the forest is closed to visitors after dark. Rock climbing and rappelling area, on Big Pine Rd., offers parking at the base of the trail leading to cliff faces. Free. (half day minimum)

★★★★ LAKE HOPE STATE PARK AND ZALESKI STATE FOREST
Lake Hope State Park, Zaleski, 740/596-5253; Zaleski State Forest, Zaleski, 740/596-5781

About 20 miles southeast of Hocking Hills State Park, this state forest and the lake within its boundaries attract swimmers, boaters, campers, and backpackers. Once the site of giant iron furnaces used to process ore extracted from the sandstone bedrock, the area has since recovered and is a prime nature and wildlife locale. A bridle camp and primitive backpacking sites, plus those with heated shower-houses and electrical hookups, are available. Ice fishing, sledding, ice-skating, and cross-country skiing are wintertime options. Contact the Division of Forestry for a backpacking trail guide that outlines the scenic and historic aspects of the forest along the 10-mile day-use trail. The main trail covers 23.5 miles.

Details: Park and forest daily 6 a.m.–11 a.m.; campers, hunters, and fishers may make extended stays. Free. (half day minimum)

ADVENTURES IN LEARNING

As if the scenery weren't enough to entice visitors to the Hocking Hills, guests can combine the outdoor activities with others planned throughout the region and seasons as part of the "Adventures in Learning" series. Classes in basket weaving, gourmet cooking, wine tasting, poetry reading and writing, photography, and hikes accompanied by state naturalists are but a few on the long list of possibilities. Advance reservations are required. Contact the Hocking County Tourism Association, 740/385-9706, to request the current schedule.

★★★★ **LAKE LOGAN STATE PARK**
30443 Lake Logan Rd., Logan, 740/385-3444, park office; 740/385-6727 boat rentals
Public swimming and prime fishing for anglers interested in catching bluegill, crappie, bass, muskie, catfish, and northern pike are available at this lake park located only a few miles north of Hocking Hills State Park. A variety of boats, including pontoons, canoes, and powerboats, are rented by the hour and day. You'll also find a portion of the Buckeye Trail running through the park and hills for winter sledding.
    Details: Daily 7 a.m.–9 a.m. Rentals range from $6 per hour for paddle boats to $15 per hour for pontoon boats. (half day minimum)

★★★ **ROBBINS' CROSSING**
Hocking Technical College, 3301 Hocking Pkwy Nelsonville, 740/753-3591
Robbins' Crossing is one of those communities where time stands still. The clock stopped somewhere in the mid-1800s in this town typical of early southeastern Ohio. Today, college students don period wardrobes to relive the pioneer era in a unique teaching laboratory—a living-history interpretation program at **Hocking Technical College** in Nelsonville. Future interpreters energetically provide a hearty sampling of the era by inviting visitors to try their skills at the various workstations in the village. Weaving, candle making, and open-hearth cooking are a few of the daily tasks. Note that Robbins' Crossing is also a stop along the **Hocking Valley Scenic Railway**

HOCKING HILLS REGION

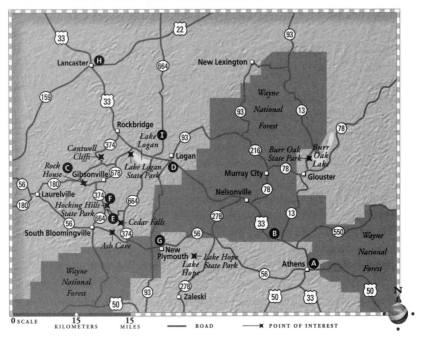

FOOD

- Ⓐ Big Chimney Baking Co.
- Ⓐ Bob Evans
- Ⓐ Casa Nueva
- Ⓑ Coffee Cup Restaurant
- Ⓒ Glenlaurel: A Scottish Country Inn and Cottages
- Ⓓ Great Expectations
- Ⓔ Hocking Hills Lodge
- Ⓕ Inn at Cedar Falls
- Ⓓ Jack's Steak House
- Ⓓ M. R. Mac's Café
- Ⓓ Olde Dutch Restaurant

FOOD (continued)

- Ⓖ Ravenwood Castle (Coach House)
- Ⓐ Seven Sauces
- Ⓗ Shaw's Restaurant and Inn

LODGING

- Ⓐ AmeriHost Inn, Athens
- Ⓓ AmeriHost Inn, Logan
- Ⓐ Ash Caves Cabins
- Ⓘ Burr Oak State Park
- Ⓘ Crockett's Run
- Ⓒ Glenlaurel: A Scottish Country Inn

LODGING (continued)

- Ⓕ Inn at Cedar Falls
- Ⓕ Log Cabins at Cedar Grove
- Ⓐ Ohio University Inn
- Ⓕ Old Man's Cave Chalets
- Ⓖ Ravenwood Castle and Olde Worlde Cottages
- Ⓑ Resort at Blackjack Crossing

Note: Items with the same letter are located in the same area.

and can be reached as well via the **Hock-Hocking Adena Bikeway**, a new, 17-mile, multipurpose recreational trail running from Athens.

Details: Educational center open Memorial Day–Oct 31 Sat–Sun noon–5. Free. (2–4 hours)

FITNESS AND RECREATION

Outdoor enthusiasts will find recreational pastimes beyond hiking and walking, although naturalists say they could direct you to a different hike each day for more than a week without repeating themselves. Even beginners who have never driven all-terrain four-wheel-drive vehicles can safely venture out on the trails constructed by the U.S. Forest Service within the **Wayne National Forest**. Some 70 miles of twisting trails wind throughout the 5,000 acres, developed specifically for use by mountain bikers and those on four wheels. During winter, the trails are perfect for snowshoes and cross-country skis. For trail information, call 740/592-6644.

Hocking State Forest contains 99 acres, located on Big Pine Road one mile east of Conkle's Hollow, where rock climbers and rappellers may test their skills. Top-rope sites for climbers of all abilities are available. For instruction and outdoor gear, contact Hocking Outdoor Sports, 12789 OH 664 S, Logan, 740/385-5312. Classes, costing $50 per person for a four-hour lesson, include all equipment. Group rates are available.

*Students in Hocking College's award-winning Culinary Arts School "learn by doing" at the **Ramada Inn**, OH 691 in Nelsonville, 740/753-3531. Students test their skills and creativity in preparing meals in the hotel's two eateries, which are owned and operated by the college: the **Garden Terrace Restaurant** for casual dining and **The Foxfire**, a gourmet restaurant.*

Depending on weather conditions, canoeing on the Hocking River usually provides a more leisurely activity. Trips range from five to seven miles, but those looking for a longer trip can book one at the Hocking Hills Canoe Livery, 12789 OH 664 S, Logan, 800/634-6820. Opt for a moonlight or dawn wildlife trip, if possible, or try your skill at tubing or kayaking. Tubs, rafts, and kayaks rent for $8, $12, and $14 at Hocking Valley Canoe Livery, 31251 Chieftain Dr., Logan, 800/686-0386.

The **Hocking Valley Scenic Railway**, P.O. Box 427, Nelsonville,

Lancaster, with a current population just over 35,000, was founded before Ohio became a state. It originated as New Lancaster, named after the early German settlers' home in Lancaster, Pennsylvania. The town's founding father, Ebenezer Zane, put the town on the map when he blazed "Zane's Trace," the first national road and the only primary entry into Ohio, in 1797. That's just the beginning of the lesson in Lancaster history.

You can learn more by borrowing an audiotape and headphones for the self-guided **Square 13 Historic Walking Tour**, which explains the city's outstanding nineteenth-century architecture. The tour takes one hour, and the tape is available at the Fairfield County Convention and Visitors Bureau, 1 N. Broad, Lancaster, 800/626-1296, or next door at Shaw's Restaurant & Inn.

Several home museums are open for tours, including the **Sherman House Museum**, 137 E. Main St., 740/654-9923, where guides tell boyhood stories of Civil War General William Tecumseh Sherman and his younger brother John, who served as U.S. senator, secretary of the treasury, and secretary of state, and wrote the Sherman Anti-Trust Act. Furnishings in the small brown frame house are in keeping with the period; some personal items are displayed. Hand-stenciled borders of a pale pink hue, made from a raspberry-juice wash, decorate the dining room, used to entertain such notable travelers as Daniel Webster and Henry Clay, en route from Washington across the National Road to Kentucky. Around the corner, you can stroll through the **Georgian Museum**, 105 E. Wheeling St., 740/654-9923, the cornerstone of the area, although technically located in Square 12. The Federal-style home, an American adaptation of English Georgian architecture, boasts five Ionic columns, curved bays, and rooms full of period furnishings. Both the Sherman House and the Georgian are open April through

800/967-7834 or 614/470-1300, departs from the U.S. Route 33 station in Nelsonville at noon on a 12-mile round-trip to nearby Haydenville. The cost is $7.50 for adults and $4.75 for children ages 2 to 11. A 2:30 p.m. train leaves on a 25-mile round-trip to Logan through the Hocking Hills; the fare is $10.50 for adults and $7.25 for children. From Memorial Day through October, the historic passenger train operates on weekends only, with Santa trips planned over Christmas.

Ride or walk the **Hock-Hocking Adena Bikeway** for 17 miles be-mid-December Tuesday through Sunday from 1 to 4 and by appointment the remainder of the year.

Antique shops and galleries add unique shopping opportunities, and a local coffee house, **Four Reasons Bakery and Deli**, 135 W. Main St., 740/654-2253, serves some 20 sandwich combinations, fresh coffee and tea, soups, salads, and desserts, including Cincinnati's Graeter's Ice Cream. Another dining and lodging choice is **Shaw's Restaurant & Inn**, 123 N. Broad St., 740/654-1842 or 800/654-2477, open for breakfast, lunch, and dinner every day. Reservations are advisable, especially on weekends. French country cooking, a wild-game menu, a connoisseur wine and cigar evening for couples, Italian specialties week, and other gastronomic feasts are planned throughout the year. Overnight accommodations come with breakfast and range from $61 to $177, depending on which of the 21 uniquely decorated rooms you choose.

Located nearby are **Rising Park** and **Mount Pleasant**, maintained by the Lancaster Parks and Recreation Department, for picnicking, fishing, walking, and hiking up the rather steep but scenic incline for an overview of the town. The music of the **Lancaster Festival** each July attracts crowds. Each fall, **Frontier Spirit 1799**, a living-history drama, is held along the two walking trails at Alley Park. Costumed actors lure walkers back in time as they tend to their pioneer chores along the guided hiking path. For quiet spots, try **Wahkeena State Nature Preserve** in Sugar Grove south of Lancaster, 740/746-8695, or **Buckeye Lake State Park**, Millersport, 740/467-2690, for fishing and picnicking. For more information, contact the Lancaster Parks and Recreation Department, 740/687-6651, and the Lancaster and Fairfield County Visitors and Convention Bureau, 800/626-1296.

tween Nelsonville and Athens. It takes its name from the Native American word for the crooked Hocking River and leads visitors past towpath remnants of the Hocking Canal, Robbins' Crossing village, Ohio University, and other scenic and historic sites. Adjacent to the trail, Wazoo Bike Rentals, 9980 Armitage Rd., Athens, 740/592-5655, offers adult and children's bicycles, including some with training wheels. Tandems are also available, and you can arrange for delivery or pick-up. Limited rentals are available at the Ramada Inn in Nelsonville.

FOOD

Cuisine in the Hocking Hills runs the gamut from picnics and campfires to up-scale dining with entrées prepared by resident chefs. In the middle is an array of eateries where the locals go.

Reservations are required at the two small inns in the Hocking Hills. **Glenlaurel: A Scottish Country Inn and Cottages**, 15042 Mount Olive Rd., Rockbridge, 800/809-REST, where Scottish bagpipe music calls you to the 7 p.m. seating and soft Celtic background music plays throughout the meal, prepares five-course meals during the week and seven-course rack of lamb dinners on the weekend. At the **Inn at Cedar Falls**, 21190 OH 374, Logan, 800/65-FALLS, culinary feasts prepared in the open kitchen of an 1840s log cabin set the ambiance for a casual yet delicious experience. Fixed prices for the five- to six-course meals are $21 during the week, $30 on weekends. Wine, beer, and box lunches are available.

At nearby **Ravenwood Castle**, visitors and guests can enjoy lunch and tea in the **Coach House**, 65666 Bethel Rd., New Plymouth, 800/477-1541. In Lancaster, about 20 minutes northeast of Logan, diners can select from a wide variety of regional favorites and unique specialties at **Shaw's Restaurant & Inn**, 123 N. Broad St., Lancaster, 800/654-2477. Special themed dinners and events are often planned.

For less expensive experiences, try **Jack's Steak House**, 35770 Hocking Dr., Logan, 740/385-9909, or, for Amish-style fare, the **Olde Dutch Restaurant**, U.S. 33 and OH 664, 740/385-1000. Both are local favorites. In downtown Logan, **M. R. Mac's Cafe** provides the refreshments in a small complex of gift and antique retailers, 4 E. Main St., 740/380-1817. You can "build-your-own" sandwich, choose a popular wrap, or opt for a homemade dessert to accompany your coffee drink. Peruse the bookstore and gifts, then stop for Italian *panini* (grilled sandwiches) at **Great Expectations**, located in a restored nineteenth-century Victorian home, 179 S. Market St., 740/380-9177. **Hocking Hills Lodge**, 740/385-6495, located inside the park, offers informal dining with nice views. Box lunches and party packs are also available.

Bob Evans, 12930 OH 664, Logan, 740/385-1878, and 357 E. State St., Athens, 740/592-3842, and other chains dot the region. If you continue further toward Athens, you'll run into unique eateries in the "uptown" neighborhood of the Ohio University community. Many of the restaurants, including **Casa Nueva**, 4 W. State St., Athens, 740/592-2016, pride themselves on their use of locally grown, organic, fresh ingredients. You might try others like **Seven Sauces**, 66 N. Court St., Athens, 740/592-5555. They offer a varied menu—steaks, pasta, and vegetarian offerings moderately priced but up-scale—and are open for dinner only.

A popular, family-owned and family-run roadside stopping place, the **Coffee Cup Restaurant**, between Athens and Nelsonville on U.S. 33, 749/753-3336, features down-home cooking from a large menu, reasonable prices, and friendly service. You'll need to take the back roads to find the **Big Chimney Baking Co.**, 8776 Mine Rd., Athens, 740/592-4147, but once you do, you'll discover dozens of European hearth breads, scones, and sweets—with many jams and olive oils to accompany them.

LODGING

Lodging choices are plentiful here. Each year more B&Bs spring up to answer the needs of additional tourists. Cabin owners keep building, and inns add to their amenities. The area has quite a reputation as a romantic getaway—if not for its natural serenity and beauty, then for the number of cozy fireplaces and decks with hot tubs in the woods. The cabins often sleep six, so if you choose to vacation with your family, you will have plenty of room. Larger rentals for multiple-family trips and family reunions are also available.

The tone is simple and authentically rustic, with no phones or TVs, at the **Inn at Cedar Falls**, 21190 OH 373, 800/65-FALLS, www.innatcedarfalls.com. You'll find beautifully renovated and fully equipped nineteenth-century log cabins nestled in the woods and nine rooms furnished with Shaker-style antiques in a barnlike structure. Several are wheelchair accessible. Rates include a gourmet breakfast.

All the luxuries of home, and then some, are found in the cabins at **Crockett's Run**, 9710 Bauer Rd., Logan, 800/472-8115. Cabins and lodge facilities, with accommodations large enough for family reunions and business retreats, are located minutes from the Buckeye Trail. A self-guided interpretative trail marks interesting wildlife habitat, local history, and significant plant life for a 1.75-mile segment of the Crockett's Run trails.

Vacation log homes are popular in the Hocking Hills. You'll find many choices and prices—hot tubs with each—at **Old Man's Cave Chalets**, 18905 OH 664 S, Logan, 800/762-9396. Try the **Resort at Blackjack Crossing**, 18170 OH 664 S, Logan, 800/504-9993, where owners have recently added a swimming pool for guests, or the **Log Cabins at Cedar Grove**, 19601 OH 664, Logan, 800/889-3397. At **Ash Cave Cabins**, 25780 Liberty Hill Rd., South Bloomingville, 800/222-4655, you select a cabin that sleeps up to 10 people or a little "lovebug" cabin, big enough for a couple yet fully equipped with fireplaces, decks, and kitchen amenities.

If you're looking for a European-style getaway, try a stay at **Glenlaurel: A Scottish Country Inn**, 15042 Mount Olive Rd., Rockbridge, 800/809-REST.

You'll find country cottages as well as rooms in the manor house and carriage house, gourmet meals, serenity, and a Scottish ambiance, all overlooking Camusfearna Gorge. A Scotch exchange student helps out each summer. Port Columbus International Airport pickup service can be arranged. Stained-glass windows, castle doors, and meals served in the Great Hall at **Ravenwood Castle and Olde Worlde Cottages**, 65666 Bethel Rd., New Plymouth, 800/477-1541, attract visitors who want to live in a castle, at least for a few days. The owners loved their treks to European castles so much that they finally built their own.

Dozens of B&Bs are located in the area. Contact the Hocking County Tourism Association, 800/HOCKING, for a list of Hocking Hills Bed and Breakfast Association members. Remember to inquire about rooms with private baths and amenities, as some establishments offer little more than home stays. If you're looking for reasonable rates, a continental breakfast, and a pool, the **AmeriHost Inn**, 12819 OH 664, Logan, 800/459-4678, may ft the bill.

Nearby, in Athens, try the **Ohio University Inn**, 331 Richland Ave., 740/593-6661, the **AmeriHost Inn**, 20 Home St., Athens, 740/594-3000, or the lodge at **Burr Oak State Park**, 30 minutes north, in Glouster, 800/282-7275.

CAMPING

Hocking Hills State Park, 740/385-6841 (park office), 740/385-6165 (camp office), offers campsites, rustic cabins, and swimming pools along with park activities. A few rent-a-camp units are available. Secluded deluxe campsites at **Crockett's Run**, 9710 Bauer Rd., Logan, 800/472-8115, feature covered picnic tables, hot tubs, hot showers, valet service (all sites are a distance from vehicle parking), and a social hall. You can rent a horse or bring your own to **Smoke Rise Ranch Resort**, Murray City, 800/292-1732, which offers campsites, bunkhouse-style cabins, a swimming pool, a hot tub, and clubhouse barbecues and dances for you, and trails, pastures, and stalls for your four-legged friends. **Palmerosa Family Campground**, 19217 Keifel Rd., Laurelville, 740/385-3799, provides miles of scenic trails for hikers and horse riders alike. Bunkhouses are available, and owners will arrange rentals for horseless guests.

9
OHIO RIVER TOWNS

From an economic point of view, the Ohio River is a passageway for millions of tons of freight. For visitors and tourists, however, the lure of the river comes in the relaxing pastimes along its banks or aboard a paddle wheeler. No matter the activity, spending time along the Ohio River is a sure cure for stress.

The river has an inviting ambiance, whether you're enjoying the river from its largest Ohio port in Cincinnati or from the small river towns—like Point Pleasant, Ripley, Manchester, Portsmouth, Gallipolis, Marietta, or Steubenville. Each has its share of antique shops and riverfront charm.

From the river, the towns evoke memories of yesteryear, with gaps of wilderness between. From scenic river routes of U.S. 52, OH 7, and others, recently designated the Ohio River National Scenic Byway, you'll cover almost 500 miles if you drive the entire route. You'll also notice the poverty of the region's Appalachian counties. As the trees change colors in fall, tobacco crops turn the landscape bright chartreuse, and weathering tobacco barns full of drying golden leaves paint pastoral scenes uncommon elsewhere in Ohio.

I suggest you stop in Marietta, dubbed the "Riverboat Town," which conjures up the Mark Twain era and riverboating at its best. You'll understand why some folks drive several hours each day to their jobs, just so they can live along the river.

OHIO RIVER TOWNS

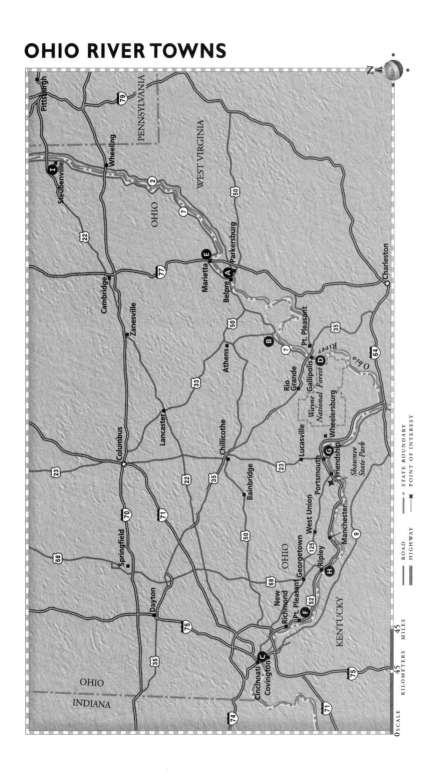

A PERFECT DAY IN THE OHIO RIVER TOWNS

If you have only one day, spend it in Marietta, where you can easily lunch next to the river, visit museums, take a packet cruise, and rent a room at a riverboat B&B. If you're lucky enough to be cruising the Ohio River, perhaps as a passenger aboard one of the Delta Queen steamboats, which recall a bygone era, you'll be greeted as you disembark for a day of sightseeing. Hour-long trolley tours provide an architectural and historical overview of the town, maps provided by the visitors bureau guide you to the county's 10 covered bridges, and antique shops and gift emporiums await in the revitalized downtown. The Ohio River Museum and Campus Martius Museum, both operated by the Ohio Historical Society, are must-dos.

SIGHTSEEING HIGHLIGHTS

★★★★ BUFFINGTON ISLAND CIVIL WAR BATTLE SITE
About 20 miles east of Pomeroy on OH 124, Portland, 800/686-1535 or 740/297-2630

Just a few miles south of Marietta, on the banks of the Ohio River, is Ohio's only Civil War battle site. At this site, in July 1863, 10,000 Union troops headed off Morgan's raiders. A memorial constructed from Ohio's glacial rock marks the spot where re-enactors gather each summer to commemorate the battle; picnic grounds are available for visitors at other times. The area north along the Ohio River is also known for Under-ground Railroad stations and "safe houses."

James Garfield, Rutherford B. Hayes, and William McKinley fought on the Buffington Island battlefield. All from Ohio, each went on to become President of the United States.

Details: *The Buffington Island Civil War Site is not on an island, but it is near the banks of the Ohio River. The parklike setting is managed*

SIGHTS

© *Marcia Schonberg*

by the Ohio Historical Society and is open year-round during daylight hours. Free. Self-guided Underground Railroad tour maps are available through the Marietta Washington County Convention & Visitors Bureau, 800/288-2577.

★★★★ DELTA QUEEN STEAMBOAT COMPANY
Robin St. Wharf, 1380 Port of New Orleans Place, New Orleans, LA 70130, 800/543-1949

Riverboating is the ideal experience for the romantic who yearns for a taste of life from a bygone era, especially on the deck of the vintage *Delta Queen* or one of her newer sisters, the *Mississippi Queen* and the *American Queen*. The *Delta Queen* still bears her Port of Cincinnati registry, although the line is now based in New Orleans. On a four-day trip between Cincinnati and Pittsburgh, you'll make friends onboard while waving to townspeople at each lock and stopping at the river towns along the way. The musician at the brass calliope serenades onlookers as the steamboat churns past each lock and landing.

Details: *Call for brochures and information about theme cruises, special packages (like free children's fares), destinations, and schedules. Fares range from $800 to $2,740 per person for the four-day trip. (4 days minimum)*

★★★★ GALLIPOLIS
County seat of Gallia County in southeastern Ohio on U.S. 35, 800/765-6482

This river town south of Marietta dates back to early French settlers who came to the New World only to find they owned false deeds to land along the Ohio River. A walking tour highlights remnants of this early "French 500" community, while an audio tour, available at the Ohio Valley Visitors Center, 45 State St., Gallipolis, 800/765-6482, will direct you through rural Gallia County in the hills along the river. Personal anecdotes and relaxing music enliven the 45-minute journey. The award-winning tape can be purchased for $5.

Points of interest along the way include the **Bob Evans Farm** on OH 588 in Rio Grande, 800/994-FARM. Here guests can canoe, ride horses, and visit the farm museum, craft barn (where you'll find more than 60 crafters year-round), and log cabin village. The farm is open daily Memorial Day through Labor Day, with special events in summer and fall. You can buy grains and flour year-round at **Jewel**

Evans Grist Mill nearby. In Gallipolis a worthwhile stop is the re-stored tavern operated by the Ohio Historical Society. Dressed in period garb, interpreters take on characters of the past, such as the tavern's founder, Henry Cushing, who speaks of the Revolutionary War heroes he has entertained in the brick, Federal-style establishment now called **Our House State Memorial**, 432 First Ave., Gallipolis, 800/752-2618. It's open Tuesday through Saturday from 10 to 4 and Sunday from noon to 4. Tours last about one hour and cost $3 for adults, $2 for seniors, and $1 for children. Antiques made by the French artisans who settled Gallipolis in 1790 are featured. The beautifully restored Victorian **Ariel Theatre**, 426 Second Ave., 740/446-ARTS, is home to the **Ohio Valley Symphony** and the **Ariel Players**, a resident community theater troupe.

Details: (full day)

★★★★ **MARIETTA**
Southeastern Ohio on the Ohio River at I-77, 800/288-2577
Marietta calls itself the "Riverboat Town"—with good cause. A visit soon reveals the town's enthusiasm for both its history and its scenic location at the confluence of the Muskingum and Ohio Rivers. Townspeople gather along the riverbank to wave at the passing steamboats; the locals happily share the nostalgia for Marietta's history. Museums, historic streets, and districts such as **Harmar Village** recall 1788, when Marietta was the first permanent settlement in the Northwest Territory. Nowadays, Marietta is a great place to find a quiet repast while enjoying the river.

The **Ohio River Museum**, 601 Front St., Marietta, 740/373-3717, and the adjacent **W. P. Snyder Jr.**, the only surviving coal-fired, steam-powered stern-wheeler in the United States, are good starting points for visitors. They detail the Ohio River's role in the formation of the United States, especially during the steamboat era. Hollowed-out canoes made by Native Americans, calliopes, and stern wheels from old riverboats are a few of the artifacts here. Museum hours are weekdays from 9:30 to 5; Sunday from noon to 5. Admission is $5 for adults and $1.25 for children 6 to 12. (2 hours)

Campus Martius: The Museum of the Northwest Territory, 601 Second St., Marietta, 800/860-0145, traces migration in Ohio and occupies the site of the first organized settlement. Part of the original fort and home of Rufus Putnam (the oldest existing residence in Ohio and home of Marietta's founding father) are the focal points. The **Ohio Land Office** is behind the museum. Admission is $5 for adults and $1.25 for children 6 to 12. The office is open in March, April, October, and November Tuesday through Saturday from 9:30 to 5, Sunday from noon to 5. Hours May to September Monday through Saturday are from 9:30 to 5, Sunday from noon to 5.

Narrated excursions on the *Valley Gem*, a 300-passenger riverboat moored at the 600 block of Front Street, 740/373-7862, remind guests of the stern-wheel packet boats that once traveled the Muskingum and Ohio Rivers (although the *Gem* was built in 1989). Trips run hourly June through August, weekends in May and September, and at 10 a.m. and 2 p.m. (by reservation only) for October fall foliage viewing. Tickets are $5.50 for adults and $3 for children. Saturday evening dinner cruises sport a buffet meal from 5:30 to 7:30. Permanently docked on the Muskingum, the **Showboat Becky Thatcher Theater**, 237 Front St., Marietta, 740/373-6033, box office 740/373-4130, toll free 877/SHO-BOAT, offers evening entertainment. Dining overlooks the river, and nineteenth-century-style melodramas and vaudeville revues encourage the audience's boos, cheers, and hisses on the first deck of the showboat. Performances run $12 for adults, $10 for seniors and students, and $5 for children under 12; dinner prices are moderate.

The showboat is listed on the National Register of Historic Places, as is the **Lafayette Hotel**, 101 Front St., Marietta, 800/331-9336 (800/331-9337 in Ohio), another of the town's landmarks. The Lafayette offers dining and overnight accommodations. A drive around Marietta College, where fraternities and sororities are housed in turn-of-the-century Victorian mansions, and a tour of **The Castle**, 418 Fourth St., 740/373-4180, an outstanding example of Gothic Revival architecture, provide a sampling of nineteenth-century Marietta. Admission to the castle is $3.50 adults, $3 for seniors, and $2 for children six and older.

The quaint shops and restaurants in **Historic Harmar Village**, in the 100 block of Maple Street, include **Harmar Station**, 220 Gilman St., 740/374-9995, where more than 250 train models are displayed and some 20 are continuously operating. It's open daily from 11 to 5; admission is $5 for adults, and children under fourth-grade age are admitted free with an adult. Nearby points of interest include the **Fenton Art Glass Company**, 420 Caroline Ave. in Williamstown, West Virginia, 304/375-7772, and the **Lee**

Middleton Original Doll Company, 1301 Washington Blvd., Belpre, 740/423-1481. Factory tours and "preferred seconds" outlet shopping are available at both. (1–2 days)

★★★★ RIPLEY
One hour east of Cincinnati on U.S. 52; Brown County Chamber of Commerce, 888/276-9664

This river town with a population around 1,800, designated as a historic district, ranks high on my list for its importance in abolitionist times and for the active restoration process under way. On a hill overlooking the town and river stands the **Rankin House**, Rankin Rd., Ripley, 800/752-2705, where John Rankin, a Presbyterian minister and founder of the Ohio Anti-Slavery Society, helped more than 2,000 slaves escape. It is open June through August Wednesday through Saturday from 10 to 5, Sunday from noon to 5, and on weekends in September and October. On Front Street, you can drive past the former home of John Parker, a freed slave who assisted many others as a conductor on the Underground Railroad. Currently under renovation, it will open for tours when renovations are completed.

The **Ohio Tobacco Festival**, held each August in Ripley, is the town's major event, but the **Dulcimer Festival**, held over Memorial Day weekend, is also gaining popularity. The **River Village Christmas** celebration brings sightseeing to the river town the second weekend in December.

One of the most unique shops in town, brimming with in-stock tiems, is the **Some Old Man**, 113 Main St., Ripley, 937/392-4221, where—you guessed it—some old man crafts custom-made leather goods. (1–2 days)

★★★ BLENNERHASSETT ISLAND STATE PARK
Between Belpre, OH, and Parkersburg, WV, in the Ohio River

I first learned of this island and its historical park during a steamboat cruise down the Ohio River. The captain decided to add an unplanned port of call midway between Belpre, in Washington County, and Parkersburg, West Virginia. The customary arrival method is aboard the *Blennerhassett* or *Centennial,* two stern-wheelers that depart Point Park in Parkersburg on a regular schedule. On the island, you can choose the mansion tour or a horse-drawn wagon ride through the shady park. Craft vendors selling regional folk art have set up a small village along a path in a wooded setting. It's the place to amble while awaiting the stern-wheeler for the return trip.

Blennerhassett Island receives much of its fame from the "Palace in the Wilderness," a Palladian-style mansion with European gardens built by owners Harman and Margaret Blennerhassett in 1800— when drab log cabins typically dotted the frontier.

The Blennerhassett story ends in poverty, with Harman serving a prison sentence for his affiliation with Aaron Burr. You may wish to begin your tour with a video about the couple at the **Blennerhassett Museum** in downtown Parkersburg. Then it's a short walk to Point Park to pick up the stern-wheeler for the ride to the island.

Details: Purchase tickets at the museum, 137 Juliana St., Parkersburg, 304/420-4800. During summer the museum is open Mon by appointment only and other days 9:30–6. The island is closed on Mon and open 10–5:30 other days. Call ahead for schedules and information on seasonal special events. The round-trip ferry costs $6 adults, $5 children 3–12. Tickets are also available at the visitors center next to Point Park. Mansion tour $3 adults, $2 children; wagon ride is $3.50 adults, $2 children. (2 hours)

★★ **POINT PLEASANT**
Southeast of Cincinnati on U.S. 52, 800/796-4282

Ulysses S. Grant, the first native Ohioan to become a U.S. president, was born in a small frame house along the Ohio River in Point Pleasant. Allow about 45 minutes for a careful look at the two-room birthplace before heading to his boyhood home some 35 miles east in Georgetown. Grant's 1823 Georgetown home, built when he was a year old, and seven other homes in that community make up the **"Land of Grant"** tour. Several homes are closed to the public, but **Grant's Boyhood Home**, 219 E. Grant Ave., Georgetown, 937/378-4222, displays many rare artifacts. **Grant's Schoolhouse**, 508 S. Water St., Georgetown, 937/378-4119, has been completely restored recently by the Ohio Historical Society.

Details: Birthplace open for touring Apr–Oct Wed–Sat 9:30–noon and 1–5, Sun noon–5. $1 adults, $.75 seniors, 50¢ children. Boyhood home open Mon–Sat 9–1 and 2–5. Free, but donations accepted. The schoolhouse is open May 22–Sept 5 Wed–Sun noon–5; mid-Sept–Oct Sat–Sun noon–5. (3 hours)

★★ PORTSMOUTH

Two hours south of Columbus on U.S. 23

The Portsmouth riverfront offers beautiful views, especially from Sawyer's Point, with benches facing west for spectacular sunset vistas. Locals describe the Front Street floodwall as "2,000 feet of art" and worth a drive-by to see it awash in murals. Portsmouth's history and famous citizens, including Roy Rogers, Branch Rickey, Jim Thorpe, and Shakespearean actress Julia Marlowe, come to life through the work of muralist Robert Dafford. Forty lifelike portrayals have been completed, with at least 10 more scheduled.

Details: Contact Portsmouth Convention and Visitors Bureau, 324 Chillicothe St., Portsmouth, OH 45662, 740/353-1116. (3–4 hours)

★★ STEUBENVILLE

On the Ohio River, bordering West Virginia and a short distance from Pennsylvania, 800/510-4442

The heritage of this river town, known as the "City of Murals," is best explained through the larger-than-life artwork around the city. The decorated walls began as a move to revitalize the downtown. More than a decade later, 26 murals are downtown and in outlying regions. Various works depict scenes from the 1800s and before, when **Fort Steuben** was built for protection against Indian sieges. Other works depict the steamboat era. You can visit eight buildings in **Old Fort Steuben**, Third and Adams Sts., Steubenville, 740/264-6304, and the **First Federal Land Office** behind it, 740/264-4534.

You'll learn everything you've ever wanted to know about Jaguars at the **Welsh Classic Car Museum**, Fifth and Washington Sts. When you spy a collection of red British telephone boxes and several Jags parked nearby, you'll know you're there. Museum entrance is free to diners at **Jaggin' Around**, located in the same complex.

Details: For a map of Steubenville, or to arrange a guided tour, call 740/282-0938. Fort open May–Sept daily 11–4; $1 adults, children free. Museum open Sun–Wed noon–6, Thu–Sat noon–8. (3–4 hours)

FITNESS AND RECREATION

The wilderness setting of **Shawnee State Park**, 4404 OH 125, Portsmouth, 740/858-6652, makes it perfect for nature hikes and other outdoor pastimes. You'll find a lake for fishing, boating, and swimming, as well as many picnic sites, an 18-hole golf course, and miles of bridle trails.

Trails lead to river views, covered bridges, and beautiful scenery in the **Wayne National Forest**. For details call 740/373-9055. **Bob Evans Farm**, Rio Grande, 800/994-FARM, has a canoe livery and horse stables for hourly trips or overnight camping combinations. The visitors center provides information on self-guided walking and hiking tours through hilly Appalachia.

FOOD

One of the highlights of a visit to Marietta is dining at the **Levee House Café**, 127 Ohio St., 740/374-CAFE. Housed in an original riverfront, Federal-style building, the restaurant serves its meals with freshly baked bran rolls and features entrées made with Rossi Pasta created down the street. The restaurant on the **Showboat Becky Thatcher** stern-wheeler, 740/373-4130, moored on the Muskingum River, offers a varied menu with after-dinner entertainment possibilities of a light vaudeville show or melodrama. For a reasonably priced yet freshly prepared and appealing selection, try **Bridgwater 1*2*3**, 130 Front St., Marietta, 740/374-6344, a bistro and coffee bar. Hand-crafted local brews (and delicious root beer) are served up with a bit of history at **Marietta Brewing Company**, 167 Front St., Marietta, 740/373-BREW. The **Gun Room** at the **Historic Lafayette Hotel**, 101 Front St., Marietta, 800/331-9336 (800/331-9337 in Ohio), serves traditional American cuisine.

In Steubenville, try **Lenora's Cafeteria**, 350 Hollywood Plaza, 740/266-6555. I don't usually recommend cafeterias, but this one is different. The food is freshly prepared, and the uniquely decorated rooms recall a Main Street past. It serves lots of homemade pies for dessert and free baby food. **Jaggin' Around Restaurant and Pub** in the Jaguar Museum building, 501 Washington Street., 740/282-1010, serves pasta, grilled entrées, burgers, and more.

About 90 minutes east of Cincinnati, you'll come to **Moyer's Vineyards Winery and Restaurant** on U.S. 52 in Manchester, 937/549-2957, overlooking the river, where delicious lunches and dinners prepared with garden-fresh herbs are served. The cheese, bean, and bacon soup and grated lemon pie are two of the signature items—and do try the local wine. Saturday reservations are recommended.

Rockin' Robin's Soda Shoppe, 8 N. Front St., 937/392-1300, is a popular spot in Ripley. The 1950s-themed shop faces the river and serves a local favorite: marshmallow Coke (too sweet for my taste, but everyone else seems to like it).

OHIO RIVER TOWNS

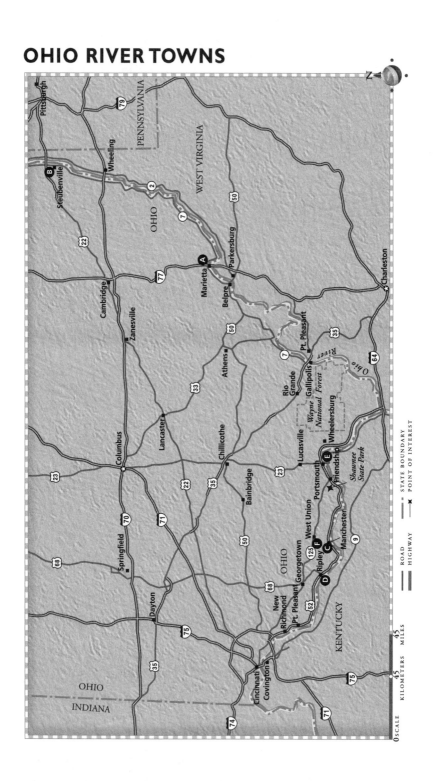

LODGING

My suggestions for overnight accommodations along the river are in restored historical settings, all of which, in one way or another, show signs of long use. However, they also feature a river ambiance, perhaps by overlooking the water or maybe as the former home of a captain. If you prefer rooms with private baths, you may not find these B&B accommodations to your liking. National chains, including a **Holiday Inn**, 701 Pike St., Marietta, 740/374-9660, dot the Marietta area and other larger towns along the river.

Though not located on the river, the **Murphin Ridge Inn**, 750 Murphin Ridge Rd., West Union, 937/544-2263, is highly recommended. Set on 140 acres at the edge of the Appalachian foothills, the inn offers queen-size beds and full baths plus walking trails, a seasonal pool, rocking chairs, and modern rooms furnished with David T. Smith reproduction pieces. Breakfast is included in the room rates, which are between $80 and $100. Dinner, prepared by the on-site chef, is available to guests every day, and to the public Wednesday through Saturday and Sunday afternoon.

The charming and freshly restored **Captain's Quarters**, 529 Sixth St., Portsmouth, 740/354-6609, provides a delightful breakfast outside in the garden patio, weather permitting.

Among the choices in river view in Ripley are **Signal House B&B**, 234 N. Front St., 937/392-1640, and **Misty River B&B**, 206 N. Front St., 937/392-1556, said to have hosted Ulysses S. Grant as a boarder while he attended Whittmore Private School across the river.

To continue the riverboat-town theme, you might consider booking a room aboard the *Claire E.*, which is permanently moored on the west bank of the Muskingum River at Noland's Landing, 900 Gilman Ave., Marietta, 740/374-CAFÉ. It is the only stern-wheeler B&B in the United States. There

---

FOOD

- Ⓐ Bridgewater 1*2*3*
- Ⓐ Gun Room at the Historic Lafayette Hotel
- Ⓑ Jaggin' Around Restaurant and Pub
- Ⓑ Lenora's Cafeteria
- Ⓐ Levee House Café

FOOD (continued)

- Ⓐ Marietta Brewing Company
- Ⓒ Moyer's Vineyards Winery and Restaurant
- Ⓓ Rockin' Robin's Soda Shoppe
- Ⓐ Rossi Pasta
- Ⓐ Showboat Becky Thatcher

LODGING

- Ⓓ Buckley House
- Ⓔ Captain's Quarters
- Ⓐ *Claire E.*
- Ⓐ Historic Lafayette Hotel
- Ⓐ Holiday Inn
- Ⓕ Murphin Ridge Inn
- Ⓓ Signal House B & B

Note: Items with the same letter are located in the same area.

are three staterooms on the 115-foot boat; it's best to rent all three or go with others with whom you are very friendly.

Landlubbers may opt for accommodations at the **Buckley House**, 332 Front St., Marietta, 740/373-3080, or the **Historic Lafayette Hotel**, 101 Front St., Marietta, 800/331-9336 (800/331-9337 in Ohio). Each of the 78 rooms in the 100-plus-year-old Lafayette is uniquely furnished.

CAMPING

You can go backpacking and camping in the **Shawnee State Forest**, 13291 U.S. 52, Portsmouth, 740/858-6685. Rustic cabins and a lodge, as well as a horse camp and electric and nonelectric sites, are found at **Shawnee State Park**, within the Shawnee State Forest. Primitive sites are located within the **Wayne National Forest**, 740/373-9055. Overnight canoe and horseback trips are popular at **Bob Evans Farm**, Rio Grande, 800/944-FARM, or campers may prefer to settle in at one of the many sites available at the farm and choose among day options.

Scenic Route: Pike Lake Loop

For the past 30 years visitors have been coming to the Appalachian foothills around Bainbridge during the Fall Festival of Leaves on the third weekend in October. But you can enjoy this scenic tour any time of year.

The 32-mile Pike Lake Loop travels through **Pike Lake State Park**, following routes taken by early settlers. From Bainbridge, head east on U.S. 50 and turn right onto Potts Hill Rd., heading toward the village of **Nipgen**. You'll pass several small old cemeteries and interesting vistas off to the left, as well as old outhouses, along the way. Look for the **Driapsa Home**, a log house built in 1866. Turning left onto OH 772, you'll see **Eggar's Inn**, a stopping place for Morgan's Raiders, a band of 2,400 Confederate cavalrymen who gave Ohio its only taste of the Civil War. You'll pass Pike Lake, created in the 1940s by the Civilian Conservation Corps. Turn north onto Greenbriar Road at **Tanglewood Acres**, a horse campground. Here the narrow roads lead through a magnificent rainbow of fall foliage. A right turn onto Jester Hill Road provides more great vistas.

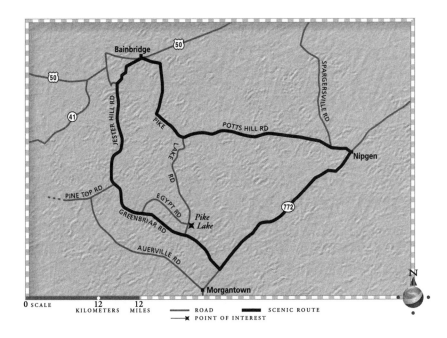

10
CINCINNATI

Cincinnati attracts tourists for many of the same reasons people like to settle there. It's not one those "nice place to visit, but I wouldn't want to live there" areas. Over the years it has lived up to its early title of "Queen City of the West" and has gone on to earn other superlative ratings. It offers big-city attributes, attracting Fortune 500 companies and retailers from both coasts. From its seat on the banks of the Ohio River, it offers scenic and leisurely activities along with a rich cultural and ethnic diversity.

The downtown boasts tall buildings, fountains, open plazas, public art, and enclosed walkways. Neighborhoods like Mount Adams, with its hilly streets lined with narrow and often colorful brownstones, remind visitors of San Francisco. City and county parks are plentiful, and rural areas and woodlands are within easy reach.

Traveling further west, nearly to the Indiana state line, leads visitors to Hamilton and then Oxford, home of Miami University (MU) and the McGuffey Museum. You can have an enjoyable leisure weekend here, whether you have a student attending MU or not.

If you're looking for world-renowned attractions or unique treasures in small museums and neighborhoods, you'll find them here. Unlike other big cities, Cincinnati does not rank high in cost of living or cost of travel. Most of my food and lodging choices fall within the moderate range, though you can spend more or less without ever losing the ambiance of this grand Queen City.

CINCINNATI

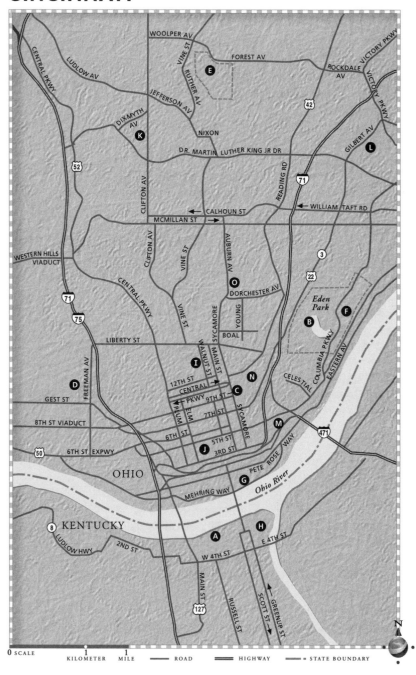

A PERFECT DAY IN CINCINNATI

Start the day at the Museum Center, then visit Krohn Conservatory and the Cincinnati Art Museum with a stop at Twin Lakes Overlook, in Eden Park. Have lunch in Mount Adams at Rookwood Pottery, then head to one of the county parks, perhaps north of I-275 to the Miami Whitewater Forest for a scenic afternoon walk along one of the Shaker Trace Multipurpose Trail loops. Try nine holes (or baskets) of Frisbee golf in the park before some last-minute shopping downtown, perhaps to pick up something to wear to dinner at one of Cincinnati's four- or five-star restaurants.

SIGHTSEEING HIGHLIGHTS

★★★★ BB RIVERBOATS
1 Madison Ave., Port of Cincinnati, Covington, KY
800/261-8586

BB Riverboats' four-craft fleet, including its authentic stern-wheeler, offers a full menu of cruise choices: harbor excursions, gambling and horse-racing junkets, overnight vacations with stops at quaint towns along the way, Sunday brunches, lunch trips, and dinner-dance tours. The multiday river hops are especially popular with seniors looking for an all-inclusive minivacation. Highlights are good food and a "river-lorian" who spices up the trip with historical anecdotes.

Details: *Reservations are required for all trips, and schedules do change, so call ahead for up-to-date information and an itinerary. Prices vary. The daytime harbor cruise starts at $9 adults, $8 seniors, $5*

SIGHTS

Ⓐ BB Riverboats
Ⓑ Cincinnati Art Museum
Ⓒ Cincinnati Fire Museum
Ⓓ Cincinnati Museum Center at Union Terminal
Ⓔ Cincinnati Zoo and Botanical Garden
Ⓕ Krohn Conservatory
Ⓖ National Underground Railroad Freedom Center

Ⓗ Newport Aquarium
Ⓘ Over-the-Rhine Historic District
Ⓙ Queen City Driving Tour
Ⓚ Skirball Museum, Hebrew Union College-Jewish Institute of Religion, Cincinnati Branch
Ⓛ Stowe House State Memorial

Ⓜ Taft Museum
Ⓝ Verdin Bell and Clock Museum
Ⓞ William Howard Taft National Historic Site

---

children 4–12 and runs as high as $34.95 adults, $33.95 seniors, $19.95 children for a Sat evening "Admiral's Dinner Dance." Wheelchair accessible. (1–2 hours for day trips)

★★★★ **CINCINNATI ART MUSEUM**
953 Eden Park Dr., 513/721-5204,
www.cincinnatiartmuseum.org
You'll find everything here you would expect from any large metropolitan museum, with a comprehensive collection covering all major periods, but this museum adds galleries devoted to important contributions of local artists and the **Rookwood Pottery Gallery**, highlighting the artists who created this renowned Cincinnati art pottery. A hall of musical instruments, a skylit gallery of modern art, and a café are also included. Printed guides designed for younger children and teens are available at the front desk.

Details: Tue–Sat 10–5, Sun noon–6. Admission free on Sat, when family tours are also offered. Other days, $5 adults, $4 seniors and college students, children under 18 free. The first Fri evening of each month Sept–May, check out TGIF ("Thank van Gogh It's Friday!"), a monthly party with music and food. (1–3 hours)

★★★★ **CINCINNATI FIRE MUSEUM**
315 W. Court St., 513/621-5553
A fire museum in Cincinnati is appropriate—the fire pole was invented and firefighters were first paid for their services here. After entering the museum, housed in the former downtown station, you can choose to reach the lower level for an introductory video via the fire pole or a ramp. Then it's off to learn about famous fires and how firefighters worked in the days when horses stood under the "Joker's Drop" for a quick hitch to the fire truck and the "Bucket Brigade" sprang into action. Life-size models of historical scenes have faces of the real Cincinnati firefighters who helped build the museum, and hands-on exhibits, such as a hand pump, give children and adults a test of their strength. A "Safe House" provides lessons in emergency know-how and fire precautions.

Details: Tue–Fri 10–4, Sat–Sun noon–4. $4.50 adults, $3 seniors, $2.50 children. Closed Mon and major holidays. (1 hour)

★★★★ **CINCINNATI MUSEUM CENTER AT UNION TERMINAL**
1301 Western Ave., 800/733-2077 or 513/287-7000

This site houses the Cincinnati History Museum, Cincinnati Historical Society Library, Museum of Natural History and Science, Robert D. Lindner Family Omnimax Theater, and Cinergy Children's Museum all under one roof.

One of the favorite areas in the history museum is the *Cincinnati Goes to War: A Community Responds to WWII* exhibit. It is touted as the nation's largest portrait of the home front during World War II, and it focuses on wartime experiences of Cincinnatians through three-dimensional interactive exhibits. Interestingly, the day-to-day vignettes are placed in the very spot where GIs boarded the trains that would take them to war. In this area you also gain a good perspective of the art deco train station before its 1990s revival. Other displays focus on early settlers and river life.

You can explore more at the Children's Discovery Center in the Museum of Natural History and Science, which also offers a simulated limestone cavern and Ice Age exhibits, and if time permits, don't miss the Omnimax production. The **Rookwood Ice Cream Parlor** provides dairy snacks in an art deco atmosphere featuring the pottery's tiles. Museum shops carry a wide range of unusual gifts.

Details: Mon–Sat 9–5, Sun 11–6. Admission per museum $6.50 adults, $4.50 children; two museums $9 adults, $6 children; three museums $12 adults, $8 children; all four museums $15 adults, $10 children. Omnimax Theater admission is $6.50 adults, $5.50 seniors, $4.50 children, $3.50 infant pass (1 and 2 year olds). (full day)

★★★★ **CINCINNATI ZOO AND BOTANICAL GARDEN**
3400 Vine St., 800/94-HIPPO

By late spring, seven-foot stork markers lead toward the zoo's new babies and those ready for their first birthdays. During other seasons, special programs highlight the botanical gardens, holidays, and the more than 750 species of animals that live on the 67-acre grounds. One of the prettiest events is the Festival of Lights celebration, running late November through early January. You'll need to bundle up to see the 2 million lights twinkle. You can ice-skate and then warm up with hot chocolate.

Details: Open 365 days a year. Memorial Day–Labor Day, gates open 9–6, park open until 8. Labor Day–Memorial Day, the park closes at dusk. Activities are free with regular admission prices: $10 adults, $7 ages 62 and over, $4.75 ages 2–12. $5 parking. (half–full day)

Shortly after leaving Cincinnati, heading northwest toward Oxford, you can easily make a day out of interesting stops in Hamilton along the way. From there, continue on to Oxford, home of Miami University, with its picture-perfect Georgian-style campus that you might expect to find in movies, especially in spring when it becomes a blooming arboretum. Here are just a few must-sees from an expansive list.

*Take a drive through the historic neighborhoods of Hamilton. Pre–Civil War era homes line the streets of Rossville Historic District, or the German Village area, where the **Lane-Hooven House**, 319 N. Third St., Hamilton, 513/863-1389, and the **Lane Public Library**, 300 N. Third St., 513/894-7156, take center stage. The latter, the first "free library" west of the Alleghenies, is built in an octagonal shape and is just one of the architectural gems you'll discover among the walking tours of Hamilton.*

*The **White Rose B&B**, 116 Buckeye St., also in German Village, 513/863-6818, provides a homespun atmosphere and a congenial, friendly innkeeper who doubles as a great cook. Rates are small-town, too—$65 and $70. For more traditional accommodations, try the **Hamiltonian Hotel**, 1 Riverfront Plaza, Hamilton, 800/522-5570. Prices here are under $100, except during special events at MU. From either spot, you can hop on the city's multiuse trail at the **Soldier, Sailors and Pioneers Monument**, for a three-and-a-half-mile jaunt past an 1804 restored log cabin and the contemporary **Fitton Center for Creative Arts**, 101 S. Monument Ave., Hamilton, 513/863-8873, toward **Joyce Park**.*

***Pyramid Hill Sculpture Park and Arboretum**, on OH 128 (Hamilton-Cleves Rd.), offers visitors a unique setting—a park with outdoor sculpture arranged throughout, trails, and a tearoom serving light luncheon fare. Admission is $3 for adults ($4 on weekends) and $1.50 for children. It's open April to November Tuesday through Saturday from 10 to 7:30 and on weekends from 10 to 4 the rest of the year.*

*Another unique must-see destination is **Jungle Jim's International Farmers Market**, 5440 Dixie Hwy., Fairfield, 513/829-1919. It offers cooking classes, guest chefs, 8,000 kinds of wine, 40 types of rice, hundreds of fresh items, thousands of imported foods, and even a monorail. Folks drive for hours to peruse this shopper-friendly megacomplex. It definitely constitutes a destination, whether you're a shopper or not. Cigar aficionados will enjoy the* lower prices and wide selection in the well-stocked humidor. Continental imports are arranged in the European Village, a gyrating Elvis sings every five minutes, and although footprints lead customers to the 30 checkouts and restrooms, it's still easy to get lost. It's open every day from 8 a.m. to 10 p.m.

The drive to **Governor Bebb Preserve**, 1979 Bebb Park Ln., Okeana, 877/PARK FUN (Metroparks of Butler County), is a little out of the way if you're driving toward Oxford, but well worth it. You'll discover a pioneer village and the 1799 log house birthplace of William Bebb, Ohio's 19th governor (from 1846 to 1848). It is run by volunteers, and you'll likely find activities of the day taking place around themed weekends throughout the summer. Eight buildings and a covered bridge are neatly arranged in the village.

Once you arrive in Oxford, choose a path on the **"Trees of Miami University"** walking tour (detailed maps are available on campus) and set out to explore the university. Stop at the **Art Museum**, open Tuesday through Sunday from 11 to 5, on the southeast corner of the campus, and also tour **McGuffey Museum** at Oak and Spring Streets The latter, a National Historic Landmark, is the restored home of William Holmes McGuffey, the professor at Miami who wrote the McGuffey Eclectic Readers of years past. It is open Saturdays and Sundays from 2 to 4 and by special arrangement. It is closed during August.

You'll find a lively mix of college stops, coffee shops, bookstores, and eateries in town. For one of the most memorable meals, reserve a table at **Kona Bistro and Coffee Bar**, 31 W. High St., 513/523-0686. The husband-wife chef-management team, Miami University grads, have perfected their eclectic recipes while keeping prices reasonable. There are only 19 tables, so you need to make reservations if you're traveling with five or more.

Overnight accommodations are hard to come by during a college event, like Parents' Weekend, but other times the options include **Marcum Conference Center & Inn**, on the campus at 100 N. Patterson, Oxford, 513/529-6911, and the **Alexander Historic Inn & Governors Room Restaurant**, 22 N. College Ave., Oxford, 513/523-1200. The new Victorian-style **White Garden Inn B&B**, 6194 Brown Rd., Oxford, 800/324-4925, is surrounded by, yes, white gardens. Nearby, camping, cabin, and lodge facilities at **Hueston Woods Resort & Conference Center**, off OH 732, five miles north of Oxford, 800/AT-A-Park, are additional options.

★★★★ KROHN CONSERVATORY
Eden Park Dr., 513/421-5707

At the conservatory, which is located in Eden Park, you'll find outdoor gardens and a floral clock amid greenhouse after greenhouse full of tropical and seasonal flora and fauna. The summertime butterfly show is especially colorful. During winter, you can escape to the warm indoor rain forest lush with orchids. This is a minivacation in itself.

Details: *Daily 10–5; free except for special exhibitions. (1–2 hours)*

★★★★ NEWPORT AQUARIUM
One Aquarium Way, Newport, KY, 800/406-FISH
606/491-FINS

This new destination is the first attraction along the "Newport on the Levee," just across from downtown Cincinnati. Visitors can take up-close looks at more than 11,000 underwater creatures from 600 species. There's a unique, state-of-the-art clear tunnel to make viewing easy. No strollers are allowed, but backpacks designed for tots are available for free.

Details: *Located on the Ohio River, across from downtown Cincinnati. Open 365 days a year. Memorial Day–Labor Day 10–9; Labor Day to Memorial Day 10–6. $13.75 adults, $11.50 seniors, $8.50 children 3–12. Wheelchair accessible. (2–3 hours)*

★★★★ OVER-THE-RHINE HISTORIC DISTRICT
Between Central Pkwy. and Liberty St. and on Main St.,
downtown Cincinnati

Here you'll find a revitalization under way that will take this neighborhood back to its 1840s roots—when German immigrants settled here to work on the Miami & Erie Canal. The district got its name from those settlers who lived "over the Rhine" (the workers' nickname for their side of the canal). You'll find remnants of the early days in the architecture and restorations of this National Historic District. Art galleries and studios, bars, jazz and blues clubs, a used bookshop, and good restaurants are located here. Final Friday Gallery Walks take place from 6 to 10 p.m. on the last Friday of each month, except during December, when the event occurs the first Friday.

Details: *For information and a map, call Merchants of Main St. Over-the-Rhine, 513/621-9508. (1–3 hours)*

★★★★ PARAMOUNT'S KINGS ISLAND
6300 Kings Island Dr., Kings Island, 513/573-5700 or 800/288-0808

Each season adds more superlative descriptions to the theme parks across the state, and Kings Island has seen more than 25 seasons, so you can expect to find some of the wettest, fastest, and tallest rides here. The 350-acre park offers nine roller coasters, plus the new Son of Beast (the world's tallest wooden coaster and the world's only looping wooden one), the world's tallest gyro-drop, an inverted coaster, a host of Hanna-Barbera characters, more than 30 restaurants and snack stands, and a wet WaterWorks area.

Details: Mid-April–mid-May Sat, Sun; Memorial Day–Labor Day daily and on selected dates in fall. International St. opens at 9 a.m., and the rides and rest of the park open at 10 a.m. Closing hours vary throughout the season. Single-day admission $35.99 ages 7–59, $20.99 seniors and children 3–6. Second-day admission $19.99, available at the park prior to leaving. Prices include WaterWorks. $6 parking. (half–2 days)

★★★★ PARKY'S FARM
10073 Daly Rd., 513/521-3276

Located in Winton Woods, one of the Hamilton County Parks, this 100-acre interpretive farm provides inexpensive recreational and educational experiences for families. It has an indoor two-story playground, a working windmill, a barn filled with animals, antique farm equipment, and $1 pony rides for children under seven—all in the midst of suburbia.

Details: Daily dawn to dusk; pony rides in the afternoon. Admission to the play barn is $1.50 children. A motor vehicle permit to enter any of the Hamilton County Parks is $1 per day or $3 for an annual sticker. (2 hours)

★★★★ QUEEN CITY DRIVING TOUR
Starts at Fountain Square, Fifth and Vine, downtown Cincinnati

Purple and gold signs with a crown logo mark more than 100 historic and architectural sites throughout downtown Cincinnati and historic neighborhoods. Follow the signs for a self-guided drive beginning downtown at Fountain Square, at Fifth and Vine. Notes describe each site, and a map keeps you headed in the right direction. You'll discover one of the best spots for a view of Cincinnati (Riverside Drive in Covington, Kentucky), drive through Eden Park, and head up to

GREATER CINCINNATI

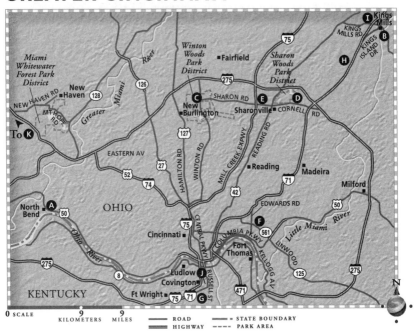

SIGHTS

- **Ⓐ** Harrison Tomb State Memorial
- **Ⓑ** Paramount's Kings Island
- **Ⓒ** Parky's Farm
- **Ⓓ** Sharon Woods Village

FOOD

- **Ⓔ** Burbank's
- **Ⓕ** Teller's Micro Pub and Eatery
- **Ⓖ** Walt's Hitching Post

LODGING

- **Ⓗ** Cincinnati Marriott Northeast
- **Ⓘ** Comfort Suites Kings Island

LODGING (continued)

- **Ⓗ** Country Hearth Inn
- **Ⓑ** Kings Island Inn & Conference Center
- **Ⓙ** Sandford House B&B
- **Ⓕ** Victoria Inn of Hyde Park
- **Ⓚ** White Garden Inn B&B
- **Ⓔ** Woodfield Suites

Note: Items with the same letter are located in the same area.

Rookwood Pottery for another view of downtown. Even if you don't complete the tour, the handy spiral-bound guide serves as a fine reference to the area.

Details: You can get a copy of the Queen City Tour Book in Cincinnati at the Cincinnati Museum Center, 1301 Western Ave., the Fountain News, Fifth and Walnut Sts., or in Covington at the Northern Kentucky Visitors Center, 605 Philadelphia St.. $4.95. (1–2 hours)

★★★★ **SHARON WOODS VILLAGE**
1 mile south of I-75 on OH 42 in Sharon Woods Park
513/563-9484

This reconstructed village is arranged to depict pioneer life in the early nineteenth century. Interpreters in period costumes relate tales of earlier times; seasonal events and Civil War reenactments take place throughout the year. Ten buildings, including a train station, doctor's office, and two-story log home, display an extensive collection of period furnishings, antique Ohio furniture, household items, and decorative art.

Details: Apr Fri 10–5, Sat–Sun 1–5; May–Oct Wed–Fri 10–4, Sat-Sun 1–5; open for "Wintry Weekends" in December. $5 adults, $3 seniors, $2 children 6–12. (1–3 hours)

★★★★ **SKIRBALL MUSEUM, HEBREW UNION COLLEGE—JEWISH INSTITUTE OF RELIGION, CINCINNATI BRANCH**
3101 Clifton Ave., 513/221-1875

On the third floor of Mayerson Hall, you'll find ceremonial and decorative objects, photographs, and memorabilia of Jewish culture. The exhibit is divided into areas that focus on immigration, the Cincinnati Jewish community, the birth of American Reform Judaism, artifacts and archaeology, the Torah, holidays and life-cycle events, the Holocaust, and Israel.

Displays include a Dead Sea Scroll urn, one of about 50 extant that contained the oldest known Biblical manuscripts, and other priceless artifacts well worth seeing. Complementing traditional items are contemporary objects, such as a brightly hand-painted wedding canopy and a modern silver Miriam Cup, used during the Passover seder.

Details: Mon–Thu 1–4, Sun 2–5. Closed Fri–Sat and on Jewish and national holidays. Free. Wheelchair accessible. (2 hours)

★★★★ TAFT MUSEUM
316 Pike St., 513/241-0343

Here is another of the unique museums you'll find in Cincinnati. Once the residence of Anna and Charles Taft (half brother of President William Howard Taft), it is now full of their art treasures—famous works by Rembrandt, Hals, Turner, and Gainsborough (among others), Chinese porcelains, European decorative arts, and a collection of French Renaissance Limoges enamels. The furnishings and restorations to the Federalist period make a tour of the home itself worthwhile. Exhibits change seasonally. Small tables in formal gardens are inviting spots for picnic lunches.

> **Details:** *Mon–Sat 10–5, Sun and some holidays 1–5. $4 adults, $2 college students and children under 18. Additional fee for some programs. (1–2 hours)*

★★★★ WILLIAM HOWARD TAFT NATIONAL HISTORIC SITE
2038 Auburn Ave., 513/684-3262

Twenty-seventh president William Howard Taft's boyhood home, a two-story, mid-nineteenth-century Greek revival in the Mount Auburn section of Cincinnati, changed ownership several times and was left in a state of disrepair before preservation efforts began in 1938. The house has been painstakingly restored with reproduction wallpaper and period, if not original, furnishings. Decorating ideas were developed from notes handwritten by Taft's mother, Louise, to her family back east. The striking gold home with deep red and green trim sits atop a hill overlooking Cincinnati. Guides offer tours of four rooms, pointing out the original pieces in each, the decorating styles of the time, and the political accomplishments of Taft—the only president who also served as a Supreme Court justice.

> **Details:** *Museum and gift shop open daily 10–4. Free. An elevator provides wheelchair accessibility. (1–2 hours)*

★★★ HARRISON TOMB STATE MEMORIAL
Cliff Rd., west of U.S. 50, North Bend

William Henry Harrison, ninth president and War of 1812 hero, was the first president to die in office—only a month after his inauguration. He was born in Virginia but came north in 1791 to become an Indian fighter. A 60-foot marble obelisk honors him at a 14-acre park in North Bend, west of Cincinnati. The tomb and surrounding grounds, managed by the Ohio Historical Society, recently underwent an extensive restoration. The tomb contains 24 vaults, including that of John Scott Harrison, the only American whose father and son were both presidents.

Details: Open during daylight hours. Free. (1 hour)

★★★ VERDIN BELL AND CLOCK MUSEUM
444 Reading Rd., 513/241-4010 or 800/543-0488

This museum is yet another unusual Cincinnati gallery, located in the restored St. Paul's Church, an 1848 landmark destined for demolition prior to its purchase by the Verdin Company. The bell and clock company makes 19th-century bells that ring worldwide. They chime at EPCOT Center in Orlando, Florida; at Busch Gardens in Williamsburg, Virginia; on college campuses; and at over half the Catholic churches in the United States—you've probably heard them before. A self-guided tour through the church's sanctuary, beneath magnificent stained-glass windows once displayed at the 1890 World's Fair, will lead you past such early inventions as the first mechanical bell ringers, huge clock faces, and a series of bells. Once your tour is over, you'll begin noticing all the bells, carillons, clocks, and *glockenspiels* in your future travels throughout Ohio, where their concentration is greatest.

Details: Museum open Mon–Fri 8:30–5. Tours of the manufacturing plant available upon request and by previous arrangement. Free. (1 hour)

★ NATIONAL UNDERGROUND RAILROAD FREEDOM CENTER
877/648-4838

This center is scheduled to open in 2003 on the riverfront and will offer exhibits and educational programming in a museum setting.

Details: Virtual tour only: check the center's Web site: www. undergroundrailroad.org for updated information and programming.

★ STOWE HOUSE STATE MEMORIAL
2950 Gilbert Ave., 513/632-5120

Harriet Beecher Stowe lived here from 1833 to 1850 with her father, Dr. Lyman Beecher, while he was president of Lane Seminary. While here, she was inspired to write her famous book *Uncle Tom's Cabin's*. The home now serves as a cultural and educational center promoting black history.

Details: Limited hours: Tue–Thu 10–4. Free admission. (30 minutes)

FITNESS AND RECREATION

All types of recreational and nature activities are available in Cincinnati parks, throughout the Hamilton County Park District, and along the Little Miami Scenic River Bike Trail. **Eden Park**, one of the city's oldest and largest, offers a self-paced Vita Course. Skating has gained popularity at the skating rink at **Sawyer Point**, Bicentennial Commons, where rentals are available.

If you've never tried Frisbee golf, you can play 9 holes at **Embshoff Woods & Nature Preserve** and **Miami Whitewater Forest** or 18 holes at **Winton Woods** and **Woodland Mound**. Bring your own disc or purchase one at the Miami Whitewater Visitor Center or Seasongood Nature Center in Woodland Mound. Otherwise, the game is free. County parks also offer fishing, skating, hiking, golfing, biking, and boating, plus many acres of nature preserves and habitats perfect for strolling. A motor vehicle permit to enter the county parks runs $1 for a day or $3 for an annual sticker. Contact the Hamilton County Park District, 10245 Winton Rd., Cincinnati, 513/521-7275 (voice/TDD) for a guide.

For sports fans, Cincinnati has the **Reds** (National League baseball), **Bengals** (NFL), and **Cyclones** (AAA hockey), along with collegiate sports at the **University of Cincinnati** and **Xavier University**. You can watch horse racing at **River Downs** and **Turfway Park Race Course**.

FOOD

Finding good restaurants in Cincinnati isn't a problem; deciding which ones to include in a few short paragraphs, however, is. Here are just a few of the many choices available.

The recipe for Cincinnati's renowned chili came not from the city's fire-fighting history but rather from a Greek immigrant who opened the original Empress Chili parlor and began the chili "ways." With over 150 chili parlors around the city, you'll have no trouble finding "three-way chili," mounded atop spaghetti and finished with shredded cheddar; "four-way chili," with chopped onions; and "five-way chili," with a scoop of kidney beans. Cinnamon, chocolate, or allspice in the "secret recipes" give Cincinnati chili a unique flavor even before the "ways" are added.

Another peculiarity you'll see on some Cincinnati breakfast tables is *goetta*, a combination of beef or pork, pinhead oats, and seasonings. I tasted it at the Amos Shinkle Townhouse B&B, but you can also find it in markets.

As you explore the shops along the hilly streets in Mount Adams, stop at **Rookwood Pottery**, 1077 Celestial St., 513/721-5456, where diners are seated in the same old kilns in which the famous collectible pottery once dried.

GOETTA

Goetta (GET-uh) is a breakfast food Cincinnati claims as original. *Goetta* dates back to the 1800s, when German immigrants might have based their version on European recipes. The breakfast accompaniment, prepared from pork, or sometimes beef, seasonings, and tiny "steel-cut" oats is loaf- or chub-shaped, sliced, and fried. To find out more, check out www.goetta.com.

The restaurant is known for burgers named after local landmarks and colorful Cincinnati characters, but other entrée choices are also available. In the Over-the-Rhine area, try one of the local brewpubs—**Main Street Brewery**, 1203 Main St., 513/665-4677, or the **Barrel House Brewing Company**, 22 E. 12th St., 513/421-2337—for hand-crafted beer, creative menus, and lively entertainment. The **Diner on Sycamore**, 1203 Sycamore St., 513/721-1212, is an original diner moved from northeast Ohio. If you're staying downtown, try a Cincy landmark, **Arnold's**, 210 E. Eighth St., 513/421-6234, for lunch or dinner; under new ownership, it still serves contemporary Italian fare along with American and vegetarian choices. **First Watch**, 700 Walnut St., 513/721-4744, offers great breakfasts and lunches served from 7 to 2:30 every day. First Watch has three locations in the suburbs, too.

A barbecue rivalry runs in Cincinnati among several restaurants, each one claiming to be the best. The **Montgomery Inn Boathouse**, 925 Eastern Ave., 513/721-RIBS, does offer a nice river view, and it has Bob Hope's endorsement. The same menu sans the view can be enjoyed at its northern location, 9440 Montgomery Rd., 513/791-3482. Over the bridge, **Walt's Hitching Post**, 3300 Madison Pike, Fort Wright, Kentucky, 606/331-0494, also lays claim to "the best." **Burbank's**, with locations scattered around the city, dishes up "real Bar-B-Q" with three sauce choices on the side.

For lively and inexpensive possibilities in the University of Cincinnati area, try **Pomi's Pizzeria and Trattoria**, 125 W. McMillan, 513/861-0080, and for the best ice cream, **Graeter's** at 332 Ludlow and a dozen other locations. North of the university in Hyde Park, I recommend **Teller's Micro Pub and Eatery**, 2710 Erie Ave., 513/321-4721, in a former bank vault, for creative pastas, pizzas, salads, and other entrées.

If you're in the mood to splurge, choose the **Maisonette**, 114 E. Sixth

CINCINNATI

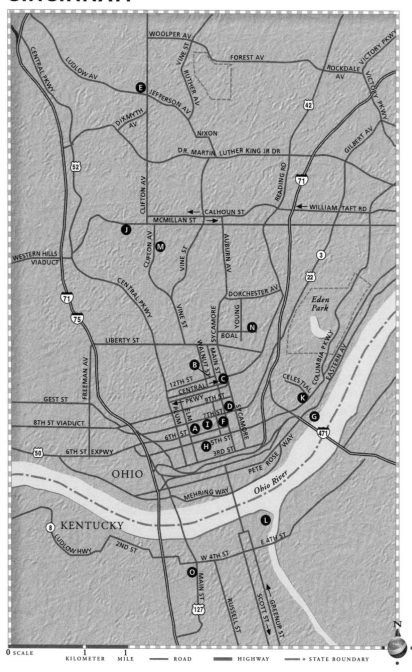

0 SCALE

KILOMETER 1   MILE 1   ▬▬ ROAD   ▬▬ HIGHWAY   ▬ ▬ STATE BOUNDARY

St., 513/721-2260, Cincinnati's five-star restaurant; **The Palace** at the Cincinnatian Hotel, 601 Vine St., 513/381-3000; or **Orchids** at the Omni Netherlands, 35 W. Fifth St., 513/421-9100, where a wonderful dinner for two with drinks averages $130.

LODGING

You'll find thousands of rooms in Cincinnati as well as some across the river in Covington, Kentucky. Choices include the **Amos Shinkle Townhouse Bed-and-Breakfast**, 215 Garrard St., 800/972-7012, a Greco-Italianate delight a few minutes from downtown Cincinnati in Covington's Riverside Historic District, and the **Sandford House B&B**, 1026 Russell St., Covington, 606/291-9133.

In Cincinnati, **Prospect Hill B&B**, 408 Boal St., 513/421-4408, over-looks the city. The **Victoria Inn of Hyde Park**, 3567 Shaw Ave., 513/321-3567, is within walking distance of eateries and shops in Hyde Park Square. The **Parker House**, 2323 Ohio Ave., 513/579-8236, is a short walk from the University of Cincinnati.

Over in Hamilton and Oxford, several more B&Bs await. The **White Garden Inn B&B**, 6194 Brown Rd., Oxford, 800/423-4925 (a short drive from Hueston Woods State Park), built its new Victorian-style inn shortly after relocating from Florida. The inn focuses on—you guessed it—an all-white garden, in memory of the innkeeper's grandmother.

The **Cincinnatian Hotel**, Sixth and Vine, 513/381-3000 or 800/942-9000, and the **Omni Netherland Plaza**, 35 W. Fifth St., 800/THE-OMNI or 513/421-9100, both offer luxurious dining and lodging downtown. The

---

FOOD

- **A** Arnold's
- **B** Barrel House Brewing Company
- **C** Diner on Sycamore
- **D** First Watch
- **E** Graeter's
- **B** Main Street Brewery
- **F** Maisonette
- **G** Montgomery Inn Boathouse

FOOD (continued)

- **H** Orchids
- **I** The Palace
- **J** Pomi's Pizzeria and Trattoria
- **K** Rookwood Pottery

LODGING

- **L** Amos Shinkle Townhouse Bed-and-Breakfast

LODGING (continued)

- **I** Cincinnatian Hotel
- **H** Omni Netherland Plaza
- **M** Parker House
- **N** Prospect Hill B&B
- **O** Quality Riverview Hotel

Note: Items with the same letter are located in the same area.

Omni's seasonal weekend packages, including breakfast and health club facilities, are a good value. If you opt for the **Quality Riverview Hotel**, 668 Fifth St., Covington, 800/292-2079, you'll be staying in a round hotel with great views of Cincinnati from the revolving dining room on the 18th floor. Reasonable packages are offered here, too.

Myriad national chains line the highways, but one of the most unique is the **Woodfield Suites**, 11029 Dowlin Dr., just off I-75 at Sharon Rd., 513/771-0300 or 800/338-0008, where suites are roomy. It has a billiard room, a beautiful indoor pool with toddler play space, and complimentary cocktails and breakfast at reasonable rates. Other motels—**Cincinnati Marriott Northeast**, 9664 Mason-Montgomery Rd. (I-71, Exit 19), Cincinnati, 513/459-9800; **Country Hearth Inn**, Fields-Ertel Rd., Cincinnati, 513/336-7911, and **Comfort Suites Kings Island**, 5457 Kings Center Dr., Kings Island, 513/459-1530—are among the newest of the area's national chains.

Families visiting Kings Island may opt for motels in that vicinity. A good choice is the **Kings Island Inn & Conference Center**, 5691 Kings Island Dr., 800/727-3050. Free shuttle service to the theme park and large rooms are available.

CAMPING

Believe it or not, you can camp in Cincinnati. Nonelectric and electric sites are available in a pine grove along the lake at **Winton Woods**; call 513/851-CAMP April through October and 513/521-PARK January through March. The **Miami Whitewater Forest**, 513/367-9632, has nonelectric wooded spots. Camping is also part of the fun at **Paramount's Kings Island**, 513/754-5901 or 800/832-1133. Cabins rent for $58 per night, and 300 campsites offer various optional amenities, like water, electricity, and sewer, ranging from $19.99 to $29.99, which includes a coupon for $8 off adult admission. Reservations are recommended.

Hueston Woods State Park, northwest of Cincinnati in College Corner, 800/282-7275, supplies wonderful scenery, including a 200-acre virgin forest, along with over 700 campsites, a lodge, and cabins.

SHOPPING

The major-league stores are downtown at **Tower Place** in Carew Tower and nearby, where you'll find a new **Lazarus Department Store**, **Tiffany & Co.**, and **Brooks Brothers** on Fountain Square. **Saks Fifth Avenue** has been in downtown Cincinnati for years.

NIGHTLIFE

Most any night you can find an exciting performance on one of the three stages at the **Aronoff Center for the Arts** in downtown Cincinnati on Walnut St. between Sixth and Seventh Streets. That's where the Broadway series touring casts perform as well as the **Cincinnati Ballet Company**, 513/621-5219, and many other companies. The **Cincinnati Symphony Orchestra's**, 513/381-3300 for ticket information, homes are the Music Hall in the Over-the-Rhine District and Riverbend Music Center, five miles east of downtown along the banks of the Ohio River, during summer. You can catch **Cincinnati Pops**, 1220 Elm St., Over the Rhine, 513/381-330, concerts, and a full schedule of other performers there, too.

To see rich talent, take in a performance of the **University of Cincinnati's College-Conservatory of Music** at the Patricia Corbett Theater or Corbett Auditorium. Some of the concerts are free; others are not and require reservations. Check their Web site, www.ccm.uc.edu, or call the ticket office, 513/556-4183. To find out who's headlining while you're in town, pick up the Friday edition of the *Cincinnati Enquirer* or one of the free weekly entertainment tabloids, *City Beat* and *Everybody's News*.

11
SOUTHWESTERN OHIO

The route between Cincinnati and Dayton leads visitors to the antique mecca of the state, the oldest inn in Ohio, and some favorite outdoor corridors perfect for canoeing or biking. Within a few miles you can visit one of the foremost modern furniture makers, who is busy making new wood look old; choose from upscale dining choices in former stagecoach stops; bike asphalt paths that follow old railroad lines; and sleep in the rooms of former presidents.

If you're looking for something old, you can find it here. Waynesville is known as the antique capital of the Midwest, and Lebanon has over 20 antique shops and boutiques. If you're in the mood for English gaiety, you can partake in an English Renaissance celebration during early fall.

Lodging and restaurant choices come in all varieties, and most are more reasonably priced than those in nearby major cities. Several of the B&Bs are perfect for special occasions, as are the dining possibilities. You can choose a steak cookout at a local winery or a picture-perfect spot for a picnic.

A PERFECT DAY IN SOUTHWESTERN OHIO

Devote a few hours to perusing the antique shops in Waynesville before lunch. You'll find several eateries, including the Hammel House Inn and Der Dutchman, an Amish-style restaurant featuring homemade pies. Save time and energy for biking along the Little Miami Scenic River Trail, and if you are so inclined, peddle or walk the trail to Fort Ancient and spend the early afternoon among true remnants of antiquity: the Hopewell prehistoric mounds and the museum that explains their significance. Try to fit in a short canoe or raft trip down the Little Miami, designated a scenic river. Head back to Lebanon for some additional shopping and dinner at the Golden Lamb Inn or drive into Morrow for a steak cookout and local wine at Valley Vineyards if you're visiting on the weekend.

SIGHTSEEING HIGHLIGHTS

★★★★ FORT ANCIENT STATE MEMORIAL
6123 Ohio 350, Oregonia, 513/932-4421 or 800/283-8904
Exploring this "Gateway to American Indian History and Culture," where the Hopewell people (100 B.C. to A.D. 500) built one of the finest prehistoric Indian hilltop enclosures, is a rare opportunity. The area along the Little Miami River was later home to the Fort Ancient Indians (A.D. 1000–1600). When you finish touring the state-of-the-art museum, complete with interactive exhibits and a mastodon, head out back to see ancient gardening techniques. Then take one of the various trails, perhaps linking up with the **Buckeye Trail**, the **Little Miami Scenic River Trail**, or the **North Country National Scenic Trail**. The park has picnic tables, outdoor interpretive stations, scenic overlooks, and a gift shop.

    Details: Park and museum open Mar–Nov daily 10–5, to 8 in summer. $5 adults, $1.25 children 6–12. (2–3 hours)

★★★★ GOLDEN LAMB INN
27 S. Broadway, Lebanon, 513/932-5065
Even if you don't book a room at this inn, the oldest in continuous operation in Ohio, it's worth a stop to stroll past the cordoned rooms where guests have yet to arrive. If sleeping in the same room, perhaps even the same bed, as a former president and other famous people sounds intriguing, then check in. Ten presidents stayed here—long before cable TVs, air conditioning, telephones, and the recent redecorating that modernized the 1815 Federal stagecoach stop. However, details of the original furnishings and well-worn handrails, for example, are still found throughout the inn and its 18 guest rooms. Each uniquely furnished room is filled with antiques and bears the name of a notable former guest. Presidents William

SOUTHWESTERN OHIO

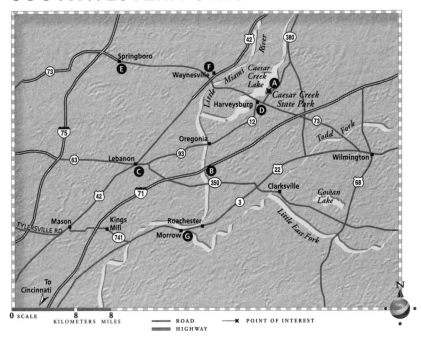

SIGHTS

A Caesar's Creek
Pioneer Village

B Fort Ancient State
Memorial

C Glendower State
Memorial

C Golden Lamb Inn

D Ohio Renaissance
Festival

E Olde Springboro
Village Walking Tour

C Turtle Creek Valley
Railway

C Warren County
Historical Society
Museum

F Waynesville: Antiques
Capital of the Midwest

G Workshops of
David T. Smith

Note: Items with the same letter are located in the same area.

Howard Taft, Warren G. Harding, James A. Garfield, Ulysses S. Grant, Benjamin Harrison, William Henry Harrison, Martin Van Buren, John Quincy Adams, and Rutherford B. Hayes, and a host of others well known in American history, have stayed here.

As you visit the upper levels of this museum inn, be aware of the Shaker collection exhibited throughout. One favorite attraction is the Charles Dickens Room, lavishly appointed with an antique copy of the Lincoln bed.

Details: *Open daily and offers special midweek packages. Regular room rates $75–$110, including continental breakfast. The dining room and tavern serve lunch and dinner to the public. (1 hour minimum)*

★★★★ OHIO RENAISSANCE FESTIVAL
Renaissance Park, 2 miles west of I-71, 15 miles east of I-75, on OH 73 in Harveysburg, 513/897-7000

Spending a day in make-believe Willy-Nilly-on-the-Wash takes visitors back to somewhere in the English countryside in 1572, on a day when the queen is touring. To commemorate her arrival, the village holds a lavish holiday celebration—one in which visitors are encouraged to participate. Some visitors come in period costume, but most step back only as far as sampling the pub food and English-style brews while joking with the performers. Over 150 performers, trained in English history, improvisation, character development, and dialect, perfect the joviality of "merrie olde England." A full-armored joust occurs three times each day. Outdoor minidramas take place in the "Theatre in the Ground," where mud beggars relate tales of Beowulf or Dante mixed with dry English humor on a stage in a wet mud pit. The Naughty Bawdy Wenches teach their merry melodies at My Dear Mother's Pub. Skilled swordsmen show off their wit and weaponry in half-hour performances, as do Robin Hood and Little John.

Details: *The festival runs for 8 weekends late Aug–mid-Oct, rain or shine. Call for specific dates. $12.95 adults, $6 children 5–12. (3–4 hours)*

★★★★ WARREN COUNTY HISTORICAL SOCIETY MUSEUM
105 S. Broadway, Lebanon, 513/932-1817

This museum isn't your typical county site. It is acclaimed as one of the finest in the United States, and you'll understand why when you visit. The major exhibit space centers around the "Village Green," where storefront shops replicate various aspects of early Americana. Lebanon has been the Warren County seat since Ohio joined the Union in 1803, but the museum collection spans a greater time period with its archaeological artifacts. Upstairs, on the mezzanine overlooking the Village Green, visitors tour an outstanding permanent exhibit in the Shaker Gallery, with remnants of Union Village, the largest Shaker community in the Midwest during the early 1800s.

Details: Tue–Sat 9–4, Sun noon–4. Closed holidays. $3 adults, $1 students through high school. (1–2 hours)

★★★★ WAYNESVILLE: ANTIQUES CAPITAL OF THE MIDWEST

Five blocks of historic buildings offer more than 65 antique shops and galleries with over 100 dealers represented. As you wander in and out of shops along Main Street between South Street and Chapman Street and along High and Miami Streets just off Main, you'll undoubtedly discover your own favorites. You might look for **Velvet Bear Antiques**, 65 S. Main St., 513/897-0709, **My Wife's Antiques**, 513/897-7455 or 937/435-8287, **Little Red Shed**, 513/897-6326, or others in the same block. Most shops are open daily 11 to 5, but some are closed on Mondays or don't open until noon. For a self-guided walking tour map, call 800/791-4386 or 513/897-8855.

You'll also find a mélange of new items, ranging from primitive country giftware to museum-quality reproductions. The **Waynesville Gallery & Garden Shoppe**, 177 S. Main St., 513/897-0888, features Amish-made American reproduction pieces. Even the rose-and-green McDonald's takes on a Victorian character, offering patrons a gazebo for dining.

Details: For shop listings and maps, contact the Waynesville Area Chamber of Commerce, 513/897-8855. (half day)

★★★★ WORKSHOPS OF DAVID T. SMITH
3600 Shawhan Rd., Morrow, 513/932-2472

If you hobnob with the rich and famous—Ralph Lauren, Connie Chung, Bill Cosby, Michelle Pfeiffer, or Julia Roberts, let's say—then David T. Smith might be a household word to you. However, most of us are unfamiliar with the cabinetmaker from the rural community of Morrow. A visit to his workplace will change that. You can see the woodworking and finishing shops, pottery studio, blacksmith shop, wood-fired kiln, and showroom where current pieces are displayed, and you'll discover for yourself why his furniture (eighteenth- and nineteenth-century American reproduction pieces) and pottery (hand-thrown American folk styles) have become so popular with decorators all over the world. Then you can relax in the herb garden. You may also meet members of Smith's family, the main forces in the business that grew from an antique furniture repair shop in the 1960s to today's business, which ships "new" antiques to 50 dealers across the country. In addition to making furniture, craftspeople at Smith's **Turtlecreek Redware Potters** personalize wedding, anniversary, and birth plates, and customize lamps for those willing to wait six weeks for their gifts. Smith's pieces are expensive; they retail in a few shops in Ohio, including the Pine Tree Barn in Wooster.

Details: Workshops and showrooms open Mon–Sat 10–5. Special events, including a spring auction and a summertime Festival of American Crafts, are scheduled. (1–2 hours)

★★★ OLDE SPRINGBORO VILLAGE WALKING TOUR
Begin the tour at the Brass Pig, 245 S. Main St.

This village advertises nineteenth-century charm and a variety of architectural styles, but most significant are the Underground Railroad stations you'll discover along the walk. The staunchly abolitionist community was founded by a Quaker pioneer in 1815. Walk past the **Wright House**, 80 State St., where hidden walls and tunnels are still part of this private dwelling. The ghost of a runaway slave who died while hiding upstairs is said to inhabit this home along with the current residents. Resident ghosts also dwell in many other tunnel-connected homes along Main Street.

Details: The walking tour brochure is available from village merchants or the Warren County Convention & Visitors Bureau, 800/791-4386. (1–2 hours)

★★★ TURTLE CREEK VALLEY RAILWAY
198 S. Broadway, Lebanon, 513/398-8584

As it leaves Lebanon on one-hour journeys, the train crosses Turtle Creek and passes the spot where Shakers settled early on. Passengers can choose coach seating or, for those who don't mind the noise from the diesel-electric locomotive's whistle, ride in the open gondola car.

Details: The 14-mile round-trips depart Apr–Nov Wed, Fri–Sun on varying schedules. Specialty excursions are planned throughout the season. $10 adults, $9 seniors, $6 children 3–12. (1 hour)

★★ CAESAR'S CREEK PIONEER VILLAGE
3999 Pioneer Village Dr., Waynesville, 513/897-1120

The activities in this reconstructed village take visitors back to pioneer times. Volunteers dressed in period costumes tend herb gardens, dip candles, and prepare open-hearth meals with the help of passersby. Guests can take self-guided tours among 20 outbuildings taken from nearby locations and rebuilt here on the edge of Caesar Creek State Park.

Details: Admission to village free. Special events $3–5 adults, $1–2 children. Donations accepted. (1–2 hours)

★★ GLENDOWER STATE MEMORIAL
105 Cincinnati Ave., Lebanon, 513/932-1817

Those who enjoy home tours won't want to miss this 1836 Greek Revival overlooking downtown from its hilltop location. The building housed the county artifacts before they were moved to a downtown location, but many items remain.

Details: An Ohio Historical Society museum, open June–Labor Day Wed–Sat noon–4, Sun 1–4. Also open selected weekends through Oct. $3 adults, $1 students through high school. (1 hour)

FITNESS AND RECREATION

No matter what your stamina, you can enjoy a ride down the **Little Miami Scenic River**. Various canoeing/camping packages are available at Morgan's Livery, 800/WE-CANOE, ranging from 3-mile brief excursions to 18-mile day trips. Regular rates vary from $21 to $37 per canoe. Morgan's Livery has three locations and also offers bike rentals, picnic grounds, a deli, campsites, and group packages. Seniors are encouraged to try a guided scenic float in an "impossible to capsize or sink" raft. Little Miami Canoe Rental, 800/634-4277, operates from both Morrow and Oregonia. Prices vary depending on the trip and day of the week. Canoeing is available April through October.

The multiuse **Little Miami Scenic River Trail**, running from Milford, near Cincinnati, to Yellow Springs, north of Dayton, provides recreation and great scenery for 70 miles. Various trail hubs and stations, including the Crown staging area near Waynesville and the Fort Ancient trail access area, provide rentals and refreshments. The trail is wheelchair accessible.

FOOD

In-line skaters, cyclists, and walkers fresh from the Little Miami Scenic River Trail are welcome at **Menker's Bikeway Café**, 819 Corwin Ave., Corwin, 513/897-0220. The café is open from 11 a.m. to 10 p.m. daily except Monday.

SOUTHWESTERN OHIO

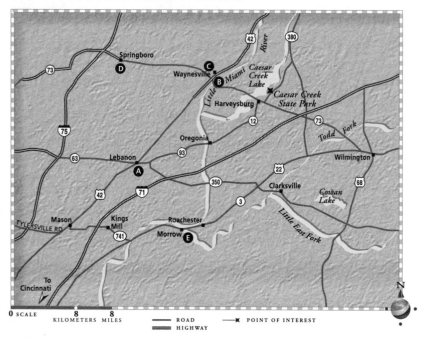

FOOD

- **A** Best Cafe
- **B** Corwin Peddler
- **C** Der Dutchman
- **A** Doc's Smoke Shop
- **A** Golden Lamb Inn
- **A** Golden Turtle
  Chocolate Factory

FOOD (continued)

- **C** Hammel House Inn
- **D** La Comedia
- **C** Menker's Bikeway Café
- **E** Valley Vineyards
  Winery
- **A** Village Ice Cream
  Parlor & Restaurant

LODGING

- **A** Artist's Cottage
- **A** Golden Lamb Inn
- **C** Hammel House Inn
- **A** Hatfield Inn B&B

Note: Items with the same letter are located in the same area.

The atmosphere here is casual; outdoor walk-up service and covered patio dining make it easily accessible for bike path users. At the trail access, 69 Maple St., **Corwin Peddler**, 513/897-3536, rents bicycles and in-line skates and sells ice cream à la Young's Dairy. The **Golden Lamb Inn**, 27 S. Broadway, 513/932-5065, and the **Best Café**, 17 E. Mulberry St., 513/932-4400, are my recommendations in Lebanon. Stop at the **Village Ice Cream**

Parlor & Restaurant, 22 S. Broadway, Lebanon, 513/932-6918, as Melanie Griffith did in the movie *Milk Money*. If you like cigar smoke (although the proprietors rave about their high-tech ventilation system), try **Doc's Smoke Shop**, 12 W. Mulberry St., Lebanon, 513/932-9939, for sandwiches, salads, and a long beer and wine list, as well as a substantial selection of single-barrel bourbons and single-malt scotches. If you'd rather indulge in chocolate, hit the **Golden Turtle Chocolate Factory**, 120 S. Broadway, Lebanon, 513/932-1990. My mouth waters just thinking about their Texas Tortoises (large turtles).

Two miles from the bike trail, **Valley Vineyards Winery**, 2276 E. U.S. 22 and OH 3, Morrow, 513/899-2485, offers wine-tastings followed by a bottle to enjoy with your steak dinner. On Friday and Saturday evenings, diners choose their own steaks and then grill them. Homemade accompaniments and desserts are included. **LaComedia**, 765 W. Central Ave., Springboro, 800/677-9505, combines professional Broadway-style musicals and revues with buffet and dinner (Wednesday through Sunday).

If you a need break from antique shopping in Waynesville, try the **Hammel House Inn**, 121 S. Main St., 513/897-2333. You can dine outdoors, weather permitting. **Der Dutchman**, 230 N. U.S. 42, Waynesville, 513/897-4716, serves Ohio Amish recipes, either family-style or from the menu.

LODGING

Accommodations in this region will fit every budget, mood, and itinerary. If you like B&Bs, try the **Hatfield Inn B&B**, 2563 Hatfield Rd., Lebanon, 513/932-3193 or 888/247-9793. This nineteenth-century farmhouse has been renovated to include vaulted ceilings with exposed beams, deluxe amenities, and beautiful hand-stenciling in each guest room. No two rooms are alike at Ohio's oldest inn, the **Golden Lamb Inn**, 27 S. Broadway, Lebanon, 513/932-5065. Some beds are so high that you may need the help of a step stool. The **Artist's Cottage**, 458 E. Warren St., Lebanon, 513/932-5938 or 888/233-2378, offers a quiet retreat that includes a swimming pool and hot tub. The resident artist adds a personal touch to "her" cottage. The **Hammel House Inn**, 121 S. Main St., Waynesville, 513/897-3779, in the heart of the antiques area, provides five guest rooms and a full country-style breakfast in the restaurant. Rooms are air-conditioned and furnished with antiques.

CAMPING

Campers have ample choices in this natural wonderland. **Morgan's Riverside Campground**, 800/932-2663, offers family riverside sites along the banks of the Little Miami Scenic River and Bike Trail. A horse camp for overnight trail rides, 280 family electrical sites, and four rent-a-camp sites with a tent, dining canopy, cooler, stove, and other necessities are the choices at **Caesar Creek State Park Campground**, Center Rd. (off OH 380), Waynesville, 937/488-4595. Family activities abound at **Hueston Woods State Park**, OH 1, College Corner, 800/282-7275 (reservations), tucked among thousands of acres for outdoor enthusiasts. Visitors staying in the rustic family and one-room efficiency cabins and the 255 family campsites can use all the park facilities, including those at the lodge. **Camp America**, with 30 campsites, all having electricity, water, a bunkhouse, cabins, and a picnic shelter, is within Hueston Woods State Park (a quarter mile past the park grocery), 513/798-2794.

SPECIAL EVENTS
This region goes all out for the Christmas holidays. The Workshops of David T. Smith hosts its Holiday Festival, Santa rides the Turtle Creek Valley Railroad on weekends, and the Golden Lamb serves special holiday menus during December. The Victorian buildings in Waynesville take on a Dickensian look, with carolers, strolling musicians, and carriage rides, for two weekends before the holiday. Call the Warren County Convention & Visitors Bureau, 800/791-4386, for more information.

12
DAYTON

Spend only a few minutes in Dayton, and you will learn that it's the birthplace of aviation. After spending a little more time in this friendly city, you'll learn why. Many of the area's major attractions salute the town's aviation history. The spirit of Orville and Wilbur Wright lives on at their cycle shop in Carillon Historical Park, where you can view their 1905 *Wright Flyer III*, and at the United States Air Force Museum, where displays of their earliest journeys share space with America's latest aviation technology. Along with several other stops, these attractions make up the Dayton Aviation Trail.

After learning all you've ever wanted to know about aviation, you can explore biking and hiking trails, nearby arboretums, and state nature preserves. SunWatch Indian Village, an archaeological site excavated and reconstructed by the Dayton Museum of Natural History, explains how the Fort Ancient Indians lived some 800 years ago. Carriage Hill, part of the Dayton Metropark system, explores the 1800s. Area museums include the Dayton Art Institute, the Paul Laurence Dunbar House State Memorial, and the National African American Museum and Cultural Center.

You'll be pleasantly surprised by the upscale caliber of dining, nightlife, and entertainment you'd expect to find only in much larger cities. With a metropolitan population of 180,000, the city has small-town friendliness, lots of free parking, and easy access to favorite destinations. You'll also find boutique shops, coffeehouses, fine dining, jazz, and comedy in the Oregon Historic District.

DAYTON

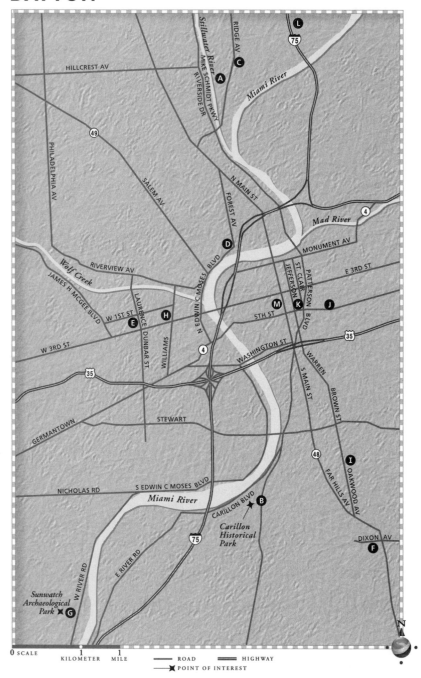

HILLCREST AV

Stillwater River

RIDGE AV

MIKE SCHMIDT PKWY

RIVERSIDE DR

A

C

L
75

Miami River

49

PHILADELPHIA AV

SALEM AV

N MAIN ST

FOREST AV

Mad River

4

MONUMENT AV

D

E 3RD ST

RIVERVIEW AV

Wolf Creek

JAMES H MCGEE BLVD

N EDWIN C MOSES BLVD

LAURENCE DUNBAR ST

ST CLAIR

JEFFERSON

PATTERSON BLVD

J

W 1ST ST

WILLIAMS

5TH ST

M **K**

E **H**

W 3RD ST

WASHINGTON ST

4

35

S MAIN ST

WARREN

US 35

35

GERMANTOWN

STEWART

BROWN ST

48

I

OAKWOOD AV

FAR HILLS AV

NICHOLAS RD

S EDWIN C MOSES BLVD

Miami River

CARILLON BLVD

B

Carillon Historical Park

DIXON AV

F

75

E RIVER RD

W RIVER RD

Sunwatch Archaeological Park **G**

N

0 SCALE

1 KILOMETER

1 MILE

ROAD HIGHWAY

POINT OF INTEREST

A PERFECT DAY IN DAYTON

Start the day with breakfast at one of the many bagel shops around town or at First Watch in suburban Kettering, before heading to the United States Air Force Museum and IMAX Theater. Don't leave without learning about the Wright Brothers and visiting the hangar for a look at a Stealth bomber from Operation Desert Storm and the Air Force One exhibit. View the IMAX production if you have an extra 40 minutes.

A picnic lunch at Carillon Historical Park and a peek at the historical buildings throughout the complex will revitalize you for an afternoon visit to the Dayton Art Institute. Afterward, take a few hours to relax at one of the Metroparks, where hiking/biking trails are available, or just watch the fishing activity in the Great Miami River below the museum.

Soon you will have to make a difficult choice among one of the city's top-notch restaurants, perhaps one of the steak houses or the Bistro at L'Auberge, before an evening walk through the lively Oregon Historical District, a few blocks from downtown.

SIGHTSEEING HIGHLIGHTS

★★★★ BLUE JACKET OUTDOOR DRAMA
Stringtown Rd., Xenia, 937/376-4318
www.bluejacketdrama.com
Amid galloping horses and cannon fire, the story of Blue Jacket, a white man adopted by the Shawnees who later led the fight to keep their land, comes to life against a backdrop of starry skies in an

---

SIGHTS
- **Ⓐ** Boonshoft Museum of Discovery
- **Ⓑ** Carillon Historical Park
- **Ⓒ** Citizens Motorcar Company: American Packard Museum
- **Ⓓ** Dayton Art Insitute
- **Ⓔ** Dunbar House State Memorial

SIGHTS (continued)
- **Ⓕ** Hawthorn Hill
- **Ⓖ** Sunwatch Indian Village
- **Ⓗ** Wright Cycle Company shop

FOOD
- **Ⓘ** Ben and Jerry's
- **Ⓙ** Blue Moon Café

FOOD (continued)
- **Ⓙ** Dublin Pub
- **Ⓙ** Pacchia
- **Ⓘ** Pine Club

LODGING
- **Ⓚ** Crowne Plaza Dayton
- **Ⓛ** Dayton Marriott Hotel
- **Ⓜ** DoubleTree Dayton Downtown

Note: Items with the same letter are located in the same area.

---

outdoor amphitheater. Natural surroundings add reality to the staged scenes as viewers find themselves back in the late 1700s, when European white settlers first came to the frontier.

The story encompasses historical elements of African American, Native American, and pioneer heritage. Take in some of the theatrics during backstage tours, which cost $3.50 for adults and $2 for seniors and children. Come early for a dinner buffet, held in a screened pavilion before the show. The main courses are chicken or ham entrées with sides and desserts ($7.95 for adults and $5.95 for children).

Details: *Summer performances Tue–Sun 8 p.m. $12 adults Tue–Thu, $14 adults Fri–Sat, $8 adults Sun, $1 discount seniors over 59 Tue–Sat, $6 children under 13. Parents are advised not to bring children under 6. (3–4 hours)*

★★★★ BOONSHOFT MUSEUM OF DISCOVERY
2600 DeWeese Pkwy., 937/275-7431

This combination of the former Dayton Museum of Natural History and the Children's Museum of Dayton focuses on natural science through interactive exhibits and programming for all ages. An indoor zoo, a space theater for stargazing, an Egyptian tomb, and the newest installation, Ecotrek (an adventure through five environments of the Western Hemisphere), invite children to use their imaginations and take a hands-on journey through both time and space. They can participate in an Ice Age Mastodon Dig or walk through the Sonoran Desert; would-be scientists can try out the equipment in a field lodge. And that's just for starters. Planetarium and laser shows are among more activities for kids and adults to enjoy. Traveling exhibits are ever changing.

Details: *Mon–Sat 9–5, Sun noon–5. $6.50 adults, $4.50 seniors, $3.50 children 2–12, free for children 2 and under. Laser show: $6 adults, $4 children 12 and under. Wheelchair accessible. (2–4 hours)*

★★★★ CARILLON HISTORICAL PARK
2001 S. Patterson Blvd., 937/293-2841,
www.activedayton.com

Fifty-seven bells ring from Deeds Carillon at the top of each hour, welcoming visitors to the charming historical park and grounds on the outskirts of downtown. The Kettering Family Education Center welcomes visitors to the park and houses a museum shop and special traveling exhibits. Twenty original buildings include the area's first tavern (circa 1796), a working 1930s print shop, and **Wright Hall**, where you'll find the original 1905 *Wright Flyer III*, considered the world's first practical airplane. A new transportation center, the John W. Berry Sr. Wright Brothers Aviation Center, is planned for 2001.

Details: May–Oct Tue–Sat 9:30–5, Sun noon–5. $2 adults, $1 ages 6–17. (1–4 hours)

★★★★ **DAYTON ART INSTITUTE**
456 Belmonte Park N, 937/223-5277, 800/296-4426
www.daytonartinstitute.org
A recent renovation of this masterpiece of an art museum makes it visitor-friendly, even for those who aren't too well versed in the fine arts. Permanent installations, from the gallery's collection of 12,000 works, are hung in chronological order within the various art periods. Important paintings by Monet, Degas, Rubens, Hopper, O'Keeffe, and Warhol, as well as special exhibitions, are displayed under natural and directed artificial light. The institute also has a Renaissance theater, a hands-on Expericenter, a museum shop with a framing service, a library, a café, and docent-led daily tours.

Details: Daily, including major holidays, 10–5, until 9 Thu. General admission is free, but some special exhibitions have a nominal fee. Wheelchair accessible. (2–4 hours)

★★★★ **GLEN HELEN NATURE PRESERVE**
405 Corry St., Yellow Springs, 937/767-7375
Nature lovers won't be satisfied until they trek the trails at this 1,000-acre preserve operated by Antioch University in Yellow Springs. All the wildlife, vegetation, and natural features are protected, but the public is welcome to stroll the 20 miles of trails. Favorite spots are the picturesque waterfalls at the Grotto and Old Dam and the raptor center at the outdoor education center.

Details: Daily dawn–dusk. Free. (2–3 hours)

★★★★ **JOHN BRYAN STATE PARK**
3790 OH 370, Yellow Springs, 937/767-1274
One of the most scenic parks in Ohio, John Bryan offers outdoor enthusiasts 10 trails from which to choose. Each overlooks beautiful vistas and unusual geological formations. All are suitable for family hiking, but use caution (especially with children) on rim trails. Clifton

Gorge, cut by the Little Miami River during the last Ice Age, is the famous highlight of the park. The magnificent limestone gorge, a national natural landmark dedicated as a nature preserve, and the surrounding woods are home to over 460 species of plants and a variety of wildlife. Trails lead past waterfalls, spectacular views of the narrow gorge, and spots such as the Blue Hole and Steamboat Rock. Portions of the Buckeye Trail wind through the park. Rappelling and rock-climbing areas are located near the main entrance, where participants and onlookers must register.

Details: *Open 24 hours, but restrictions may apply in some areas. Admission to Ohio state parks is free. (2–5 hours)*

★★★★ NATIONAL AFRICAN AMERICAN MUSEUM AND CULTURAL CENTER
1350 Brush Row Rd., Wilberforce, 937/376-4944

This museum, on the original site of Wilberforce University, where African American students were educated beginning in 1856, is adjacent to Central State University and provides exhibition space for traveling art displays. A permanent exhibit, *From Victory to Freedom*, highlights post–World War II years, while *Music as a Metaphor*, a video presentation, traces African American music from its African roots to the present day. Ask guides to point out Shorter Hall, once a station along the Underground Railroad.

Details: *Tue–Sat 9-5, Sun 1–5. Closed Mon and holidays except Martin Luther King Jr. Day. $4 adults, $1.50 students with ID. Wheelchair accessible. (1–2 hours)*

★★★★ NEIL ARMSTRONG AIR AND SPACE MUSEUM AND FORT RECOVERY
500 S. Apollo Dr., Wapakoneta, 419/738-8811

Aviation buffs will want to continue along the aviation trail with an hour's drive northwest to Wapakoneta, birthplace of Neil Armstrong, to peruse this collection managed by the Ohio Historical Society.

The Neil Armstrong Air and Space Museum, located about 30 miles northwest of Bellefontaine on U.S. 33, opened in 1972 but was restored and expanded in 1999. The museum offers an easily understood introduction to aviation and space exploration through well-designed displays. The contemporary structure, with a large Earth-like dome, reflects the boldness of space exploration. The

© Marcia Schonberg

entry hall exhibits portraits of Ohio's 23 astronauts, including Armstrong, with brief explanations of their accomplishments.

The first gallery of the museum salutes Armstrong with a collection of childhood memorabilia highlighting his interest in flight. New exhibits, like the Orbit Table explaining how and why objects circle the earth, move visitors through the various types of space exploration with hands-on experiences. You'll learn about women in space, along with Ohio's contributions to research and development of the space program. Even the evolution of space underwear is on display. Exhibits include model airplanes, the *Gemini VII* craft, the backup suit worn by Armstrong during his historic flight, lunar drills, space food, and a passive seismic experiment package. Many National Air and Space Administration items are on loan from the Smithsonian, while hometown memorabilia, such as newspapers collected by Armstrong's mother about her son's historic achievements, personalizes the exhibit.

The Moon Rock Gallery houses a sample of vesicular basalt—the moon's 4.5-billion-year-old crust—that Armstrong and Buzz Aldrin removed from the Sea of Tranquillity. In the Astro-Theater, you can view original NASA footage filmed during the lunar landing. The movie includes views from Columbia, the *Apollo 11* command module, as the Eagle departed the moon for its return flight. The Infinity Room, with a unique mirror arrangement, shows what Earth looks like from outer space. At the gift shop, you can replenish your freeze-dried space-food supply.

Continuing farther west, stop at **Fort Recovery State Memorial**, 1 Fort Site St., Fort Recovery, 800/551-FORT, near the intersection of OH 119 and OH 49. Here you'll catch a glimpse of the 1790s in the reconstructed blockhouses, a stockade built by Major General "Mad Anthony" Wayne's legionnaires, and a monument and museum that commemorate Ohio's Indian wars.

Details: Mon–Sat 9:30-5, Sun 12–5, closed Christmas Eve, Christmas Day, New Year's Eve, and New Year's Day. $5 adults, $1.25 children 6–12, children 5 and under free. (half day)

★★★★ **SUNWATCH INDIAN VILLAGE**
2301 W. River Rd., 937/268-8199
In the 1970s, emergency excavations at this prehistoric Indian site uncovered a village built by the Fort Ancients during the thirteenth century. The land, slated for development as a sewage treatment

facility, was spared by the discovery, and now visitors can walk along a quarter-mile village trail on a self-guided tour, stopping at the reconstructed homes, ceremonial house, and solar calendar posts. A gift shop, movie, and indoor exhibit area are available as well.

Details: *Mid-Mar–Nov Tue–Thu 9–5, Sat–Sun noon–5. $5 adults, $3 seniors and ages 6–17, children 5 and under free. (1–2 hours)*

★★★★ UNITED STATES AIR FORCE MUSEUM AND IMAX THEATER
Springfield St. (OH 444) at Gate 28B, Wright-Patterson Air Force Base, Fairborn, 937/255-3284, www.wpafb.af.mil/museum/

This museum is unique in many respects. Photography is actually encouraged here. Its size is incomparable. It's the largest and oldest military museum in the world, and (except for the IMAX theater presentation) it's free. Something eye catching is here for everyone, no matter what age. Don't miss the modern flight hangar filled with World War II aircraft and newer, state-of-the-art examples, including a Lockheed F-117A (Stealth bomber). Guests can shuttle to the museum annex for tours of a collection of presidential aircraft at the Air Force One display. If you take time to see everything, you'll view 300 aircraft and missiles. In the Modern Flight Hangar, visitors ride Morphis, an exciting space age movie ride simulating the sensations of flying.

Details: *Daily 9–5 except Thanksgiving, Christmas, and New Year's Day. Free admission and parking; a charge for the IMAX Theatre and Morphis. Wheelchair accessible. (2–6 hours)*

★★★★ WRIGHT CYCLE COMPANY SHOP
22 S. Williams St., 937/443-0793

A National Historic Landmark, this restored building once housed the bicycle shop and printing business where the Wright brothers first began their powered-flight experiments. A re-created shop exhibit contains period artifacts, bicycles, and machinery. Drive by the Hoover Block, part of the West Third Street National Historic District, where Wilbur and Orville Wright operated a printing business in the late 1800s. The old buildings come alive with mural-like paintings of the era.

Details: *Memorial Day–Labor Day Mon–Fri 8–5, Sat 10–4, Sun noon–4. Weekend hours and tours by appointment the rest of the year. Free. (1 hour)*

★★★★ YOUNG'S JERSEY DAIRY
6880 Springfield–Xenia Rd., Yellow Springs, 937/325-0629

A restaurant rarely lands on a sightseeing list, but Young's is different. You can choose breakfast, lunch, and dinner items at the walk-up counters, where you will also find long lists of homemade ice-cream concoctions in every variety and size. Fancier meals are found at the full-service Golden Jersey Inn. Portions are hearty, and prices are reasonable whatever you choose, but the rest of the working farm also attracts families. For a fun-filled family outing, choose among Udders and Putters miniature golf course, a driving range, batting cages, wagon rides around the working farm, a popular petting zoo, and a children's play area where farm machinery fascinates youngsters.

Details: *Dairy open for walk-up service 6 a.m.–1 a.m., except Christmas (shortened hours on Christmas Eve), to 10 p.m. at the inn. (2–3 hours)*

★★★ CITIZENS MOTORCAR COMPANY: AMERICA'S PACKARD MUSEUM
420 S. Ludlow St., 937/226-1917

Housed in an authentic restored dealership, this museum takes visitors back to an earlier time. You'll see about 20 models covering the company's heyday (1899–1956) in the art deco showroom and working service department. You can climb inside several models for an imaginary ride down memory lane.

Details: *Mon–Fri noon–5, Sat–Sun 1–5. $5 adults, $3 seniors and children. Wheelchair accessible. (1 hour)*

★★★ DUNBAR HOUSE STATE MEMORIAL
219 N. Paul Laurence Dunbar St., 937/224-7061

This small museum, the first African American home listed as a National Historic Landmark, honors Dayton's African American poet laureate, Paul Laurence Dunbar. A guided tour of the restored home where he lived with his mother, a former Kentucky slave, tells of his humble childhood and rise to fame as the first African American to attain international literary acceptance. Many of his works are displayed. His bedroom and study remain unchanged, and original furnishings are noted throughout the home.

Details: *Memorial Day–Labor Day Wed–Sat 9:30–4:30, Sun noon–5; Labor Day–Oct Sat–Sun 9:30–4:30; Nov–Memorial Day Mon–Fri 9:30–4:30. $3 adults, $2.50 seniors, $1.25 children. (1–2 hours)*

★★ AULLWOOD AUDUBON CENTER AND FARM
1000 Aullwood Rd., 937/890-7360

Naturalists and conservationists will enjoy this park, where trails wind through prairies, deep woods, pastures, and sugar bush lands. Other paths follow the banks of ponds and streams in this 358-acre sanctuary that serves as an educational center for the National Audubon Society. Seasonal classes and workshops are offered for children and adults, along with full-moon walks each month.

From November 29 through December 29, over a million lights decorate Clifton Mill. It's a holiday photo opportunity or a scenic stop if you're in the area. Visit the Santa collection on the premises.

Details: *Mon–Sat 9–5, Sun 1–5 except some holidays. $4 adults, $2 ages 2–18. (2–3 hours)*

★ HAWTHORN HILL
901 Harmon Ave., Oakwood

Although this pillared, Georgian-style home isn't open to the public, it is worth driving by. It was built by the Wright brothers and their sister, Katherine, after the three made a pact never to marry and to live together in this Oakwood mansion. Wilbur died before its completion, Orville lived here until his death in 1948, and Katherine married in 1926. Now NCR Corporation, started by Daytonians, uses it as a guest house.

Details: *Drive-by only.*

FITNESS AND RECREATION

The **Five Rivers Metroparks** offer 20 public sites for various outdoor activities. Gentle, wooded nature trails wind through **Cox Arboretum**; strolls through the specialty gardens offer additional outdoor experiences. At **Carriage Hill**, E. Shull Rd., 937/879-0461, in the city's northeast quadrant, you can walk through an operating 1880s-style farm, where monthly activities change with the season's farming chores. During winter you can go sledding and skating. **Englewood Metropark Bikeway**, a one-and-one-half-mile asphalt trail; the 26-mile **River Corridor Bikeway**; and the 13-mile crushed limestone **Wolf Creek Bikeway**, a rails-to-trails project, all offer biking, cross-country skiing, and walking. Fishing, canoeing, and other outdoor

DAYTON REGION

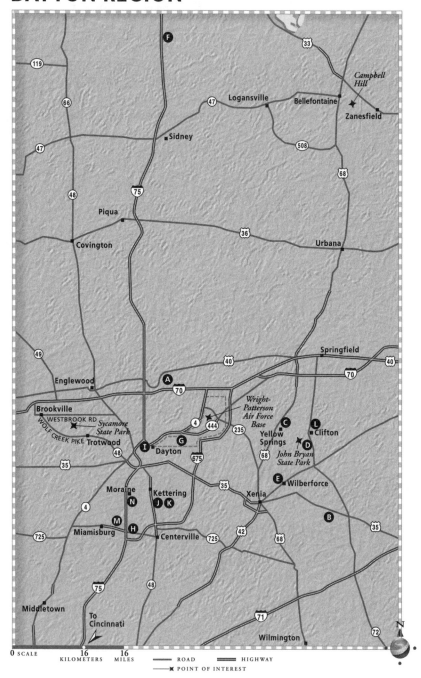

119

66

47

48

F

47 Logansville   Bellefontaine   33
Campbell
Hill
Zanesfield

Sidney   508

68

75

Piqua   36   Urbana

Covington

49
40   Springfield   40
Englewood   70
A
70
Brookville   Wright-
WESTBROOK RD   Sycamore   4   Patterson
State Park   444   Air Force   C   L Clifton
WOLF CREEK PIKE   235   Base
Trotwood   I   G   Yellow   D
48   Dayton   675   Springs   John Bryan
68   State Park
35
Moraine   35   E Wilberforce
N   Kettering   Xenia
4   J K   B
M   35
725   Miamisburg   H   42   68
Centerville   725
75   48
Middletown
71   72
To   Wilmington
Cincinnati

0 SCALE   16   16
KILOMETERS   MILES   ROAD   HIGHWAY
POINT OF INTEREST

N

r activities provide more recreational opportunities for visitors and residents alike. For additional information about specific sights, call the Metroparks office at 937/275-PARK.

FOOD

An ample number of restaurant selections are available in Dayton. Visitors can choose among national franchises or pick some of the local favorites. Begin the day with breakfast at **First Watch**, 4105 E. Town & Country Rd., Kettering, 937/643-4077, and end at one of the popular coffeehouses or **Ben and Jerry's**, 1934 Brown St., 937/461-1888. Locals have been enjoying breakfast at the **Golden Nugget Pancake House**, Dorothy Ln. and S. Dixie, 937/298-0138, and their other location, 1510 N. Keowee St., 937/228-2977, for more than 30 years—and they still rave. You'll encounter lines, but they move quickly. Only breakfast and lunch are served Monday through Friday from 6 a.m. to 3 p.m. and on Saturday and Sunday from 7 a.m. to 3:30 p.m.

The **Pine Club**, 1926 Brown St., 937/228-7463, has been a steakhouse mainstay for 50 years. You'll wait in line (often for two hours on weekends) even if your name is Clinton or Bush, but the steaks—especially the filet—are worth it. (Note: They don't accept plastic.) You can make a reservation at

SIGHTS	FOOD	LODGING
Ⓐ Aullwood Audubon Center and Farm	Ⓗ Bravo! Italian Kitchen	Ⓖ DoubleTree Guest Suites
Ⓑ Blue Jacket Outdoor Drama	Ⓗ Carvers	Ⓜ English Manor B&B
Ⓒ Glen Helen Nature Preserve	Ⓘ El Meson/Macarena	Ⓖ Holiday Inn Dayton Mall
Ⓓ John Bryan State Park	Ⓙ First Watch	Ⓝ Holiday Inn Hotel and Suites Dayton South
Ⓔ National African American Museum and Cultural Center	Ⓘ Garstka's Café & Catering	Ⓖ Homewood Suites Dayton South
Ⓕ Neil Armstrong Air and Space and Fort Recovery	Ⓓ Golden Nugget Pancake House	
Ⓖ United States Air Force Museum and IMAX Theater	Ⓙ L'Auberge	
Ⓓ Young's Jersey Dairy	Ⓚ Mamma Disalvo's Ristorante	
	Ⓛ Millrace Restaurant at the Clifton Mill	
	Ⓓ Young's Jersey Dairy and Golden Jersey Inn	

Note: Items with the same letter are located in the same area.

Carvers, 1535 Miamisburg Centerville Rd., Centerville, 937/433-7099, a newer, upscale steak-and-chop house chain that also features a delicious roasted chicken breast entrée, house au gratin potatoes, and a cigar-smoking area. **L'Auberge**, 4120 Far Hills Ave., 937/299-5536, provides gourmet dining along with fresh flowers and French decor in the main dining room, and lighter, less expensive yet sophisticated fare in its Bistro and Patio. Whatever you choose, leave room for an elegant dessert.

If you're in the mood for Italian cuisine, here are three favorites: **Pacchia**, 410 E. Fifth St., 937/341-5050, in Dayton's historic Oregon District, where you'll find bistro-style wood-fired pizzas, pastas, and unusual entrées; **Mamma Disalvo's Ristorante**, 1375 E. Stroop Rd., Kettering, 937/299-5831, for hearty portions of Northern Italian specialties; and **Bravo! Italian Kitchen**, 2148 Centerville Rd. (near the Dayton Mall), 937/439-1398, where families can enjoy grand portions at reasonable prices. Wood-grilled entrées and wood-fired pizzas are specialties at this chain.

For a true getaway experience, visit **El Meson/Macarena**, 903 E. Dixie Dr., West Carrolton. Owners call authentic selections on the huge menu "Hispanic" to cover South and Central America, Spain, the Mediterranean, and more. Items change depending on availability, and diners can choose between a myriad of small, cozy rooms or the outdoor patio. In another suburban community, Bellbrook, you'll find more ethnic dishes, mainly of Greek and Polish origin, at **Garstka's Café & Catering**, 129 W. Franklin St., 937/848-2226.

If you like a diner atmosphere, then you'll love the **Diner on St. Clair**, 101 S. St. Clair St., 937/228-2201, where the blue-plate specials take on a gourmet flair. Nearby in the Oregon Historic District, try the **Blue Moon Café**, 325 E. Fifth St., 937/586-4250, for upscale seafood, homemade breads, and desserts, or the **Dublin Pub**, Fifth and Wayne Ave., 937/224-7822, for Irish pub food and entertainment.

The **Millrace Restaurant at the Clifton Mill**, 75 Water St., Clifton, 937/767-5501, serves breakfast and lunch daily. Visit **Young's Jersey Dairy** and **Golden Jersey Inn**, north of Yellow Springs on U.S. 68, 937/325-0629, for homemade ice cream and freshly baked pastries, a hearty farm-style breakfast (served until 2 p.m.), sandwiches, and full-service dining.

LODGING

Dayton doesn't offer much in the way of bed-and-breakfasts, but there is one, **English Manor B&B**, 505 E. Linden Ave., 800/676-9456, in nearby Miamisburg. Several downtown hotels provide outstanding accommodations near the Dayton Convention Center, often at discount rates on weekends.

These include the **Dayton Marriott Hotel**, 1414 S. Patterson Blvd., 937/223-1000, the **Crowne Plaza Dayton**, Fifth and Jefferson Sts., 937/224-0800, and the **DoubleTree Dayton Downtown**, 11 S. Ludlow St., 937/461-9160.

Holiday Inn Dayton Mall, 31 Prestige Plaza Dr., Miamisburg, 937/434-8030, offers a Holidome recreational area near lots of shopping and restaurants. You'll also find the **DoubleTree Guest Suites**, 300 Prestige Place, 937/436-2400, adjacent to the shopping area.

For families or those desiring a little more room, opt for an overnight stay at **Homewood Suites Dayton South**, 3100 Contemporary Ln., Miamisburg, 937/432-0000. Suite-style lodging includes complimentary breakfast, dinner, and refreshments, along with kitchens and laundry facilities. Newly renovated **Holiday Inn Hotel and Suites Dayton South**, 455 Dryden Rd., Moraine, 937/294-1471, provides a Holidome facility and room options including 23 suites that are often on special for under $100 per night.

CAMPING

Just east of Dayton, in Yellow Springs, 937/767-1274, camping enthusiasts will find 100 family sites at **John Bryan State Park**. They are nonelectric, partially shaded, and close to scenic hiking trails, canoeing, bike trails, and nature preserves. Another choice, **Sycamore State Park** (named for the giant trees found along the trails) has wheelchair-accessible group-camping sites. Located in the Wolf Creek Valley, the park and surrounding area are richly steeped in Indian history. A ceremonial mound belonging to the prehistoric Adena Indians is on the grounds, which later served as a stronghold of the Shawnee and Miami tribes. You can enjoy year-round picnicking at **Overlook Picnic Area**, where an enclosed shelter with double fireplaces warms winter hikers, snowmobilers, and cross-country skiers.

Marmon Valley Farm, 5807 County Rd. 153, Zanesfield, 937/593-8000, a Christian retreat center with horseback riding, hayrides, and western cookouts, offers unique family camping experiences. You can bunk in the farmhouse, hayloft, covered-wagon cabins, or your own tent or trailer. Meals, hayrides, and horseback riding are extra, but campfire programs, a farm park, a children's wooden play area, sledding, and ice-skating are free.

NIGHTLIFE

The **Victoria Theatre**, 138 N. Main St., 937/228-3630, has been the center of performing arts in Dayton for over a century. The restored theater hosts

Broadway series and film festivals and lends its stage to the **Dayton Philharmonic Orchestra**, the **Dayton Contemporary Dance Company**, **CITYFOLK**, and other performers. For more casual ambiance try live jazz at **Gilly's**, 132 S. Jefferson St., in the Neon District, the comedy show at **Wiley's Comedy Club**, 101 Pine St., 937/224-5653, in the Oregon Historic District, or a 1950s **New Neon Movies Cinerama** flick at Showcase Cinema, 6751 Loop Rd., Centerville, 937/434-0144.

During warm months, take in a performance at the **Fraze Pavilion**, 695 Lincoln Park Blvd., Kettering, 937/297-3720, www.fraze.com. Whatever your music preference, you'll likely find a suitable concert. Some are especially well suited for a family outing. Call TicketMaster, 937/228-2323, for charge-by-phone.

13
TOLEDO

Toledo, in Ohio's northwest corner where the Maumee River meets Lake Erie, was first claimed by both Michigan and Ohio. In the 1830s an act of Congress placed the city in Ohio, just in time for the canal-era heyday. Toledo began a close trading relationship with Chicago and Detroit and remains a major Great Lakes port.

For early pioneers, traversing the "Great Black Swamp" region south and west of Toledo was often difficult, and farming was almost impossible; so the area was one of Ohio's last to see settlers. Modern travelers can learn the details of those early days with visits to Sauder Farm and Village in Archbold and to Grand Rapids, where scenic railways, canal boat rides, an old mill, and seasonal festivals celebrate life in the slow lane.

Toledo itself offers big-city culture with its art museum, symphony, and ballet, while nearby small towns mix in substantial doses of down-home friendliness. Several new additions, including the Center of Science and Industry (COSI) and the revitalization of the riverfront, give this fourth largest city in Ohio a pleasing skyline and some upscale charisma.

A PERFECT DAY IN TOLEDO
Stop at Fort Meigs and Fallen Timbers State Memorials on the way to Grand Rapids, a sleepy canal town that's big on antique shops and offers a host of

TOLEDO

N

Detwiler Park

Ravine Park

Pearson Park

Ottawa Park

International Park

Maumee River

BAY SHORE RD
CEDAR POINT RD
OTTER CREEK RD
YORK ST
CORDUROY RD
SEAMAN ST
NAVARRE AV
BROWN RD
LALLENDORF RD
WHEELING ST
CONSAUL RD
COLUMBUS ST
RAVINE PARK DR
FRONT ST
MAIN ST
STARR AV
WOODVILLE RD
E BROADWAY
OAKDALE AV
OAK ST
FASSETT
1ST ST
SUMMIT ST
CENTRAL AV
CHERRY ST
MICHIGAN ST
ADAMS ST
1ST ST
11TH ST
14TH ST
WASHINGTON ST
MIAMI ST
SUPERIOR ST
COLLINGWOOD BLVD
ASHLAND AV
21ST ST
13TH ST
11TH ST
WESTERN AV
ANTHONY WAYNE TR
BROADWAY
DETROIT AV
MONROE ST
BANCROFT ST
DORR ST
WESTWOOD AV
DOUGLAS RD

0 SCALE 1 KILOMETER
0 SCALE 1 MILE

▬▬▬ HIGHWAY   ▬▬▬ ROAD   ---- PARK AREA

A B C D E F G H I K L

canal-related festivals. Crossing the bridge at the edge of Grand Rapids will take you to the restored Isaac Ludwig Mill, a general store, and a mule-drawn boat ride along the canal towpath. Take a 1930s-era passenger train trip on the *Bluebird* before driving to downtown Toledo, where you can enjoy lunch along the river at the Cousino's Navy Bistro. Spend your remaining time exploring Center of Science and Industry (COSI) Toledo, a hands-on science museum, then enjoy a dinner cruise aboard the *Arawanna Belle*.

SIGHTSEEING HIGHLIGHTS

★★★★ **CEDAR BOG STATE NATURE PRESERVE**
980 Woodburn Road, Urbana, 937/484-3744
A visit to Cedar Bog, which is really a fen, shows off Ohio's geological history. You'll find rare plant life that usually thrives in Canada growing next to species found in Kansas and other parts of the Midwest, each reaching the area during different times and temperatures in Ohio's glacial history. The seasons bring different blooms and color; Terry Jaworski, preserve manager who built the four-fifths-mile wooden boardwalk through the park, notes specific times for the most profuse color: April 10, June 10, mid-July, mid-August, early October, Christmas, and February, when the skunk cabbage blooms. Volunteers provide insect repellent during the summer months if you forget yours.
Details: *Apr–Sept Wed–Sun 9–4:30; Oct–Mar by reservation. $3 adults, $1.25 children 6–12. Detailed guidebooks are $3. (1–3 hours)*

★★★★ **CENTER OF SCIENCE AND INDUSTRY (COSI) TOLEDO**
1 Discovery Way, 419/244-COSI
This museum is different from its sister science center in Columbus and any others you've visited. Here, in redesigned retail space along

SIGHTS	FOOD	LODGING
Ⓐ *Arawanna Belle*	Ⓕ Ciao!	Ⓙ Wyndham Toledo
Ⓑ COSI Toledo	Ⓖ Cousino's Navy Bistro	Ⓚ Mansion View B&B
Ⓒ SS *Willis B. Boyer* Museum Ship	Ⓗ Maumee Bay Brewing Company	Ⓛ Radisson Hotel
Ⓓ Toledo Museum of Art	Ⓘ Tony Packo's	
Ⓔ Toledo Zoo		

the Maumee River in downtown Toledo, children and adults alike will enjoy hands-on exhibits. You can feel what it's like to be a roller-coaster designer in full-motion simulator theaters. You'll get wet in the interactive water area while exploring such topics as maritime shipping and rainstorms. In the outdoor park children can explore sounds in the garden, compose a tune on the Musical Fence, and feel the power of the sun. My all-time favorite exhibit is the High Wire Cycle, a bike ride on a one-inch steel cable 20 feet above the ground. You can continue the educational experience at the Atomic Café and museum gift shop.

Details: *Mon–Sat 10–5, Sun noon–5:30. $25 per family, $7 ages 19–64, $5.50 seniors and ages 2–18. (2–4 hours)*

★★★★ **FORT MEIGS STATE MEMORIAL**
29100 W. River Road, Perrysburg 419/874-4121 or 800/283-8916

William Henry Harrison, commander of the Northwest Army, built the original fort here in 1813 to defend northwest Ohio from the British and Tecumseh's warriors. The seven blockhouses, five artillery batteries, two underground powder magazines, and garrison of soldiers brought him victory over the British in the War of 1812. The Ohio Historical Society has reconstructed the site and placed original artifacts on display. Revolutionary War reencampments and battle reenactments take place throughout the season.

Details: *Park open Apr–Oct during daylight hours. Free. Museum and exhibits open Memorial Day–Labor Day Wed–Sat 9:30–5, Sun and holidays noon–5; shortened early spring and late fall hours. $5 adults, $1.25 children 6–12. Wheelchair accessible. (1–2 hours)*

★★★★ **GRAND RAPIDS**
30 minutes southwest of Toledo

The peaceful river town of Grand Rapids is one of those small midwestern towns (population less than 1,000) in which time seems to stand still. Unless you visit this rural community during a seasonal event such as the **Applebutter Festival** (the second Sunday in October, when an estimated 80,000 people converge on the town), you'll feel like you've ventured back to the leisurely days of the canalboat era.

Browse the antique shops and specialty stores while waiting for the Lake Erie & Western **Bluebird Passenger Special**, 419/878-

2177, a vintage passenger train that runs Tuesday through Sunday between Grand Rapids and Waterville. Round-trip fares for the 20-mile ride are $8 for adults, $7 for seniors, and $4.50 for children 3 to 12.

Overnight guests should check into the charming **Mill House B&B**, 24070 Front St., Grand Rapids, 419/832-6455. The innkeeper, Marsha Frost, has added her creative touches to each room, while her husband, Dave, has constructed furnishings and continuously works to keep the gardens splendid. They offer "Rapids Rendezvous" packages that include dinner, a ride on the canal boat, and overnight accommodations during selected weekends. Guests can walk or bike along the towpath a short distance from the B&B or hike the eight-mile trail leading to Toledo's **Farnsworth Metropark**.

One of Ohio's few true spas, the **Kerr House**, 17777 Beaver St., Grand Rapids, 419/832-1733, is tucked away in a brick Victorian mansion a few blocks from the canal. You can opt for day treatments (one-hour massages are $50), weekend sessions, or a week's worth of gourmet meals (breakfast is served in bed) and 15 different spa services ($2,150 to $2,250 for five nights).

Walk-in tent camping and nonelectric sites are available at **Mary Jane Thurston State Park**, 1-466 OH 65, McClure, 419/832-7662, just west of Grand Rapids. A day-use lodge, stream fishing, multiuse trails (including a portion of the Buckeye Trail), and picnicking are also available—all within a scenic river setting. Winter recreational activities are permitted.

On the other side of the Maumee River, along Lock 44 on the Miami & Erie Canal, you'll find the village of **Providence**, once the most rowdy stop along the canal. Today few remnants of the town's colorful past—which featured saloons, brothels, and brawls—remain, but you can stop at the general store, watch the restored lock, visit the 1846 Isaac Ludwig Mill, and take a ride down the canal in a replica of a mule-drawn canal barge. Milling and craft demonstrations take place on Sunday. Canal boats leave on the hour May through October, Wednesday through Friday from 10 to 4, weekends and holidays from 11 to 5. Fares are $4 for adults, $3 for ages 60 and over, and $2 for children 3 to 12. Providence Village is part of the Providence/Toledo Metroparks restoration initiative and is the terminus for the eight-mile Towpath Hiking Trail.

★★★★ **SAUDER VILLAGE**
22611 OH 2, Archbold, 800/590-9755

This living-history village one hour's drive southwest of Toledo features home life and craft shops typical of the mid-1800s, when the stretch of land known as the Great Black Swamp was first settled by the Amish and the Mennonites. At 34 visitor stops, costumed interpreters, historic traders, and contemporary craftspeople tell their stories. The re-created town consists of restored buildings, some of which were moved to the site from nearby locations. A 136-year-old barn with original hand-hewn timbers is now the Barn Restaurant.

The village was planned and developed by Erie Sauder, founder of Sauder Woodworking. After many schoolchildren toured his modern factory, he decided to create a hands-on living museum that would reflect the work and labor of the area's early settlers and also exhibit a collection of hand tools that belonged to his grandfather. An enormous collection of Americana fills the museum building in the village, and a playground and barnyard animals are children's favorites. Visitors can stay as long as they wish at any spot.

Overnight guests can stay at the luxurious, 35-room Sauder Heritage Inn, where rooms run about $98 (suites $129) and include continental breakfast featuring fresh bakery items from the Doughbox Bakery on the premises. Hand-wrought ironwork, glass, and pottery created by village craftspeople complement the inn's massive timber-framed lobby and atriums. Sauder Village Campground accommodates campers with 37 sunny sites.

Details: *Village open mid-Apr–Oct Mon–Sat 10–5, Sun 1–5. $9.50 adults, $9 seniors, $4.75 children 6–16. The inn, restaurant, and bakery are open year-round. Wheelchair accessible. (half–full day at village)*

★★★★ **TOLEDO MUSEUM OF ART**
2445 Monroe St. at Scottwood Ave., 419/255-8000 (TDD) or 800/644-6862

This renowned museum, considered one of the top 10 in the country, offers 35 galleries filled with art from ancient times through the twentieth century. The museum's permanent exhibits include a two-level gallery with an outstanding glass collection, appropriate to a museum built from endowments by Libby Glass founder Edward Drummond Libby and his wife, Florence Scott Libby.

Children especially like to visit the Classic Court, which exhibits ancient art, including an Egyptian coffin and mummy. "Hands-on Egypt," a new interactive gallery, takes visitors on a minitrip down the

Nile River. The travel guide, a cat named Miu (meaning "cat" in ancient Egyptian) leads the way, stopping along the journey for touching (usually taboo in an art museum) and participating in craft activities.

Other highlights are the Libby punch bowl—the largest piece of cut glass in the world when it was created in 1903—and Peter Paul Rubens's *The Crown of Saint Catherine*. For a more lively tour, visit during "It's Friday!" evenings between 6:30 and 10. You'll find live music, guided tours, dinner in the café, and a children's studio where kids can make art with or without their parents.

Details: Tue–Thu, Sat 10–4; Fri 10–10; Sun 11–5. Free. Wheelchair accessible. Wheelchairs and strollers are available. (2 hours)

★★★★ **TOLEDO ZOO**
2700 Broadway, 419/385-5721
Among the newest exhibits at the Toledo Zoo are Arctic Adventure, the primate forest, and the bird aviary. The Hippoquarium, the only one in the world, is always a hit, as is the great ape exhibit, "Kingdom of the Apes," which features naturalistic settings for the zoo's chimpanzee, gorilla, and orangutan families, as well as the outdoor Gorilla Meadow. A unique dining experience is in store for zoo-goers at the Carnivore Café, a full-service eatery and old-fashioned dairy that has taken over the cages of the original 1927 Carnivora Building. The Toledo Concert Band holds summer concerts in the zoo's outdoor amphitheater, and "Lights before Christmas" celebrates the holiday season November 20 through January 3 from 5 to 8:30 p.m. (the cost is $6 for adults and $3 for children and seniors). Recent expansion projects have increased the zoo's exhibits and improved wheelchair accessibility.

Details: Apr–Sept 10–5; Oct–Mar 10–4. $6 adults, $3 children 2–11. (2–4 hours)

★★★★ *ARAWANNA BELLE*
International Park, 419/691-7447
Here's your chance to cruise aboard the stern-wheeler that was used in the Disney classic *Huck Finn*. It's moored at International Park in Toledo now and paddles up the Maumee River, passing the Toledo Zoo and riverfront scenery along the way. Informational narration highlights the trip.

Details: Trips offered May–Oct with special cruises for July 4, fall foliage viewing, and Halloween. Two-hour lunch cruises Thu–Sun; $23.50 adults, $16.50 children under 12. Three-hour dinner cruises Thu–Sun;

$39.50 adults, $28 children under 12. Meals served buffet-style. Moonlight cruises are offered Fri and Sat 11 p.m. to 1 a.m., cost $16.50. Cruises, including some special mystery trips, by reservation only. (2–3 hours)

★★★ FALLEN TIMBERS STATE MEMORIAL
3 miles southwest of Maumee, north of U.S. 24, 419/535-3050
Recent archaeological findings place the actual site of this 1794 Indian battle one-half mile away in a farmer's bean field, but this small park with a monument honoring Major General "Mad Anthony" Wayne, as well as the soldiers and Native Americans who died in the battle, is still worth a stop. Fallen Timbers is considered a sacred place by Native Americans, and memorial tokens are often left in remembrance. Walk along the trail from the monument to the canal locks in Side Cut Metropark and enjoy a picnic with beautiful scenery along the way.
   Details: *Daily 7 a.m.–dusk. Free. (1 hour)*

★★ SS *WILLIS B. BOYER* MUSEUM SHIP
International Park, 419/936-3070
Guided tours of this restored Great Lakes freighter take visitors behind the scenes to the engine room and captain's quarters.
   Details: *One-hour tours May–Sept daily 10–5; Oct–Apr Wed–Sun 10–5. $5 adults, $3 children. (1 hour)*

★ HIGHEST, SHORTEST, FIRST
Bellefontaine
If you find yourself commenting about the view, you may be passing Campbell Hill, which, at 1,550 feet above sea level, is the highest spot between the Appalachian Mountains and the Mississippi River. Hi Point Career Center is built on the site, a few miles east of Bellefontaine along OH 540. Bellefontaine also boasts the world's shortest street (McKinley St., 17 inches long) and the first concrete street in the United States (Court St., located downtown).
   Details: *(1 hour)*

FITNESS AND RECREATION
Toledo's nine Metroparks offer a wide range of recreational opportunities. Birders and naturalists will choose **Oak Openings Preserve** not only for

its rich bounty and diversity of wildlife but also because it is a rare "oak opening" with more than 1,000 plants and one-third of Ohio's threatened and endangered species. The preserve is a globally threatened area, so walk softly on its miles of trails. **Wildwood Preserve** offers trails, a fitness station, and playground equipment along with free tours of the 35-room **Manor House**. A regularly scheduled tea time is one of the special events at this eighteenth-century Georgian Colonial.

Anglers won't want to miss **Side Cut Park**, 1025 River Rd., Maumee, 419/893-2789, for the spring walleye run. Check with the Metroparks office, 419/535-3050, for additional tips and a guide.

Maumee Bay State Park adds its 18-hole Championship Scottish Link golf course to the long list of outdoor activities available in this waterfront area, noted for its walleye fishing and sandy beach.

FOOD

Tony Packo's, 1902 Front St., 419/691-6054 (800/366-4218 for retail product information), is the local Toledo tradition made famous by Corporal Klinger's reference to his hometown watering hole on *M*A*S*H*. Patrons walk up to the counter to order various Hungarian hot dog and chili concoctions during daytime hours, but the restaurant is full-service evenings and weekends. Newer locations have sprung up around town. The friendly atmosphere is spiced up with Dixieland jazz and magic acts on weekends. The **Barn Restaurant at Sauder Village**, OH 2, Archbold, 800/590-9755, where you'll get your fill of hearty down-home cooking at moderate prices, is another good family choice. At the **Doughbox Bakery** on-site, you can load up on delicious sweet rolls.

The **Maumee Bay Brewing Company**, 27 Broadway, 419/241-1ALE, serves an eclectic menu featuring wood-fired pizzas and house-brewed beers in the restored Oliver House, Toledo's oldest hotel. For riverfront al fresco dining and indoor dining with a nautical theme, try the seafood or hearty sandwiches at **Cousino's Navy Bistro**, 30 Main St., 419/697-NAVY. Cousino's features an extensive wine list. Nearby, the Docks, a newly refurbished area that's right along the river, promises more dining and entertainment opportunities.

For lunch or dinner with a historical flavor, dine at the **Linck Inn**, 301 River Rd., Maumee, 419/893-5255. The inn, located along a former stagecoach route, was an Underground Railroad stop during the Civil War and was popular with politicians such as Rutherford B. Hayes. These days, a lunch buffet is featured Tuesday through Friday and Sunday. Full dinners are also served

TOLEDO REGION

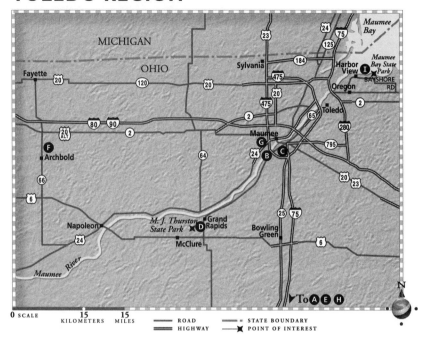

SIGHTS

A Cedar Bog State Nature Preserve
B Fallen Timbers State Memorial
C Fort Meigs State Memorial
D Grand Rapids
E Highest, Shortest, First
F Sauder Village

FOOD

B Barn Restaurant at Sauder Village
G Linck Inn
H Vintage Inn

LODGING

D Kerr House
I Maumee Bay Resort and Conference Center
D Mill House
F Sauder Heritage Inn

Note: Items with the same letter are located in the same area.

Tuesday through Saturday. In the suburb of Sylvania, locals rave about the Italian cuisine and service at **Ciao!**, 6064 Monroe St., 419/882-2334.

Travelers in the southern portion of the northwest quadrant can dine at the **Vintage Inn**, at OH 508 and 68, W. Liberty, 937/465-5010, where the local catch and locally raised ostrich meat are featured. A full menu, including selections for children and seniors and homemade desserts, is available. Ask for seating in the cabin, an 1880s log home.

LODGING

Sauder Heritage Inn, OH 2, Archbold, 800/590-9755, offers oversized rooms, breakfast, and the amenities of a pricey hotel without the crowds, traffic, or prices. If you're after a B&B experience above and beyond most others, I recommend the **Mill House**, 24070 Front St., Grand Rapids, 419/832-MILL. A former flour mill, this inn has also seen days as a hat factory. Its current incarnation, with hand-painted designs in each room—many with hand-crafted furnishings and gardens overlooking the canal—is the most noteworthy. Choose a spa-week stay at the **Kerr House**, 17777 Beaver St., Grand Rapids, 419/832-1733, if you're in need of restoration. A variety of spa treatments and programs will fix you up in a week's time ($2,150 to $2,550 for five nights).

Ohio's newest state-owned resort, **Maumee Bay Resort and Conference Center**, 1750 Park Road #2, Oregon, 419/836-1466, provides guest rooms overlooking Lake Erie, resort activities, nature trails, and outdoor events. Because Toledo is only 10 miles away, this resort offers perhaps the best of both the urban and natural worlds. Visitors who want to be within walking distance of the Toledo Art Museum while relaxing in antique furnishings can opt for **Mansion View B&B**, 2035 Collingwood Ave., 419/244-5676. The inn is child friendly, with some adjoining rooms. The **Wyndham Toledo**, 2 SeaGate, 419/241-1411, and **Radisson Hotel**, 101 N. Summit St., 419/241-3000, put you in the center of downtown activity.

CAMPING

Maumee Bay Resort and Conference Center, 1400 Park Road #1, Oregon, 419/836-8828, has 256 modern, mostly sunny, sites as well as rent-a-camp units, five miles of multiuse trails, and many other outdoor amenities. Travel south to reach **Marmon Valley Farm**, 5807 County Rd. 153, Zanesfield, 937/593-8000, a Christian retreat center with horseback riding, hayrides, and western cookouts, offers unique family camping experiences. You can bunk in the farmhouse, hayloft, covered-wagon cabins, or your own tent or trailer. Meals, hayrides, and horseback riding are extra, but campfire programs, a farm park, a children's wooden play area, sledding, and ice-skating are free.

PERFORMING ARTS

You can easily find live entertainment throughout the city during any weekend, but for advance tickets and information about specific performances it's best to call ahead. Organizations include the **Toledo Ballet Association**, 406 Adams St., 419/255-9000, the **Toledo Symphony Orchestra**, 2 Maritime Plaza, 800/348-1253, the **Toledo Repertoire**, 16 10th St., 419/243-9277, and the **Toledo Cultural Arts Center** at the **Valentine Theater**, 425 N. St. Clair St., 419/242-2787 (the theater has recently been restored to its 1890s grandeur). The **Toledo Museum of Art**, 800/644-6862, hosts the five-concert Peristyle Series. **Village Players Theatre**, 2740 Upton Ave., 419/472-6817 or 419/472-6827, Toledo's only professional, all-volunteer playhouse, produces five shows a year.

14
LAKE ERIE TOWNS

Ohioans live far from oceans, but they are not landlocked. The state is bordered on both the north and the south by water and is interwoven with lakes and rivers. Lake Erie on the north not only provides industrial strength but also offers a vast variety of tourist and recreational opportunities.

Driving OH 2 along Lake Erie between Toledo and Cleveland will lead you through the lake cities and towns in this chapter. However, don't skip the interesting side trips to the Lake Erie Islands or to intriguing towns inland. You may drive the whole route at once or select one or two towns and settle in for a while. Either way, places will be left unexplored for a return visit.

Don't forget to get out onto the water. Nearly every port has a nearby landing where you can arrange ferry rides to the islands, fishing excursions, and sightseeing cruises. The beach facing the Breaker's Hotel at Cedar Point is perhaps the best along Lake Erie. Once you get out onto the water, when the weather's clear and the zebra mussels are thriving, the lake takes on a Caribbean blue appearance, and if you let your mind drift with the waves, you can almost hear a steel-drum band.

A PERFECT DAY ALONG LAKE ERIE
A perfect day at the lake would last at least a week. Board the Island Rocket for a windswept ride to Kelleys Island. Bicycle around the island with stops at

LAKE ERIE TOWNS

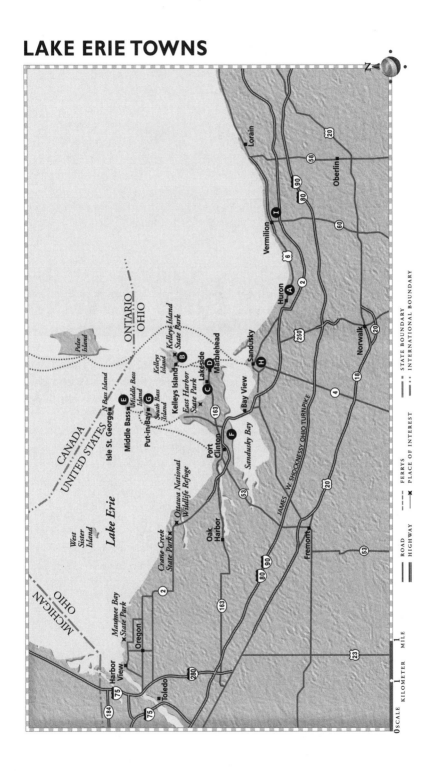

Glacial Grooves, Inscription Rock, and the Butterfly Box. Enjoy lunch at one of the lake-view restaurants before reboarding for the trip to Put-in-Bay. Rent a golf cart at the boat landing for a leisurely spin around the island. Stop at Perry's Victory and International Peace Memorial and take the elevator to the top for a 360-degree view of Lake Erie. Shop the resort-style boutiques before returning to Sandusky. Enjoy the sunset from the outdoor deck of a waterfront restaurant, perhaps in Vermilion or Huron.

SIGHTSEEING HIGHLIGHTS

★★★★ HURON

10 miles east of Sandusky

This small lake town, with a population of just 7,000, has more to offer visitors than you might imagine. **Lakefront Park** and **Nickel Plate Beach**, one on each side of the Huron River, are good picnic spots, and you can walk for a mile on the city's fishing pier to the **Huron Lighthouse**. Boat and Jet Ski rentals are available at Cranberry Creek Marina at **Ruggles Beach**, 4319 Cleveland Rd. E, 419/433-3932. Activities at the **Huron Boat Basin** bring townspeople as well as visitors to the marina area, and productions of the **Huron Playhouse**, Ohio St., 419/433-4744, during summer, or 419/433-3503 at other times, are held in an air-conditioned school when you need to beat the heat. Bordering Huron are the **Old Woman Creek National Estuarine Research Reserve and State Nature Preserve** and **Sheldon Marsh State Nature Preserve**.

Details: (half–full day)

★★★★ KELLEYS ISLAND

You can bike or get around via rented golf carts on Kelleys Island, where vacationers have been relaxing for over a century. You can see the historic charm of the island, which is designated a National Historic Landmark. New restorations meet traditional standards of

SIGHTS

- Ⓐ Huron
- Ⓑ Kelleys Island
- Ⓒ Lakeside
- Ⓓ Marblehead Peninsula
- Ⓔ Pelee and Middle Bass Islands
- Ⓕ Port Clinton
- Ⓖ Put-in-Bay/South Bass Island
- Ⓗ Sandusky
- Ⓘ Vermilion

white facades and black shutters. Abundant birding opportunities, marinas, and waterfront activities, as well as quaint shops, eateries, and weekend events, make the island a desirable getaway for romantics and naturalists. It's the largest American island in Lake Erie, covering about 2,800 acres, one-third of which is owned by the state. Flowering grottoes and natural areas can be explored, and you can view pictographs left by the Erie Indians at **Inscription Rock State Memorial** on the south shore. The very faint carvings of men, birds, and animals relate messages left by tribe members atop the limestone boulder 300 to 400 years ago. On the opposite side of the island, **Glacial Grooves State Memorial** represents the world's largest example of glacial scouring. Cordoned by fencing, the study site allows visitors to walk around the deep limestone grooves formed as recently as 30,000 years ago when mile-thick glaciers scraped the area. Fossil formations are also visible and described along the self-guided tour. You can explore the area around the grooves by taking the North Shore Loop Trail, one of the hiking trails in **Kelleys Island State Park**.

Downtown, with its eateries and shops, is a short walk from the ferry landings and bike and golf cart rentals.

Either a short ride across the island, or a longer one around Lakeshore Dr., will take you to another island treasure, **Butterfly Box Enterprises**, 604 Division St., 419/746-2454, where visitors can take a leisurely stroll through a butterfly greenhouse. North American varieties, many indigenous to Ohio, flit about in a garden of bright flowers during daylight hours. Interpreters relate facts about the various life cycles and dietary preferences of the butterflies and provide tips for attracting them to your home garden. A gift shop carries interesting T-shirts and botanical souvenirs.

Details: (1–2 days)

★★★★ **LAKESIDE**
On the Marble Head Peninsula
Lakeside, the Chautauqua on Lake Erie, was founded by Methodists in the mid-1800s as a cultural, religious, conference, and entertainment center. Today the town still offers seminars and entertainment in summer, including symphony concerts, marching bands, and an Elvis impersonator. Performances take place in the 3,000-seat Hoover Auditorium.

The community is unlike any other place on Lake Erie. Family activities include shuffleboard, swimming, boating, and basketball. Ice-cream stands, gift and antique shops, and plenty of benches slow the walking pace, and expensive bikes are left unlocked. Rocking chairs line sweeping porches, and sailboats line the beach in front of the hotel. Often the only sounds are conversations and music wafting from the auditorium through the Victorian streets. Guests can stay in private cottages, B&Bs, guest houses, the **Fountain Inn**, and the historic 1875 **Hotel Lakeside**. About 250 residents live here year-round. Comfortable, restored rooms range from $65 to $120 per night at the hotel.

Details: For information on accommodations as well as entertainment, recreation, and seminars, contact the Lakeside Association, 236 Walnut Ave., 419/798-4461. You will pay a fee (from $2 per person for a short visit to $9 for an overnight stay with a $2 car fee) to enter the gated community of less than a mile. (full day)

★★★★ **MARBLEHEAD PENINSULA**
10–15 miles east of Port Clinton
Bring your camera to the historic and picturesque 1821 **Marblehead Lighthouse** on Bayshore Road, the oldest continuously operating lighthouse on the Great Lakes. Free tours are given June 1 to September 3, Monday through Friday from 1 to 5; every second Saturday in June, July, August, and September from 10 to 3; and during the annual Autumn Lighthouse Festival in October. The original Fresnel lens from the lighthouse is on display at the **U.S. Coast Guard Station**, 606 Prairie St., 419/798-4444; the station also gives tours. To pick up nautical gifts in Marblehead, stop at the **Schoolhouse Gallery**, 111 W. Main St., 419/798-8332, or at **Richmond Galleries**, 417 W. Main St., 800/441-5631, for originals, limited editions, and prints by local artist Ben Richmond. **Just for Ewe**, 9523 E. Harbor Rd., 800/798-4EWE, is a little group of casual shops.

You may be surprised to discover a Confederate cemetery at **Johnson's Island**, off the tip of Marblehead peninsula, on Gaydos Road. After paying $1 to cross the causeway, you can look at more than 200 tombstones and the partially intact prison forts that housed as many as 9,000 Confederate officers during the Civil War. If you drive through the Byzantine cemetery near the village of Marblehead, you'll overlook a quarry, still active after nearly 150 years.

Details: (full day)

SIDE TRIPS FROM THE LAKESHORE

Within a half hour's drive of Lake Erie, you'll find the **Rutherford B. Hayes Presidential Center**, *Spiegel Grove, at the corner of Hayes and Buckland Avenues, Fremont, 800/998-PRES, which includes the gardens, home, and library of the 19th president. Gates from the White House surround the stately Victorian home and will whet your appetite for the other White House artifacts, including china and furniture, displayed in the mansion. More than 75,000 volumes are housed in the adjacent presidential library, the first of its kind. Because Hayes was a Civil War hero, much of the center's ground floor is devoted to that period. The first president to travel to the West Coast, Hayes collected many Native American artifacts, which are also included in the exhibition. You'll find more than a mile of wheelchair-accessible walking trails, Victorian high teas, and horse-drawn carriage rides here. The 25-acre estate is known as Spiegel Grove.*

A short drive south on OH 13 from Huron leads you to the quaint town of **Milan**, *birthplace of Thomas Edison. His home, 9 Edison Dr., 419/499-2135, is now the* **Thomas Edison Birthplace Museum**, *open for touring April, May, September, and October, Tuesday through Saturday from 1 to 5 and June through August, Tuesday through Saturday from 10 to 5 and Sunday from 1 to 5. It is open at other times by appointment. You can also visit eight original buildings, including a country store and blacksmith shop, at the* **Milan Historical Museum**, *10 Edison Dr., 419/499-2968. Admission is free, but donations are accepted. Browse several shops around the public square and dine at the popular and historic* **Homestead Inn**, *U.S. 250, Milan, 419/499-4271.*

★★★★ PORT CLINTON
Midway between Cleveland and Toledo

With Lake Erie rated as the "Walleye capital of the world," you won't be surprised to hear about soaring tackle and marine equipment sales at the local Wal-Mart or to learn that 2 million walleye were hooked in the lake last season. It seems only appropriate to see a huge fiberglass walleye dropping to count off the seconds to the new year. What you may not know is that Port Clinton and the ad-

One more must-see spot is **Oberlin**, a charming college town with monuments to its abolitionist background. Oberlin College is noted for its music conservatory and outstanding art collection. You can often hear music as you stroll the campus. For a concert and recital schedule, write to the Office of Outreach Programs, Oberlin Conservatory of Music, Oberlin, OH 44074, or call 216/775-8044. The Conservatory Concert Hotline, 216/775-6933, also provides performance information.

On the third Saturday and first Sunday of each month, the Frank Lloyd Wright–designed **Weltzeimer/Johnson House**, 127 Woodhaven Dr., is open for public tours. Leave your shoes at the door for the hourly tour given by architectural historian Steven Rugare. Although Ohio has about 11 Wright homes, this house is the only one open to the public. Tickets are $5, available at the **Allen Memorial Art Museum**, 216/775-8665, located in the center of town and also well worth visiting.

No tour of Oberlin is complete without noting the town's role in the Underground Railroad and the Civil War. A controversial sculpture on the campus represents the tumultuous times with actual railroad tracks elevating skyward. Many other sites are included on an **African American Heritage Tour** available through the Lorain County Visitors Bureau, 611 Broadway, Lorain, 800/334-1673. These sites include homes and churches of leading abolitionists, the **Westwood Cemetery**, where many former slaves and abolitionists are buried, and monuments to residents who marched with John Brown to Harpers Ferry in 1859.

joining peninsula, known as Catawba Island, are also popular with the rest of us who like to sightsee, shop, eat, and boat. You can hop aboard the **Bay Area Trolley**, 220 W. Perry St., 419/734-9530, to learn the history of the area or stop at some of the sites yourself. **Betsy-Mo-John's Cabin**, residence of the last known Ottawa Indian in the area, is located next to the historic **Mon Ami Winery**, 2845 E. Wine Cellar Rd., 800/777-4266, where you can sample wine and tour at 2 and 4 daily for $1.50. On the varied menu, look for local walleye, perch, and farm-raised trout, all of which are moderately priced. The restaurant serves lunch, dinner, Sunday brunch, and weekend buffets. Besides Victorian gift items, you'll find homemade fudge and cookies, gourmet coffee, spinning and weaving supplies, and garden gifts.

Details: *(full day)*

★★★★ SANDUSKY

On the mainland, halfway between Toledo and Cleveland

Make sure to drive through Sandusky's downtown public gardens in **Washington Park**, where palm trees are as profuse as indigenous species. A floral clock with a calendar is freshly planted each day. A walking tour of the area is available by calling 800/255-ERIE.

The **Merry-Go-Round Museum** is located in the old post office downtown, a 1927 building with a round facade at West Washington and Jackson Streets, 419/626-6111. The museum, which features master carvers at work and an operating carousel, is open Memorial Day through Labor Day Monday through Saturday from 11 to 5 and Sunday from noon to 5. It's open weekends January and February, and Wednesday through Sunday other months. Admission is $4 for adults, $3 for seniors, $2 for children 4 to 14, and free for children under 4. The museum is just a few blocks from **Jackson Street Pier**, where ferries and cruises depart for the islands.

Cedar Point Amusement Park is the main draw in this area. It's open daily mid-May through Labor Day and then weekends until mid-October. Along with 14 famous roller coasters and Camp Snoopy in the main park, you'll find two 18-hole miniature-golf courses and go-cart tracks at Challenge Park, and wave pools, slides, bodysurfing, and inner-tubing at Soak City, the park's separate entertainment facilities. One-day regular park admission is $18.95 for seniors, $27.95 for those 48 to 54 inches tall, and $32.95 for those over 54 inches tall. Bonus weekends ($26.95) and other packages are also available. There are additional fees for entrance to Soak City and Challenge Park. Parking is $6. For more information call 419/627-2350.

Details: *(1–2 days)*

★★★★ VERMILION

A quaint lakeside community west of Lorain

When traveling along Lake Erie, stop at the **Inland Seas Maritime**

Museum, 480 Main St., Vermilion, 800/893-1485, to find answers to all your maritime questions. Built on two levels, the museum was literally constructed around the engine of a tug. It is dedicated to preserving stories of the Great Lakes and displays model ships, nautical memorabilia, and a pilothouse. Family admission is $10, or $5 for adults, $4 for seniors, $3 for ages 6 to 16. The museum is open from 10 to 5 daily. You can also take a walking tour of Vermilion's historic "Harbour Town," which today includes mostly private residences. In its heyday during the 1800s, this area was called the "Village of Lake Captains." Along Liberty Avenue you'll find small gift stores, **Ednamae's Ice Cream Parlor**, 440/967-7733, and the **Old Prague Restaurant**, 440/967-7182, where goulashes and other Czechoslovakian favorites highlight the menu.

Details: (half–full day)

★★★ PUT-IN-BAY/SOUTH BASS ISLAND

Guests enjoy a faster, louder, and generally more crowded pace here. **Put-in-Bay** is bustling with activity during the high season between Memorial Day and Labor Day, when watercraft of every size, description, and price fill the marinas. Boats may dock overnight in designated anchorage sites. Parasailing and picnicking, music, and overflowing restaurants, bars, and boutiques complete the scene. Visitors who aren't arriving by private means usually board a ferry or cruise from Port Clinton, Sandusky, Catawba Island, or Kelleys Island and rent bicycles or a golf cart at the landing. Although cars are allowed on the island, carts are the most popular means of mobility. At **Island Bike Rental**, two-seaters cost $10 an hour or $30 to $45 for the day, depending on the season. Four-seaters are $12 an hour or $35 to $60 per day. Children especially enjoy the backward view they get from the rear seat of a cart. While taking the streets at a leisurely pace, notice the historical markers on many private homes. A variety of ice-cream shops, fudge houses, and T-shirt shops add to the island atmosphere. The calliope at **Kimberly's Carousel**, 419/285-4741, will beg you and the kids to stop for a ride on the 1917 wooden merry-go-round. The restored ride includes whimsical creatures, such as a fish wearing a hat and eating a worm.

For a pleasant ride and an overview, take the **Island Tour**, 419/285-4855, available at the ferry landing. The conductor on the trainlike ride provides lively narration and stops at some attractions, including **Heineman's Winery**, **Perry's Cave**, and **Perry's**

Monument. Rides last about one hour and run $8 for adults and $1.50 for children. Often, performers re-enact Oliver Hazard Perry's victory over the British in the War of 1812 on the steps below **Perry's Victory and International Peace Memorial**. A $3 elevator ride to the top of the 352-foot pink granite pillar offers a 360-degree panorama of the lake and its islands.

Details: *(half–full day)*

★★★ PELEE AND MIDDLE BASS ISLANDS

Plan ahead for a trip to Pelee Island, located in Canada. It's the largest of the Lake Erie Islands, but transportation and accommodations are limited. **Pelee Island Transportation**, 1060 W. Shore Rd., Pelee Island, Ontario N0R 1M0, 800/661-2220, will take you there. **Pelee Island Winery**, 455 Seacliffe Rd., County Rd. 20, Kingsville, Ontario, Canada N9Y 2K5, 519/724-2469 or 519/733-6551, offers guided tours, tastings, and other activities. For an overnight stay, opt for one of a few B&Bs, like the **Tin Goose Inn**, 1060 E. West Rd., Pelee Island, and have dinner at the adjoining restaurant, **Gooseberry's Island Cuisine**, 519/724-2223. Pelee is a good spot for a tranquil getaway, and if you enjoy nature, bird-watching, and swimming, this may be the island for you.

On the other hand, Middle Bass Island is easy to get to. Most ferries travel there regularly. Many visitors spend an afternoon on the island touring historic **Lonz Winery**, 419/285-5411. Tours are given every half hour beginning at 12:30 p.m. daily from Memorial Day through Labor Day and for limited hours a few weeks before and after. Admission is $1.50 for ages 21 and over and 50 cents for ages 20 and under. The winery, originally called Golden Eagle Winery, first opened during the Civil War and soon became the largest wine producer in the United States. Wine is no longer produced here, but the Catawba and Concord vineyards are harvested for other wine producers.

Details: *(1 day)*

FITNESS AND RECREATION

Fishing and boating are the two top recreational activities in these parts. A few of the many charter services include Tibbels Charter Service, 6965 E. Harbor Rd., Marblehead, 419/734-1143; Dunlap's Charter Service, 4255 Chatham Dr., Port Clinton, 800/797-4824; BC Charters, 2790 N. First St., Martin, 419/CHARTER; Trophy Hunter Charter Services, Inc.; Channel Grove

Marina, Marblehead, 419/732-2663; Holiday Village, 3247 NE Catawba Rd., Port Clinton, 800/493-7003; and Shore Nuf Charters, 247 Lakeshore Dr., Port Clinton, 419/734-9999. Rental rods are usually available, and "walk-on" headboats provide an economical opportunity for individual anglers. Reservations are recommended. The captains operating these charters are Coast Guard-licensed and will assist in booking overnight accommodations, providing bait, and cleaning fish. However, anglers must have an Ohio fishing license, available at most bait shops ($15 annually for residents, $24 annually for nonresidents, $15 for a three-day nonresident license, and $7 for a one-day resident or nonresident permit). For information about ice fishing in January and February, contact the **Ottawa County Visitors Bureau**, 800/441-1271, or the **Sandusky/Erie County Visitors & Convention Bureau**, 800/255-ERIE. These numbers also provide weather and fishing reports and help with accommodations. The **Ohio Department of Natural Resources** provides a fishing report at 888/HOOK-FISH.

Ohio's north coast encompasses more than 18,000 acres and 45 miles of trails for bird-watchers and nature lovers. **Lake Erie Wing Watch**, a consortium of public and private agencies with a common conservation interest, offers a variety of educational programs about birds, including a free publication describing areas from Oak Harbor to Lorain, where over 300 species make their homes. Here are my favorite easily accessible areas along the shore: **Magee Marsh Wildlife Area**, 13229 W. Route 2, Oak Harbor, 419/898-0960, is part of the marsh region, where ducks, swans, and geese migrate in early spring, followed by raptors. From mid-April through early June, more than 35 species of warblers and other songbirds fill the area. An observation tower and the **Sportsmen's Migratory Bird Center** (where a "touch table" invites children to feel fur, skeletal remains, and feathers of wildlife found in the marsh) embellish the site. Enter at the ornate iron gates, remnants of the original auto entrance to Cedar Point, then follow a scenic paved trail that is also part of the turn-of-the-century amusement park road through the **Sheldon Marsh State Nature Preserve**, 2715 Cleveland Rd. W (U.S. 6), Huron, 419/433-4919, passing woods, marsh areas, natural beach, and patches of wildflowers, especially in early spring. Over 300 species have been identified in this preserve.

Further east, the **Old Woman's Creek National Estuarine Research Reserve and State Nature Preserve**, 2514 Cleveland Rd. E (U.S. 6), Huron, 419/433-4601, a wetlands habitat, provides waterfowl glimpses via an indoor viewing area and an observation deck. You may also see bald eagles and ospreys here. For the Lake Erie Wing Watch handbook, with hours of operation, map, and birding list, call 800/255-ERIE. Also ask for a list of

LAKE ERIE TOWNS

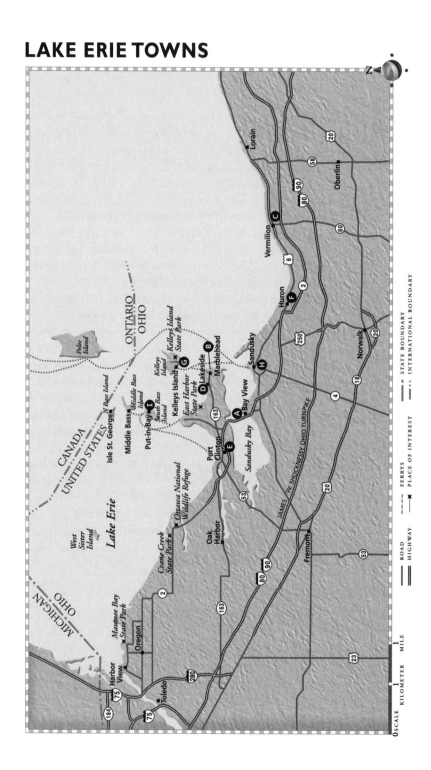

accommodations that give discounts to bird-watchers. Hiking and biking opportunities abound throughout the eight counties bordering Lake Erie. Lorain County offers 6,200 acres of Metroparks for an extensive selection of activities.

FOOD

For fresh fish and seafood, try the **Angry Trout**, 505 E. Bay View Dr., Bay View, 888/TROUT-99. Further west, in Port Clinton, are several dining options, including the **Garden at the Lighthouse**, Perry and Adams Sts., 419/732-2151, on the site of Port Clinton's first lighthouse, and **Mon Ami Restaurant & Historic Winery**, off OH 53 north of OH 2, 419/797-4445 or 800/777-4266. Continuing east to Marblehead, you'll find the award-winning **Frontwaters Restaurant and Brewing Co.**, 8620 E. Bayshore Rd., 419/798-8058, for locally crafted beers and innovative foods. The **Crow's Nest Restaurant**, 2170 N. Buck Rd., Lakeside/Marblehead, 419/734-1742, is famous for its ribs (hickory-smoked in the restaurant's own smokehouse) and house salad. Locals rave about the chili at **Big Bopper's**, 7581 E. Harbor, Ohio 163, Marblehead, 419/734-4458. For an Italian dining choice in Huron try **Marconi's**, 424 Berlin Rd., 419/433-4341. In Vermilion, try the **Old Prague Restaurant**, 5586 Liberty Ave., 440/967-7182, for authentic Czechoslovakian cuisine, and **Chez François**, 555 Main St., 440/967-0630, for expensive French fare. Chez François is the only restaurant I've found on the lake that requests "proper attire" for men. You'll find a lighter menu at slightly reduced prices and a relaxed dress code outdoors at their Riverfront Café. Both are closed Monday and in January and March.

FOOD

- **Ⓐ** Angry Trout
- **Ⓑ** Big Bopper's
- **Ⓒ** Chez François
- **Ⓓ** Crow's Nest Restaurant
- **Ⓔ** Frontwaters Restaurant and Brewing Co.
- **Ⓔ** Garden at the Lighthouse
- **Ⓕ** Marconi's

FOOD (continued)

- **Ⓖ** Mon Ami Restaurant & Historic Winery
- **Ⓒ** Old Prague Restaurant

LODGING

- **Ⓕ** Captain Montague's B&B
- **Ⓕ** Clarion Inn Twine House
- **Ⓗ** Holiday Inn Holidome
- **Ⓗ** Hotel Breakers

LODGING (continued)

- **Ⓘ** Islander Inn
- **Ⓕ** The Lodge at Sawmill Creek
- **Ⓑ** Old Stone House on the Lake
- **Ⓔ** OurGuest Inn
- **Ⓘ** Parker's Inn
- **Ⓗ** Radisson Harbour Inn
- **Ⓗ** Sandcastle Suites
- **Ⓔ** SunnySide Tower
- **Ⓖ** Water's Edge Retreat

Note: Items with the same letter are located in the same area.

LODGING

If you think Holiday Inn has no surprises, you haven't seen the "kid suites" at the **Holiday Inn Holidome**, 5513 Milan Rd., Sandusky, 419/626-6671. For about $30 extra, the kids get their own bedroom furnished with bunk beds, a VCR, Nintendo, and a CD player. Overnight lakeside accommodations at Cedar Point in Sandusky are **Hotel Breakers**, 419/627-2106, **Sandcastle Suites**, 419/627-2106, and the park's newest property, the **Radisson Harbour Inn**, 419/627-2500 or 800/333-3333.

OurGuest Inn, 2039 E. Harbor Rd., Port Clinton, 419/734-3000, a motel near the entrance to Catawba Island, offers some rooms that sleep up to six people and include a kitchenette. You can also find some kid-friendly B&Bs such as **SunnySide Tower**, 3612 NW Catawba Rd., Port Clinton, 419/797-9315; and for children 10 and older, **Old Stone House on the Lake**, 133 Clemons St., Marblehead, 419/798-5922.

In Huron, Irish scones, an outdoor swimming pool, and a romantic bridal suite are among the special features at **Captain Montague's B&B**, 229 Center St., 800/276-4756. You might also try the **Clarion Inn Twine House**, overlooking Lake Erie at the Huron River Landing, 132 N. Main St., 419/433-8000 or 800/947-3400, and **The Lodge at Sawmill Creek**, 2401 Cleveland Rd. W, 800/SAWMILL, with golf, tennis, swimming, hiking, a beach, and a marina.

Rooms on Kelleys Island are at a premium, but several B&Bs, offer private baths and luxurious amenities. Delicious breakfasts are served on the covered veranda at **Water's Edge Retreat**, 827 E. Lakeshore Dr., 419/746-2455, on the far end of the island. Innkeepers will arrange pickup from the ferry docks as well as sightseeing and excursions, and they have designed their vacation spot as an adult retreat.

Put-in-Bay on South Bass Island is adding lodging rooms, but it still doesn't have enough to accommodate the crowds. However, the addition of two new inns, **Parker's Inn**, 432 Catawba Ave., 419/285-5555, and the **Islander Inn**, 225 Erie St., 877/500-STAY or 419/285-STAY, is helping.

A free, 88-page guide, Buckeye North, is available to help in choosing transportation, lodging, fishing charters, and other island activities. Call 800/225-ERIE for a guide to sights in Erie County and 800/441-1271 for information on activities in the Lake Erie Islands region.

CAMPING

The largest campsite area in the Ohio state park system is found in the Lakeside/Marblehead area at **East Harbor State Park**, 1169 N. Buck Rd.,

419/734-4424, with 570 electric and nonelectric sites, a hiking trail system, hunting, fishing, swimming, and boating. Campers with RVs can book one of the 224 full-service sites at **Cedar Point's Camper Village**, 419/627-2106. Amenities include free shuttle service to the park and the nearby Breakwater Cafe. One of the state's prime properties, **Maumee Bay Resort and Conference Center**, 1400 Park Rd. #1, Oregon, 419/836-8828, offers 256 modern, mostly sunny sites as well as rent-a-camp units, five miles of multiuse trails, and many outdoor amenities.

Campers may choose sites with a wonderful lake view from the cliffside sites at **South Bass Island State Park**, 419/285-2112, or at **Kelleys Island State Park**, 419/746-2546. More than 200 sites are located within the parks, but they're quickly filled, especially on weekends. A beach and hiking, fishing, and boating facilities are nearby.

LAKE TRANSPORTATION

All along the lake you can catch ferries to the islands and take cruises, charters, and sailing trips. The *Red Witch*, 419/798-1244, a 77-foot wooden schooner that got its name from an old John Wayne movie, debuted in 1997 with two-hour trips departing from Toledo, Port Clinton, Lakeside, Huron, and Cleveland. Rates are $18 for adults and $12 for children. Passengers can help the crew or just watch. The *Goodtime I*, 800/466-3140, provides similar trips and is available for private charters. The *Express Shuttle*, 800/245-1538, ferries between Put-in-Bay and Kelleys Island.

The *Island Rocket I and II*, 419/627-1500 or 800/854-8121, are official Cedar Point ferries and the newest and fastest way to get from Sandusky's Jackson Street Pier to Kelleys Island and Put-in-Bay. Round-trip fare to both islands and back to Sandusky is $30. Catch the *Jet Express*, 800/245-1538, Port Clinton to Put-in-Bay, for about $20 round-trip; the **Neumann Cruise and Ferry Line**, 800/876-1907, Marblehead to Kelleys Island, $8 for round-trip (cars and bikes can also be transported); and the **Miller Boat Line**, 800/500-2421, Catawba to Put-in-Bay, for $10 round-trip. These companies offer reduced children's fares as well as other destinations and amenities. For additional assistance, call the Sandusky/Erie County Visitors and Convention Bureau, 800/255-ERIE, or the Ottawa County Visitors Bureau, 800/441-1271.

APPENDIX

Consider this appendix your travel tool box. Use it along with the material in the Planning Your Trip chapter to craft the trip you want. Here are the tools you will find inside:

1. **Planning Map.** Make copies of this map and plot various trip possibilities. Once you've decided on your route, you can write it on the original map and refer to it as you're traveling.

2. **Mileage Chart.** This chart shows the driving distances (in miles) between various destinations throughout the state. Use it in conjunction with the Planning Map.

3. **Special Interest Tours.** If you would like to plan a trip around a certain theme—such as nature, history, or art—one of these tours may work for you.

4. **Calendar of Events.** Here you'll find a month-by-month listing of major area events.

5. **Resources.** This guide lists various regional chambers of commerce and visitors bureaus, state offices, bed-and-breakfast registries, and other useful sources of information.

PLANNING MAP: Ohio

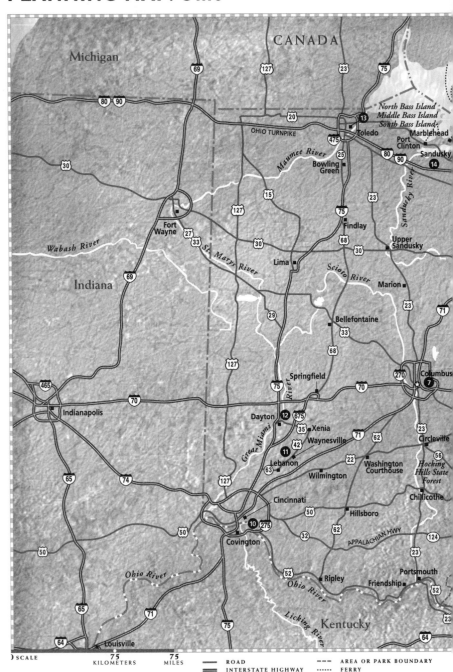

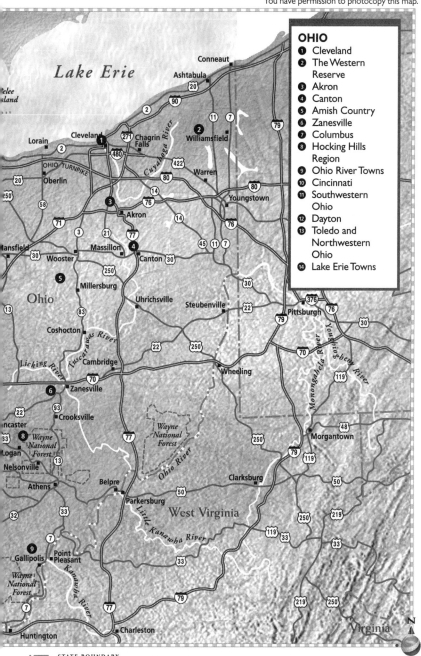

OHIO
1. Cleveland
2. The Western Reserve
3. Akron
4. Canton
5. Amish Country
6. Zanesville
7. Columbus
8. Hocking Hills Region
9. Ohio River Towns
10. Cincinnati
11. Southwestern Ohio
12. Dayton
13. Toledo and Northwestern Ohio
14. Lake Erie Towns

Lake Erie

Conneaut
Ashtabula
20
90
Pelee Island
2
11 7
79
Lorain
Cleveland 271 Chagrin Falls 422 Williamsfield 2
480
OHIO TURNPIKE Cuyahoga River Warren
20 Oberlin 14
80 80
250 58 76 Youngstown
71 3 Akron 14 76
Mansfield 3 21 77 45 11 7
30 Wooster Massillon Canton 30
250 30
Ohio 5 Millersburg Uhrichsville Steubenville 22 Pittsburgh 76
13 83 250 79 30
Coshocton Tuscarawas River 22 250 70 Youghiogheny River
Licking River Cambridge Wheeling Monongahela River 119
70 376
6 Zanesville 48
22 93 Crooksville Morgantown
ncaster Wayne National Forest 250 79 119
33 8 Wayne National Forest 77 Ohio River Clarksburg 50
Logan 13 Belpre 50 219
Nelsonville Parkersburg 50
Athens West Virginia 250 219
32 33 Little Kanawha River 119 33
7 33
9 Gallipolis Point Pleasant 33
Wayne National Forest Kanawha River 219 250
7 79
7 77
Huntington Charleston Virginia N

STATE BOUNDARY
INTERNATIONAL BOUNDARY

OHIO MILEAGE CHART

	Cleveland	Ashtabula	Akron	Canton	Mansfield	Zanesville	Columbus	Lancaster	Portsmouth	Cincinnati	Lebanon	Dayton	Toledo
Ashtabula	61												
Akron	39	85											
Canton	58	107	20										
Mansfield	80	137	669	65									
Zanesville	145	206	106	87	123								
Columbus	1428	199	128	127	67	56							
Lancaster	172	229	158	133	97	46	30						
Portsmouth	232	290	219	218	158	139	91	85					
Cincinnati	252	309	238	234	176	163	111	135	120				
Lebanon	244	301	225	223	165	160	103	134	147	27			
Dayton	217	2747	198	196	138	133	76	107	127	55	27		
Toledo	119	1637	138	161	104	200	144	174	235	206	181	154	
Sandusky	65	109	85	120	54	210	112	142	203	223	210	183	54

SPECIAL INTEREST TOURS

With *Ohio Travel•Smart* you can plan a trip of any length—a one-day excursion, a weekend getaway, or a three-week vacation—around any special interest. To get you started, the following pages contain six tours geared toward a variety of interests. For more information, refer to the chapters listed— chapter names are bolded and chapter numbers appear inside black bullets. You can follow a suggested itinerary in its entirety or shorten, lengthen, or combine parts of each, depending on your planned starting and ending points.

Discuss alternative routes and schedules with your travel companions— it's a great way to have fun, even before you leave home. Remember: Don't hesitate to change your itinerary once you're on the road. Careful study and planning ahead of time will help you make informed decisions as you go, but spontaneity is the extra ingredient that will make your trip memorable.

ACTIVE TRAVELER'S TOUR

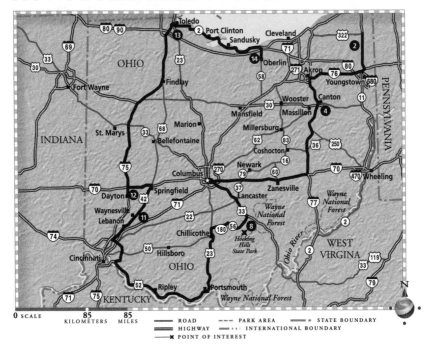

Get out on the water, trails, and hills for an energetic and revitalizing experience. Ohio's state park system, voted the best state park system in the nation for 1998, comprises 73 parks and hundreds of miles of multiuse trails, many of which are accessible to those with physical disabilities.

❷ Western Reserve (Nelson-Kennedy Ledges, and other state parks)
❹ Canton (Canal Fulton canoeing, walking, horse trails)
❽ Hocking Hills Region (Hocking Hills State Park, Hocking State Forest for rappelling and rock climbing, Lake Hope State Park, Lake Logan State Park, Hock-Hocking Adena Bikeway, canoeing)
⓫ Southwestern Ohio (canoeing, biking)
⓬ Dayton (John Bryan State Park for rappelling, rock climbing, and hiking)
⓭ Toledo (fishing)
⓮ Lake Erie Towns (water sports, boating, fishing)

Time needed: 2 weeks

ARTS AND CULTURE TOUR

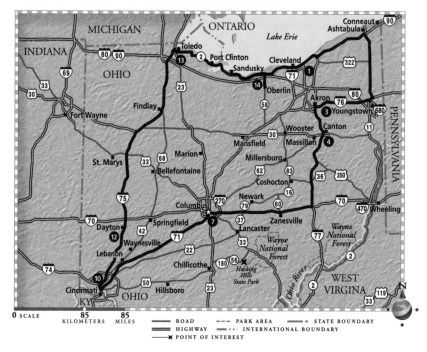

You won't find the arts only in the state's major cities. Ohio is known for its support of smaller communities, as you will notice on this tour.

❶ Cleveland (University Circle Museums, Cleveland Orchestra, Cleveland Play House, Playhouse Square, Rock and Roll Hall of Fame and Museum)

❸ Akron (Akron Museum of Art, Kent State University Museum)

❹ Canton (Canton Civic Center, Zoar, Massillon Museum)

❼ Columbus (Columbus Museum of Art, King Arts Complex, Ohio Historical Society, and Ohio Village)

❿ Cincinnati (Skirball Museum, Cincinnati Museum Center, Cincinnati Museum of Art)

⓬ Dayton (Dayton Art Institute, SunWatch Indian Village)

⓭ Toledo (Museum of Art)

⓮ Lake Erie Towns (Oberlin)

Time needed: 2 to 3 weeks

FAMILY FUN TOUR

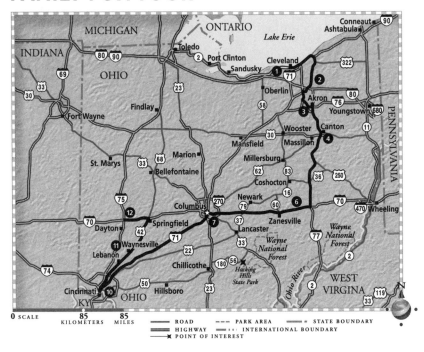

Many Ohio sights are family-friendly without screaming "kids only."

❶ Cleveland (museums, Cleveland Indians tour, Lake Erie Science Center)

❷ Western Reserve (Sea World of Ohio, Holden Arboretum)

❸ Akron (Metroparks, Cuyahoga Valley National Recreation Area)

❹ Canton (Massillon Museum, Pro Football Hall of Fame, McKinley Museum)

❻ Zanesville (Blackhand Gorge State Nature Preserve, The Wilds, parks)

❼ Columbus (*Santa Maria*, COSI, Columbus Zoo, Capitol, Metroparks)

❿ Cincinnati (Cincinnati Fire Museum, Cincinnati Museum Center, Paramount's Kings Island, Parky's Farm, Sharon Woods Village)

⓫ Southwestern Ohio (Lebanon/Waynesville, Little Miami Scenic River Trail, rafting Little Miami, Fort Ancient State Memorial Ohio Renaissance Festival)

⓬ Dayton (U.S. Air Force Museum, SunWatch Indian Village, Young's Jersey Dairy,)

Time needed: 3 weeks

NATURE LOVER'S TOUR

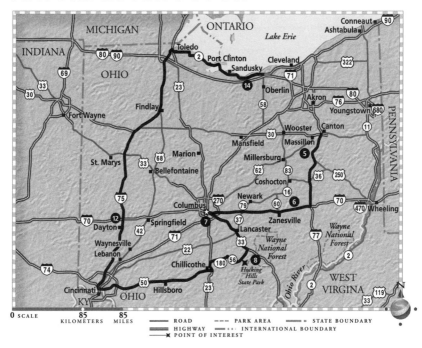

You can circle the whole state on foot by following the blue blazes of the 1,200-mile Buckeye Trail or head to specific areas that match your interests—whether they be bird-watching, wildflowers, waterfalls, or frozen ice formations.

⑤ Amish Country (Mohican State Park, Kingwood Center, Gorman Nature Center, Malabar Farm State Park, Johnson Woods State Nature Preserve)

⑥ Zanesville (Blackhand Gorge State Nature Preserve, Dawes Arboretum)

⑦ Columbus (Inniswood Metropark Gardens)

⑧ Hocking Hills region (Hocking Hills State Park, Hocking State Forest, Conkle's Hollow State Nature Preserve)

⑫ Dayton (John Bryan State Park, Glen Helen Nature Preserve)

⑭ Lake Erie Towns (Lake Erie Wing Watch)

Time needed: 2 to 3 weeks

OHIO'S PRESIDENTS' TOUR

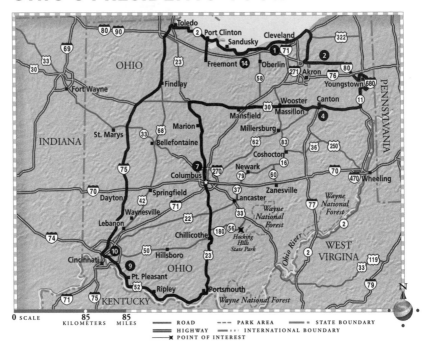

Ohio gave birth, so to speak, to seven presidents (including William Henry Harrison, who came to Ohio as a soldier and stayed). Follow the presidential path around Ohio to help shed light on our favorite and not-so-favorite sons.

❶ **Cleveland** (Garfield Monument)

❷ **Western Reserve** (James A. Garfield National Historic Site and Lawnfield, National McKinley Birthplace Memorial, Hiram)

❹ **Canton** (William McKinley National Monument, McKinley Museum, Ida Saxton McKinley Home, National First Ladies' Library)

❼ **Columbus** (Lucy Hayes Heritage Center, Warren G. Harding Memorial, Harding Home State Memorial, Harding Cabin at Deer Creek State Park)

❾ **Ohio River Towns** (Grant's Birthplace, Boyhood Home, and Schoolhouse)

❿ **Cincinnati** (William Howard Taft National Historic Site)

⓮ **Lake Erie Towns** (Rutherford B. Hayes Presidential Center)

Time needed: 1 to 1 1/2 weeks

UNDERGROUND RAILROAD TOUR

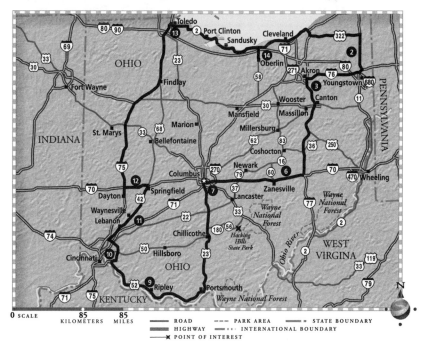

Ohioans played a significant role during the Civil War era, offering their homes and assistance to runaway slaves. Here are a few stops along the Underground Railroad to whet your appetite for further investigation.

❷ **Western Reserve** (Hubbard House Underground Railroad Museum)
❸ **Akron** (John Brown's Home)
❻ **Zanesville** (Stone Academy and Historic Putnam District)
❼ **Columbus** (Kelton House, Hanby House, Chillicothe)
❾ **Ohio River Towns** (Ripley, Buffington Island Civil War Battle Site)
❿ **Cincinnati** (National Underground Railroad Freedom Center)
⓫ **Southwestern Ohio** (Walking tour of Springboro)
⓬ **Dayton** (National African American Museum and Cultural Center)
⓭ **Toledo** (Linck Inn)
⓮ **Lake Erie Towns** (Oberlin)

Time needed: 2 weeks

CALENDAR OF EVENTS

January
Winter Hike, Hocking Hills, 740/385-6841
Lebanon Antique Show, Lebanon, 513/932-1817
Classic Sled Dog Race, Punderson State Park, Newbury, 440/888-9585
Ohio Championship Cross-Country Ski Race, Punderson State Park,
  Newbury, 440/564-2279

February
Ice Carving Festival, Medina, 800/4-MEDINA, 330/723-8773
Traditional Butchering, Carriage Hill Metropark and Farm, Dayton,
  937/879-0461
Longhorn World Championship Rodeo, The Crown, Cincinnati,
  615/876-1016
Winter Hike, Wellman Meadows, Waynesville, 513/897-2437

March
Moondog Coronation Ball, Gund Arena, Cleveland, 216/420-2000
Great Midwest Quilt Show & Sale, Lebanon, 513/932-1817
Maple Syrup Festival, Indian Lake State Park, 937/843-2717
Annual Poetry Competition, Old Dublin fire station, Dublin, 614/889-7444

April
Geauga County Maple Festival, Chardon, 440/286-3007
John Bryan Walkfest, John Bryan State Park, Yellow Springs, 937/864-5738
Annual Trout Derby, Turkey Creek Lake/Roosevelt Lake, 740/858-6652

May
Spring Library Festival, Ohio University, Athens, 800/878-9767
International Street Fair, Athens, 800/878-9767
Athens International Film & Video Festival, Athens, 800/878-9767
Moonlight Tour, Hocking Hills Canoe Livery, Logan, 740/385-0523
Artifact Identification Day, Museum at Fort Ancient, Oregonia,
  513/932-4421
Dulcimer Festival, Ripley, 937/392-9274
Old Main Street Antiques Festival, Waynesville, 513/897-8855

June

Juneteenth, Tappan Square, Oberlin, 440/774-6262

Great Ohio Bicycle Adventure (GOBA),Columbus, 614/447-0971, www.goba.com

Vintage Columbus, Coffman Park, Dublin, 800/227-6972, www.ohiowines.org

Columbus Arts Festival, Columbus, 800/354-2657

Parade the Circle, University Circle, Cleveland, 216/791-3900

Keeping the Traditions Native American Pow-Wow, Blue Jacket Outdoor Drama grounds, Xenia, 937/376-4318

Annual Northeast Ohio Polka Fest, Old Firehouse Winery, Geneva-on-the-Lake, 440/466-8650

Troy Strawberry Festival, Troy, 937/339-7714

July

United States Air and Trade Show, Dayton, 937/898-5901

Hall of Fame Festival, Canton, 800/533-4302

Pottery Week, Zanesville, 740/454-8687

Lancaster Festival, Lancaster, 740/687-4808

August

Bucyrus Bratwurst Festival, Bucyrus, 419/562-2728

Ohio Renaissance Festival, Harveysburg, 513/897-7000

Coshocton Canal Festival, Historic Roscoe Village, 800/877-1830, www.roscoevillage.com

Irish Festival, Dublin, 614/761-6500, www.dublin.oh.us

Zoar Harvest Festival, Zoar, 330/878-3011

Jubilee! African-American Life in the 19th Century, Columbus, 614/297-2606

Vintage Ohio, Lake Farmpark, Kirkland, 800/227-6972

September

DamFest, Great Miami River, Hamilton, 513/867-2287

Yankee Peddler Festival, Canal Fulton, 330/239-2554

German Village Octoberfest, Columbus, 800/354-2657, www.columbuscvb.org

Milan Melon Festival, Milan, 419/499-2766

Ohio River Sternwheel Festival, Marietta, 740/373-5178

Old Time Music Fest, Historic Roscoe VillageCoshocton, 800/877-1830

Ohio Honey Festival, Oxford, 888/53-HONEY, www.ohiohoneyfest.org

Marion Popcorn Festival, Marion, 740/387-FEST

Reynoldsburg Tomato Festival, Reynoldsburg, 614/866-2861

October

Halloween Weekend, Athens, 800/878-9767
Paul Bunyan Show, Nelsonville, 740/753-3591, ext. 2112
Covered Bridge Festival, Ashtabula County, Jefferson, 440/576-3769
Underground Railroad Pilgrimage, Ashtabula County, Ashtabula, 800/DROP-IN
Autumn Lighthouse Festival, Marblehead, 800/441-1271
Woollybear Festival, Vermilion, 216/432-4246
Hayes Civil War Encampment, Hayes Presidential Center, Fremont,
    800/998-7737
Circleville Pumpkin Show, Circleville, 740/474-7000, www.pumpkinshow.com
All Hallow's Eve, Ohio Village, Columbus, 614/297-2606

November

Columbus Marathon, 800/345-4FUN
Buckeye Book Fair, Wooster, 330/264-1125, ext. 317
Ohio Swiss Festival, Sugarcreek, 330/852-4113
Festival of Lights, Cincinnati Zoo & Botanical Gardens, 800/94-HIPPO or
    513/281-2700, ext. 2
Madrigal Dinners, Stan Hywet Hall & Gardens, Akron, 330/836-5533

December

River Village Christmas, Ripley, 888/BROWNOH
Christmas in Spiegel Grove at Hayes Presidential Center, Fremont,
    800/998-7737
Christmas at Malabar, Malabar Farm State Park, Lucas, 419/892-2784
Holidays at Ohio Village, Columbus, 800/653-6446
Christmas in the Village, Waynesville, 513/897-8855
I-X Indoor Winter Carnival, I-X Center, Cleveland, 216/265-2657
Kwanzaa Workshop, National African-American Museum and Cultural Center,
    Wilberforce, 937/376-4944

RESOURCES

In addition to the following resources, many other addresses and phone numbers are found accompanying specific listings in the destination chapters.

Akron/Summit Convention and Visitors Bureau, 77 East Mill Street, Akron, OH 44308, 800/245-4254, www.visitakron/summit.org

Ashtabula County Convention and Visitors Bureau, 1850 Austinburg Road, Austinburg, OH 44010, 440/275-3202 or 800/337-6746, www.accvb.org

Buckeye Trail Association, P.O. Box 254, Worthington, OH 43085, membership information, trail maps, and guidebooks

Canton/Stark County Convention and Visitors Bureau, 229 Wells Avenue NW, Canton, OH 44708-2630, 330/454-1439 or 800/533-4302, www.visitcantonohio.com

Greater Cincinnati Convention and Visitors Bureau, 300 West Sixth Street, Cincinnati, OH 45202, 513/621-2142 or 800/246-2987, www.cincyusa.com

Convention & Visitors Bureau of Greater Cleveland, 50 Public Square, Suite 3100, Cleveland, OH 44113, 216/621-4110 or 800/321-1004, www.travelcleveland.com

Greater Columbus Convention & Visitors Bureau, 90 North High Street, Columbus, OH 43215, 614/221-6623 or 800/345-4FUN, www.SurpriseItsColumbus.com

Dayton/Montgomery County Convention & Visitors Bureau, Chamber Plaza, Suite A, Dayton, OH 45402-2400, 937/226-8211 or 800/221-8234 in Ohio, 800/221-8235 outside Ohio, www.daytoncvb.com

Gallia County/Ohio Valley Visitors Center, 45 State Street, Gallipolis, OH 45631-1131, 740/446-6882 or 800/765-6482, www.eurekanct.com/~ovvc

Greater Hamilton Convention & Visitors Bureau, 1 Riverfront Plaza, Hamilton, OH 45011, 513/844-8080 or 800/311-5353, www.hamilton-cvb.com

Hocking County Tourism Association, 13178 State Route 664 South, Logan, OH 43138, 740/385-9706 or 800/462-5464, www.hockinghills.com

Lake County Visitors Bureau, 1610 Mentor Avenue, Room 2, Painesville, OH 44077, 440/354-2424 or 800/368-5253, www.lakevisit.com

Marion Area Convention & Visitors Bureau, 1952 Marion–Mount Gilead Road, Room 121, Marion, OH 43302, 614/389-9770 or 800/371-6688, www.mariononline.com

Ohio Arts Council, 727 East Main Street, Columbus, OH 43205-1796, 614/466-2613 for the free Ohio Arts Guide for Travelers

Ohio Bicentennial Commission, Statehouse, Room 21 North, Columbus, OH 43215, 888/OHIO-200, www.bicentennial@winslo.state.oh.us

Ohio Department of Natural Resources, 1930 Belcher Drive, Columbus, OH 43224, 614/265-6565, www.dnr.state.oh.us

Ohio Historical Society, 1982 Velma Avenue, Columbus, OH 43211, 800/686-1545, www.ohiohistory.org

Ohio Hotel & Lodging Association, 800/BUCKEYE, www.ohla.worldres.com

Ohio Rails-to-Trails Conservancy, 692 North High Street, Suite 211, Columbus, OH 43215, 614/224-8707

Ohio Tourism Hotline, 800/BUCKEYE, www.ohiotouism.com

Oxford Visitors & Convention Bureau, 118 W. High Street, Oxford, OH 45056, 513/523-8687

Portage County Convention & Visitors Bureau, 173 S. Chillicothe Street, Aurora, OH 44202, 800/648-6342

Portsmouth Convention & Visitors Bureau, 324 Chillicothe Street, Portsmouth, OH 45662, 740/353-1116, pcvb@zcomnet.net

Sandusky/Erie County Visitor & Convention Bureau, 4424 Milan Road, Suite A, Sandusky, OH 44870, 419/625-2984 or 800/255-ERIE, www.buckeyenorth.com

Summit County Metroparks, 975 Treaty Line Road, Akron, OH 44313, 330/867-5511 or 330/865-8060 for seasonal information

Greater Toledo Office of Tourism & Convention, 401 Jefferson Avenue, Toledo, OH 43604, 419/321-6404 or 800/243-4667

University Circle, 10831 Magnolia Drive, Cleveland, OH 44106, 216/791-3900, www.universitycircle.org

Zanesville Muskingum County Convention & Visitors Bureau, 205 North Fifth Street, Zanesville, OH 43701, 740/455-8282 or 800/743-2303, www.zanesville-ohio.com

INDEX

243

Map Index

Toledo: sights, food, lodging, 200
Toledo Regoin: sights, food, lodging, 208

University Circle: sights, food, lodging, 22

Western Reserve: food, lodging, 36
Western Reserve: sights, 37

Zanesville Region: food, lodging, 100
Zanesville Region: sights, 90

Guidebooks that really *guide*

City•Smart™ Guidebooks
Pick one for your favorite city: *Albuquerque, Anchorage, Austin, Calgary, Charlotte, Chicago, Cincinnati, Cleveland, Denver, Indianapolis, Kansas City, Memphis, Milwaukee, Minneapolis/St. Paul, Nashville, Pittsburgh, Portland, Richmond, Salt Lake City, San Antonio, San Francisco, St. Louis, Tampa/St. Petersburg, Tucson.*
US $12.95 to 15.95

Retirement & Relocation Guidebooks
The World's Top Retirement Havens, Live Well in Honduras, Live Well in Ireland, Live Well in Mexico.
US $15.95 to $16.95

Travel•Smart® Guidebooks
Trip planners with select recommendations to *Alaska, American Southwest, Arizona, Carolinas, Colorado, Deep South, Eastern Canada, Florida, Florida Gulf Coast, Hawaii, Illinois/Indiana, Kentucky/Tennessee, Maryland/Delaware, Michigan, Minnesota/Wisconsin, Montana/Wyoming/Idaho, New England, New Mexico, New York State, Northern California, Ohio, Pacific Northwest, Pennsylvania/New Jersey, South Florida and the Keys, Southern California, Texas, Utah, Virginias, Western Canada.* US $14.95 to $17.95

Rick Steves' Guides
See *Europe Through the Back Door* and take along guides to *France, Belgium & the Netherlands; Germany, Austria & Switzerland; Great Britain & Ireland; Italy; Scandinavia; Spain & Portugal; London; Paris;* or *Best of Europe.* US $12.95 to $21.95

Adventures in Nature
Plan your next adventure in *Alaska, Belize, Caribbean, Costa Rica, Guatemala, Hawaii, Honduras, Mexico.*
US $17.95 to $18.95

Into the Heart of Jerusalem
A traveler's guide to visits, celebrations, and sojourns.
US $17.95

The People's Guide to Mexico
This is so much more than a guidebook—it's a trip to Mexico in and of itself, complete with the flavor of the country and its sights, sounds, and people. US $22.95

**JOHN MUIR PUBLICATIONS
A DIVISION OF AVALON TRAVEL PUBLISHING
5855 Beaudry Street, Emeryville, CA 94608**

Please check our web site at www.travelmatters.com for current prices and editions, or see your local bookseller.

MARCIA SCHONBERG

Doug Wolfe

ABOUT THE AUTHOR

When Marcia Schonberg writes about Ohio, she's doing what she knows best. She has spent her life in Ohio and has been offering readers getaway ideas for nearly a decade. She writes regularly for Ohio newspapers, including the *Columbus Dispatch*, the Mansfield *News Journal*, and the Medina *County Gazette*, and for regional publications such as *Over the Back Fence* and *Country Living Magazine*. She is an active member of the Midwest Travel Writers Association and the International Food, Wine, and Travel Writers Association. Her award-winning photographs are often exhibited and sought out for commercial purposes, but her photographic specialty lies in illustrating travel features.

An Ohio State University graduate, Schonberg lives in Mansfield, Ohio, with her husband, Bill, also a born and raised Buckeye. They have two grown children, Adam and Lisa, a teenage son, David, and a grandson, Brandon.